AF656125

Reader's Guide

to

THOMAS STEARNS ELIOT

Reader's Guide
to
THOMAS STEARNS ELIOT

John T. Nichol

CENTRUM PRESS
NEW DELHI-110002 (INDIA)

CENTRUM PRESS
H.O.: 4360/4, Ansari Road, Daryaganj,
New Delhi-110 002 (India)
Ph.: 23278000, 23261597

B.O.: No. 1015, Ist Main Road, BSK IIIrd Stage
IIIrd Phase, IIIrd Block,
Bangalore - 560 085 (India)
Tel.: 080-41723429
Visit us at: www.centrumpress.com

Reader's Guide to Thomas Stearns Eliot

© Reserved

First Edition, 2009

ISBN 978-93-80106-65-6

PRINTED IN INDIA

Printed at Salasar Imaging Systems, Delhi-110035 (India)

Contents

Preface

Thomas Stearns Eliot (1888-1965) was born in St. Louis, Missouri, of an old New England family. He was educated at Harvard and did graduate work in philosophy at the Sorbonne, Harvard, and Merton College, Oxford. He settled in England, where he was for a time a schoolmaster and a bank clerk, and eventually literary editor for the publishing house Faber & Faber, of which he later became a director. He founded and, during the seventeen years of its publication (1922-1939), edited the exclusive and influential literary journal Criterion.

In 1927, Eliot became a British citizen and about the same time entered the Anglican Church. Eliot has been one of the most daring innovators of twentieth-century poetry. Eliot's poetry from *Prufrock* (1917) to the *Four Quartets* (1943) reflects the development of a Christian writer: the early work, especially *The Waste Land* (1922), is essentially negative, the expression of that horror from which the search for a higher world arises. In *Ash Wednesday* (1930) and the *Four Quartets* this higher world becomes more visible; nonetheless Eliot has always taken care not to become a religious poet and often belittled the power of poetry as a religious force.

In his essays, especially the later ones, Eliot advocates a traditionalism in religion, society, and literature that seems at odds with his pioneer activity as a poet. But although the Eliot of *Notes towards the Definition of Culture* (1948) is an older man than the poet of *The Waste Land,* it should not be forgotten that for Eliot tradition is a living organism comprising past and present in constant mutual interaction.

Author

Chapter 1

Introduction

Thomas Stearns Eliot, OM (September 26, 1888 – January 4, 1965), was a poet, dramatist, and literary critic. He received the Nobel Prize in Literature in 1948. Among his most famous writings are the poems *The Love Song of J. Alfred Prufrock, The Waste Land, The Hollow Men, Ash Wednesday* and *Four Quartets;* the plays *Murder in the Cathedral* and *The Cocktail Party*; and the essay "Tradition and the Individual Talent". Eliot was born in the United States, moved to the United Kingdom in 1914 (at age 25), and became a British subject in 1927 at the age of 39.

Of his nationality and its role in his work, Eliot said: "[My poetry] wouldn't be what it is if I'd been born in England, and it wouldn't be what it is if I'd stayed in America. It's a combination of things. But in its sources, in its emotional springs, it comes from America."

LIFE AND EDUCATION

Eliot was born into the prominent Eliot family of St. Louis, Missouri. His father, Henry Ware Eliot (1843–1919), was a successful businessman, president and treasurer of the Hydraulic-Press Brick Company in St. Louis; his mother, born Charlotte Champe Stearns (1843–1929), wrote poems and was also a social worker. Eliot was the last of six surviving children; his parents were both 44 years old when he was born. His four sisters were between eleven and nineteen years older than he; his brother was eight years older. Known to family and friends as Tom, he was the namesake of his maternal grandfather, Thomas Stearns.

From 1898 to 1905, Eliot was a day student at Smith Academy, a preparatory school for Washington University. At the academy, Eliot studied Latin, Greek, French, and German. Upon graduation, he could have gone to Harvard University, but his parents sent him to Milton Academy (in Milton, Massachusetts, near Boston) for a preparatory year. There he met Scofield Thayer, who would later publish *The Waste Land.*

He studied at Harvard, where he earned an A.B., from 1906 to 1909. During this time, he read Arthur Symons's The Symbolist Movement in Literature, where, by his own admission, he first came across Laforgue, Rimbaud, and Verlaine. The *Harvard Advocate* published some of his poems, and he became lifelong friends with Conrad Aiken. The next year, he earned a master's degree at Harvard. In the 1910–1911 school year, Eliot lived in Paris, studying at the Sorbonne and touring the continent. Returning to Harvard in 1911 as a doctoral student in philosophy, Eliot studied the writings of F. H. Bradley, Buddhism and Indic philology (learning Sanskrit and Pâli to read some of the religious texts). He was awarded a scholarship to attend Merton College, Oxford, in 1914, and, before settling there, he visited Marburg, Germany, where he planned to take a summer programme in philosophy.

When the First World War broke out, however, he went to London and then to Oxford. In a letter to Aiken late in December 1914, Eliot, aged 26, wrote "I am very dependent upon women (I mean female society)" and then added a complaint that he was still a virgin. Less than four months later, he was introduced by Thayer, then also at Oxford, to Cambridge governess Vivienne Haigh-Wood. Eliot was not happy at Merton and declined a second year there. Instead, on 26 June 1915, he married Vivienne in a register office.

After a short visit, alone, to the U. S. to see his family, he returned to London and took a few teaching jobs such as lecturing at Birkbeck College, University of London. He continued to work on his dissertation and, in the spring of 1916, sent it to Harvard, which accepted it. Because he did not appear in person to defend his dissertation, however, he was not awarded his PhD. (In 1964, the dissertation was published as *Knowledge and Experience in the Philosophy of F. H. Bradley.*) During Eliot's university career, he studied with George Santayana, Irving Babbitt, Henri Bergson, C. R. Lanman, Josiah Royce, Bertrand Russell, and Harold Joachim.

Bertrand Russell took an interest in Vivien (the spelling she preferred while the newlyweds stayed in his flat. Some scholars have suggested that Vivien and Russell had an affair, but these allegations have never been confirmed. Eliot, in a private paper, written in his sixties, confessed: "I came to persuade myself that I was in love with Vivienne simply because I wanted to burn my boats and commit myself to staying in England. And she persuaded herself (also under the influence of Pound) that she would save the poet by keeping him in England. To her, the marriage brought no happiness. To me, it brought the state of mind out of which came *The Waste Land.*"

A plaque at SOAS's Faber Building, 24 Russell Square commemorating T S Eliot's years at Faber and Faber. After leaving Merton, Eliot worked as a schoolteacher, most notably at Highgate School where he taught the young John Betjeman, and later at the Royal Grammar School, High Wycombe. To earn extra money, he wrote book reviews and lectured at evening extension courses.

In 1917, he took a position at Lloyds Bank in London, where he worked on foreign accounts. In August 1920, Eliot met James Joyce on a trip to Paris, accompanied by Wyndham Lewis. After the meeting, Eliot said he found Joyce arrogant (Joyce doubted Eliot's ability as a poet at the time), but the two soon became friends with Eliot visiting Joyce whenever he was in Paris.

In 1925, Eliot left Lloyds to join the publishing firm Faber and Gwyer (later Faber and Faber), where he remained for the rest of his career, becoming a director of the firm. Wyndham Lewis and Eliot became close friends, a friendship leading to the well-known painting produced in 1938.

LATER LIFE IN ENGLAND

In 1927, Eliot took two important steps in his self-definition. On 29 June he converted to Anglicanism and in November he dropped his American citizenship and became a British subject.

In 1928, Eliot summarised his beliefs when he wrote in the preface to his book, *For Lancelot Andrewes* that "the general point of view [of the book's essays] may be described as classicist in literature, royalist in politics, and anglo-catholic in religion." Eliot was a vestryman of his parish church, Saint Stephen's, Gloucester Road, London, and a life member of the Society of King Charles the Martyr.

By 1932, Eliot had been contemplating a separation from his wife for some time. When Harvard University offered him the Charles Eliot Norton professorship for the 1932-1933 academic year, he accepted, leaving Vivien in England. Upon his return in 1933, Eliot officially separated from Vivien. He avoided all but one meeting with his wife between his leaving for America in 1932 and her death in 1947.

(Vivien died at Northumberland House, a mental hospital north of London, where she was committed in 1938, without ever having been visited by Eliot, who was still her husband.)

From 1946 to 1957, Eliot shared a flat with his friend, John Davy Hayward, who gathered and archived Eliot's papers and styled himself *Keeper of the Eliot Archive.*[13] He also collected Eliot's pre-"Prufrock" verse, commercially published after Eliot's death as *Poems Written in Early Youth*. When Eliot and Hayward separated their household in 1957, Hayward retained his collection of Eliot's papers, which he bequeathed to King's College, Cambridge in 1965.

Eliot's second marriage was happy but short. On 10 January 1957, he married Esmé Valerie Fletcher, to whom he was introduced by Collin Brooks. In sharp contrast to his first marriage, Eliot knew Miss Fletcher well, as she had been his secretary at Faber and Faber since August 1949. Like his marriage to Vivien, the wedding was kept a secret to preserve his privacy.

The ceremony was held in a church at 6.15 a.m. with virtually no one other than his wife's parents in attendance. Valerie was 37 years younger than her husband. Since Eliot's death she has dedicated her time to preserving his legacy; she has edited and annotated *The Letters of T. S. Eliot* and a facsimile of the draft of *The Waste Land*.

Eliot died of emphysema in London on 4 January 1965. For many years, he had health problems owing to his heavy smoking, often being laid low with bronchitis or tachycardia. His body was cremated at Golders Green Crematorium and, according to Eliot's wishes, the ashes taken to St Michael's Church in East Coker, the village from which Eliot's ancestors emigrated to America.

There, a simple wall plaque commemorates him with a quote from his poem, "East Coker": "In my beginning is my end. In my end is my beginning." On the second anniversary of his death, a large stone placed on the floor of Poets' Corner in London's Westminster Abbey was dedicated to Eliot. This commemoration contains his name, an indication that he had received the Order of Merit, dates, and a quotation from his poem, "Little Gidding": "the communication / Of the dead is tongued with fire beyond / the language of the living."

ELIOT'S POETRY

For a poet of his stature, Eliot's poetic output was small. Eliot was aware of this early in his career. He wrote to J. H. Woods, one of his former Harvard professors, that "My reputation in London is built upon one small volume of verse, and is kept up by printing two or three more poems in a year. The only thing that matters is that these should be perfect in their kind, so that each should be an event." Typically, Eliot first published his poems in periodicals or in small books or pamphlets consisting of a single poem (e.g., the Ariel poems) and then adding them to collections. His first collection was *Prufrock and Other Observations*.

In 1920 Eliot published more poems in *Ara Vos Prec* (London) and *Poems: 1920* (New York). These had the same poems (in a different order) except that "Ode" in the British edition was replaced with "Hysteria" in the American edition. In 1925 Eliot collected *The Waste Land* and the poems in *Prufrock* and *Poems* into one volume and added "The Hollow Men" to form *Poems: 1909–1925*. From then on he updated this work (as *Collected Poems*). Exceptions are:

- *Old Possum's Book of Practical Cats* (1939)—a collection of light verse.
- *Poems Written in Early Youth* (posthumously published in 1967)—consisting mainly of poems published between 1907 and 1910 in *The Harvard Advocate*, the student-run literary magazine at Harvard University.
- *Inventions of the March Hare: Poems 1909–1917* (posthumously published in 1997)—poems, verse and drafts Eliot never intended to be published. Densely annotated by Christopher Ricks.

THE LOVE SONG OF J. ALFRED PRUFROCK

In 1915, Ezra Pound, overseas editor of Poetry magazine, recommended to Harriet Monroe, the magazine's founder, that she publish "The Love Song of J. Alfred Prufrock". Although Prufrock seems to be middle-aged, Eliot wrote most of the poem when he was only 22. Its now-famous opening lines, comparing the evening sky to "a patient etherised upon a table," were considered shocking and offensive, especially at a time when the poetry of the Georgians was hailed for its derivations of the 19th century Romantic Poets.

The poem then follows the conscious experience of a man, Prufrock (relayed in the "stream of consciousness" form indicative of the Modernists), lamenting his physical and intellectual inertia, the lost opportunities in his life and lack of spiritual progress, with the recurrent theme of carnal love unattained.

Critical opinion is divided as to whether the narrator even leaves his own residence during the course of the narration. The locations described can be interpreted either as actual physical experiences, mental recollections or even as symbolic images from the sub-conscious mind, as, for example, in the refrain "In the room the women come and go."

Its mainstream reception can be gauged from a review in *The Times Literary Supplement* on 21 June 1917: "The fact that these things occurred to the mind of Mr Eliot is surely of the very smallest importance to anyone, even to himself. They certainly have no relation to *poetry...*"

The poem's structure was heavily influenced by Eliot's extensive reading of Dante Alighieri (in the Italian). References to Shakespeare's Hamlet and other literary works are present in the poem: this technique of allusion and quotation was developed in Eliot's subsequent poetry.

THE WASTE LAND

In October 1922, Eliot published The Waste Land in The Criterion. Composed during a period of personal difficulty for Eliot—his marriage was failing, and both he and Vivien suffered from disordered nerves —The Waste Land is often read as a representation of the disillusionment of the post-war generation.

Even before The Waste Land had been published as a book (December 1922), Eliot distanced himself from the poem's vision of despair: "As for The Waste Land, that is a thing of the past so far as I am concerned and I am now feeling toward a new form and style" he wrote to Richard Aldington on 15 November 1922.

Despite the alleged obscurity of the poem—its slippage between satire and prophecy; its abrupt changes of speaker, location, and time; its elegiac but intimidating summoning up of a vast and dissonant range of cultures and literatures—it has become a touchstone of modern literature, a poetic counterpart to a novel published in the same year, James Joyce's Ulysses. Among its famous phrases are "April is the cruellest month"; "I will show you fear in a handful of dust"; and "Shantih shantih shantih," the utterance in Sanskrit which closes the poem.

THE HOLLOW MEN

The Hollow Men appeared in 1925, and marked, for Edmund Wilson, 'the nadir of the phase of despair and desolation given such effective expression in "The Waste Land."' It is Eliot's major poem of the late twenties, and, like many of his others, its themes are overlapping and fragmentary; it is, however, widely recognized to be concerned with: post-War Europe under the Treaty of Versailles (which Eliot despised—compare 'Gerontion'); the difficulty of hope and religious conversion; and, as some critics argue, Eliot's failed marriage.

Allen Tate, reviewing the 1926 volume, perceived a shift in Eliot's method and noted that, "The mythologies disappear altogether in *The Hollow Men'*—a striking claim for a poem as indebted to Dante as anything else in Eliot's early work, to say little of the modern English mythology — the 'Old Guy [Fawkes]' of the Gunpowder Plot—or the colonial and agrarian mythos of Conrad and Frazer, which, at least for reasons of textual history, echoes *The Waste Land*. The 'continuous parallel between contemporaneity and antiquity' that is so characteristic of his mythical method remains in fine form.

The Hollow Men contains some of Eliot's most famous lines, most notably its conclusion:

This is the way the world ends
This is the way the world ends
This is the way the world ends
Not with a bang but a whimper.

ASH WEDNESDAY

Ash Wednesday is the first long poem written by Eliot after his 1927 conversion to Anglicanism. Published in 1930, this poem deals with the struggle that ensues when one who has lacked faith in the past strives to move towards God. Sometimes referred to as Eliot's "conversion poem", *Ash Wednesday,* with a base of Dante's *Purgatorio,* is richly but ambiguously allusive and deals with the aspiration to move from spiritual barrenness to hope for human salvation. The style is different from his poetry which predates his conversion. *Ash Wednesday* and the poems that followed had a more casual, melodic, and contemplative method.

Many critics were "particularly enthusiastic concerning *Ash Wednesday.*" Edwin Muir maintained that "*Ash Wednesday* is one of the most moving poems he has written, and perhaps the most perfect." while in other quarters it was not well received. The poem's groundwork of orthodox Christianity did discomfit many of the more secular literati.

FOUR QUARTETS

Although many critics preferred his earlier work, Eliot and many other critics considered Four Quartets his masterpiece and it is the work which led to his receipt of the Nobel Prize. The *Four Quartets* draws upon his knowledge of mysticism and philosophy.

It consists of four long poems, published separately: *Burnt Norton* (1936), *East Coker* (1940), The *Dry Salvages* (1941) and *Little Gidding* (1942), each in five sections. Although they resist easy characterisation, each begins with a rumination on the geographical location of its title, and each meditates on the nature of time in some important respect—theological, historical, physical—and its relation to the human condition. Also, each is associated with one of the four classical elements: air, earth, water, and fire. They approach the same ideas in varying but overlapping ways, and are open to a diversity of interpretations.

Burnt Norton asks what it means to consider things that might have been. We see the shell of an abandoned house, and Eliot toys with the idea that all these "merely possible" realities are present together, but invisible to us: All the possible ways people might walk across a courtyard add up to a vast dance we can't see; children who aren't there are hiding in the bushes.

East Coker continues the examination of time and meaning, focusing in a famous passage on the nature of language and poetry. Out of darkness Eliot continues to reassert a solution ("I said to my soul, be still, and wait without hope").

The Dry Salvages treats the element of water, via images of river and sea. It again strives to contain opposites ("...the past and future/Are conquered, and reconciled").

Little Gidding (the element of fire) is the most anthologized of the Quartets. Eliot's own experiences as an air raid warden in The Blitz power the poem, and he imagines meeting Dante during the German bombing. The beginning of the Quartets

("Houses.../Are removed, destroyed") had become a violent everyday experience; this creates an animation, where for the first time he talks of Love—as the driving force behind all experience. From this background, the Quartets end with an affirmation of Julian of Norwich "all shall be well and/All manner of thing shall be well".

The Four Quartets cannot be understood without reference to Christian thought, traditions, and history. Eliot draws upon the theology, art, symbolism and language of such figures as Dante, St. John of the Cross and Julian of Norwich. The "deeper communion" sought in East Coker, the "hints" and whispers of children, the sickness that must grow worse in order to find healing, and the exploration which inevitably leads us home all point to the pilgrim's path along the road of sanctification.

ELIOT'S PLAYS

With the important exception of his magnum opus, Four Quartets, much of Eliot's creative energies after Ash Wednesday were spent in writing plays in verse, mostly comedies or plays with redemptive endings. He was long a critic and admirer of Elizabethan and Jacobean verse drama (witness his allusions to Webster, Middleton, Shakespeare and Kyd in *The Waste Land.*) In a 1933 lecture he said: *"Every poet would like, I fancy, to be able to think that he had some direct social utility.... He would like to be something of a popular entertainer, and be able to think his own thoughts behind a tragic or a comic mask. He would like to convey the pleasures of poetry, not only to a larger audience, but to larger groups of people collectively; and the theatre is the best place in which to do it."*

After writing *The Waste Land* (1922) Eliot wrote that he was "now feeling toward a new form and style." One item he had in mind was writing a play in verse with a jazz tempo with a character that appeared in a number of his poems, Sweeney. Eliot did not finish it. He did publish two pieces of what he had separately. The two, "Fragment of a Prologue" (1926) and "Fragment of an Agon" (1927) were published together in 1932 as *Sweeney Agonistes*. Although noted that this was not intended to be a one-act play, it is sometimes performed as one.

In 1934 a pageant play called *The Rock* that Eliot authored was performed. This was a benefit for churches in the Diocese of London. Much of the work was a collaborative effort and Eliot only accepted authorship of one scene and the choruses. The pageant would have a sympathetic audience but one largely consisting of the common churchman, a new audience for Eliot who had to modify his style, often called "erudite."

George Bell, the Bishop of Chichester, who was instrumental in getting Eliot to work as writer with producer E. Martin Browne in producing the pageant play *The Rock* asked Eliot to write another play for the Canterbury Festival in 1935. This play, *Murder in the Cathedral,* was more under Eliot's control.

Murder in the Cathedral is about the death of Thomas Becket. Eliot admitted being influenced by, among others, the works of 17th century preacher Lancelot Andrewes. *Murder in the Cathedral* has been a standard choice for Anglican and Roman Catholic curricula for many years.

Following his ecclesiastical plays Eliot worked on commercial plays for more general audiences. These were *The Family Reunion* (1939), *The Cocktail* Party (1949), The Confidential Clerk (1953) and The Elder Statesman (1958). The dramatic works of Eliot are less well known than his poems.

ELIOT AS CRITIC

Although best known as a poet, Eliot also made significant contributions to the field of literary criticism. In particular, Eliot strongly influenced the school of New Criticism. While somewhat self-deprecating and minimizing of his work as a critic—he once said his criticism was merely a "by-product" of his "private poetry-workshop"—Eliot is considered by some to be one of the greatest literary critics of the 20th century. The critic William Empson once said, "I do not know for certain how much of my own mind [Eliot] invented, let alone how much of it is a reaction against him or indeed a consequence of misreading him. He is a very penetrating influence, perhaps not unlike the east wind." In his critical essay "Tradition and the Individual Talent," Eliot argues that art must be understood not in a vacuum, but in the context of previous pieces of art: "In a peculiar sense [an artist or poet]... must inevitably be judged by the standards of the past."

This essay was one of the most important works of the school of New Criticism. Specifically, it introduced the idea that the value of one work of art must be viewed in the context of all previous work—a "simultaneous order" or works. It has also been argued that "Tradition and the Individual Talent" served to keep out the public at large from engaging in literature (or having literature in engage in them): "T.S. Eliot's insistence in essays such as 'Tradition and the Individual Talent' (1917) that the young poet need only assimilate the (all-male) canon of established authors contributed to public definitions of literary modernism that would exclude mass culture."

Conversely, Eliot's work regarding music—particularly his article "Marie Lloyd"—may have actually helped lead to the idea that popular culture could be the subject of criticism.

Also extremely important to New Criticism was the idea—as articulated in Eliot's essay "Hamlet and His Problems"—of an "objective correlative," which posits a connection among the words of the text and events, states of mind, and experiences. This notion concedes that a poem means what it says, but suggests that there can be a non-subjective judgment based on different readers' different—but perhaps corollary—interpretations of a work.

More generally, New Critics took a cue from Eliot in regards to his "'classical' ideals and his religious thought; his attention to the poetry and drama of the early seventeenth century; his deprecation of the Romantics, especially Shelley; his proposition that good poems constitute 'not a turning loose of emotion but an escape from emotion; and his insistence that 'poets...at present must be difficult.'"

Eliot's essays were also a major factor in the revival of interest in the metaphysical poets. Eliot was particularly favorable to the metaphysical poets' ability to show experience as both psychological and sensual, while at the same time infusing this portrayal with—in Eliot's view—wit and uniqueness.

Eliot's essay "The Metaphysical Poets," along with giving new significance and attention to metaphysical poetry, introduced his now well known definition of "unified sensibility," which is considered by some to mean the same thing as the term "metaphysical." Some have argued that Eliot can be best understood as critic through his poetry—that one reflects the other and that Eliot has a unique perspective as a poet-critic.

In his "Four Quartets," a series of poems, is self-aware in a way that "open the poem up to modern critical movements in which understanding is made contingent on the perspective in which it is installed." Eliot's self-examination through poetry reflects his belief in the objective correlative. Eliot's 1922 poem *The Waste Land*—which at the time of its publication, many critics believed to be a joke or hoax—also can be better understood in light of his work as a critic.

Eliot had argued that a poet must write "programmatic criticism"—or the idea that a poet should write to advance his own interests than to advance "historical scholarship". Viewed from Eliot's own critical lens, *The Waste Land* likely shows his personal distaste for World War I rather than an objective historical understanding of it. Some have argued that late in his career, Eliot recanted much of his earlier work as a critic. However, this is disputed. At that time, Eliot stressed the importance of every poet creating his or her own unique personality through his work.

OTHER WORKS

In 1939, Eliot published a book of light verse, Old Possum's Book of Practical Cats — "Old Possum" being a name Ezra Pound had bestowed upon him. This first edition had an illustration of the author on the cover. In 1954 the composer Alan Rawsthorne set six of the poems for speaker and orchestra, in a work entitled *Practical Cats*. After Eliot's death, it became the basis of the West End and Broadway hit musical by Andrew Lloyd Webber, *Cats*. In 1958 the Archbishop of Canterbury appointed Eliot to a commission which resulted in "The Revised Psalter" (1963). A harsh critic of Eliot's, C. S. Lewis, was also a member of the commission but their antagonism turned into a friendship.

CRITICISM OF ELIOT

LITERATURE AND LITERARY CRITICISM

Eliot's poetry was first criticized as not being poetry at all. Another criticism has been of his widespread interweaving of quotations from other authors into his work. "Notes on the Waste Land," which follows the poem, gives the source of many of these, but not all.

This practice has been defended as a necessary salvaging of tradition in an age of fragmentation, and completely integral to the work, adding richness through unexpected juxtaposition. It has also been condemned as showing a lack of originality, and for plagiarism. The prominent critic F. W. Bateson published an essay called 'T. S. Eliot: The Poetry of Pseudo-Learning'. Eliot wrote in *The Sacred Wood*: "Immature poets imitate; mature poets steal; bad poets deface what they take, and good poets make it into something better, or at least something different."

Canadian academic Robert Ian Scott pointed out that the title of *The Waste Land* and some of the images had previously appeared in the work of a minor Kentucky poet, Madison Cawein (1865–1914). Bevis Hillier compared Cawein's lines "... come and go/Around its ancient portico" with Eliot's "... come and go/talking of Michelangelo". (This line actually appears in Eliot's "The Love Song of J. Alfred Prufrock", and not in *The Waste Land*.) Cawein's "Waste Land" had appeared in the January 1913 issue of Chicago magazine *Poetry* (which contained an article by Ezra Pound on London poets). But scholars are continually finding new sources for Eliot's *Waste Land*, often in odd places.

Many famous fellow writers and critics have paid tribute to Eliot. According to the poet Ted Hughes, "Each year Eliot's presence reasserts itself at a deeper level, to an audience that is surprised to find itself more chastened, more astonished, more humble."

Hugh Kenner commented, "He has been the most gifted and influential literary critic in English in the twentieth century." However, other writers have not supported this view. In one of his criticisms, Samuel Beckett suggests that Eliot's work belongs in what the reverse of "T. Eliot" spells.

C. S. Lewis, however, thought his literary criticism "superficial and unscholarly". In a 1935 letter to a mutual friend of theirs, Paul Elmer Moore, Lewis wrote that he considered the work of Eliot to be *"a very great evil"*. Although, in a letter to Eliot written in 1943, Lewis showed an admiration for Eliot along with his antagonism toward his views when he wrote: "I hope the fact that I find myself often contradicting you in print gives no offence; it is a kind of tribute to you—whenever I fall foul of some widespread contemporary view about literature I always seem to find that you have expressed it most clearly. One aims at the officers first in meeting an attack!"

CHARGES OF ANTI-SEMITISM

Eliot has sometimes been charged with anti-Semitism. Biographer Lyndall Gordon has noted that many in Eliot's milieu successfully eschewed such views.

PUBLIC EXPRESSIONS

The poem "Gerontion" contains a depiction of a landlord referred to only as the "jew [who] squats on the window sill." Another much-quoted example is the poem, "Burbank with a Baedeker: Bleistein with a Cigar", in which a character in the poem implicitly blames the Jews for the decline of Venice ("The rats are underneath the piles/ The Jew is underneath the lot"). In "A Cooking Egg", Eliot writes, "The red-eyed scavengers are creeping/ From Kentish Town and Golder's Green" (Golders Green was a largely Jewish suburb of London). It has been noted, on the other hand, that the publisher of "Gerontion" and "Burbank" was John Rodker. Additionally,

Eliot mailed a draft of "Gerontion" to his friend Sidney Schiff for pre-publication editing and commentary. A third and perhaps most frequently cited "anti-semitic" poem, "Sweeney Among the Nightingales," was published by Eliot's friend Leonard Woolf. None of these three men, who were all Jewish, considered the poems in question anti-semitic.

In a series of lectures given at the University of Virginia in 1933 and later published under the title "After Strange Gods" (1934), Eliot said, regarding a homogeneity of culture (and implying a traditional Christian community), "What is still more important is unity of religious background, and reasons of race and religion combine to make any large number of free-thinking Jews undesirable." The philosopher George Boas, who had previously been on friendly terms with Eliot, wrote to him that, "I can at least rid you of the company of one." Eliot did not reply. In later years Eliot disavowed the book, and refused to allow any part to be reprinted.

Eliot also wrote a letter to the *Daily Mail* in January 1932 which congratulated the paper for a series of laudatory articles on the rise of Mussolini. In *The Idea of a Christian Society* (1939) he says "...totalitarianism can retain the terms 'freedom' and 'democracy' and give them its own meaning: and its right to them is not so easily disproved as minds inflamed by passion suppose." In the same book, written before World War II, he says of J. F. C. Fuller, who worked for the Policy Directorate in the British Union of Fascists:

Fuller... believes that Britain "must swim with the out-flowing tide of this great political change". From my point of view, General Fuller has as good a title to call himself a "believer in democracy" as anyone else. ...I do not think I am unfair to [the report that a ban against married women Civil Servants should be removed because it embodied Nazism], in finding the implication that what is Nazi is wrong, and need not be discussed on its own merits.

PROTESTS AGAINST

One of the first and most famous protests against Eliot on the subject of anti-Semitism came in the form of a poem from the Anglo-Jewish writer and poet Emanuel Litvinoff, at an inaugural poetry reading for the Institute of Contemporary Arts in 1951.

Only a few years after the Holocaust, Eliot had republished lines originally written in the 1920s about 'money in furs' and the 'protozoic slime' of Bleistein's 'lustreless, protrusive eye' in his *Selected Poems* of 1948, angering Litvinoff. When the poet got up and announced his poem, entitled 'To T. S. Eliot', the event's host, Sir Herbert Read, declared 'Oh Good, Tom's just come in'. Litvinoff proceeded in evoking to the packed but silent room his work, which ended with the lines "Let your words/tread lightly on this earth of Europe/ lest my people's bones protest". Many members of the audience were outraged; Litvinoff said "hell broke loose" and that no one supported him. One listener, the poet Stephen Spender, claiming to be as Jewish as Litvinoff, stood and called the poem an undeserved attack on Eliot. However, Litvinoff says that Eliot was heard to mutter, 'It's a good poem'.

REBUTTALS

Leonard Woolf, husband of Virginia Woolf, who was himself Jewish and a friend of Eliot's, judged that Eliot was probably "slightly anti-Semitic in the sort of vague way which is not uncommon. He would have denied it quite genuinely." In 2003, Professor Ronald Schuchard of Emory University published details of a previously unknown cache of letters from Eliot to Horace Kallen, which reveal that in the early 1940s Eliot was actively helping Jewish refugees from Germany and Austria to re-settle in Britain and America.

In letters written after the war, Eliot also voiced support for modern Israel.

RECOGNITION

Formal Recognition

- Order of Merit (awarded by King George VI (United Kingdom), 1948)
- Nobel Prize for Literature "for his outstanding,

pioneer contribution to present-day poetry" (Stockholm, 1948)

- Officier de la Legion d'Honneur (1951)
- Hanseatic Goethe Prize (Hamburg, 1955)
- Dante Medal (Florence, 1959)
- Commandeur de l'ordre des Arts et des Lettres, (1960)
- Presidential Medal of Freedom (1964)
- 13 honorary doctorates (including Oxford, Cambridge, the Sorbonne, and Harvard)
- Two posthumous Tony Awards (1983) for his poems used in the musical *Cats*
- Eliot College of the University of Kent, England, named after him
- Celebrated on commemorative postage stamps
- Has a star on the St. Louis Walk of Fame

PEOETRY

- *Prufrock and Other Observations* (1917)
  - *The Love Song of J. Alfred Prufrock*
  - *Portrait of a Lady (poem)*
- *Poems* (1920)
  - *Gerontion*
  - *Sweeney Among the Nightingales*
- *The Waste Land* (1922)
- *The Hollow Men* (1925)
- *Ariel Poems* (1927-1954)
  - *The Journey of the Magi* (1927)
- *Ash Wednesday* (1930)
- *Coriolan* (1931)
- *Old Possum's Book of Practical Cats* (1939)
- *The Marching Song of the Pollicle Dogs* and *Billy M'Caw: The Remarkable Parrot* (1939) in *The Queen's Book of the Red Cross*
- *Four Quartets* (1945)

PLAYS

- *Sweeney Agonistes* (published in 1926, first performed in 1934)
- *The Rock* (1934)
- *Murder in the Cathedral* (1935)
- *The Family Reunion* (1939)
- *The Cocktail Party* (1949)
- *The Confidential Clerk* (1953)
- *The Elder Statesman* (first performed in 1958, published in 1959)

NONFICTION

- *The Second-Order Mind* (1920)
- *Tradition and the Individual Talent* (1920)
- *The Sacred Wood: Essays on Poetry and Criticism* (1920)
  - "Hamlet and His Problems"
- *Homage to John Dryden* (1924)
- *Shakespeare and the Stoicism of Seneca* (1928)
- *For Lancelot Andrewes* (1928)
- *Dante* (1929)
- *Selected Essays, 1917–1932* (1932)
- *The Use of Poetry and the Use of Criticism* (1933)
- *After Strange Gods* (1934)
- *Elizabethan Essays* (1934)
- *Essays Ancient and Modern* (1936)
- *The Idea of a Christian Society* (1940)
- *A Choice of Kipling's Verse* (1941) made by Eliot, with an essay on Rudyard Kipling, London, Faber and Faber.
- *Notes Towards the Definition of Culture* (1948)
- *Poetry and Drama* (1951)
- *The Three Voices of Poetry* (1954)
- *The Frontiers of Criticism* (1956)
- *On Poetry and Poets* (1957)

POSTHUMOUS PUBLICATIONS

- *To Criticize the Critic* (1965)

- *The Waste Land: Facsimile Edition* (1974)
- *Inventions of the March Hare: Poems 1909-1917* (1996)

ON THE COMPOSITION OF THE WASTE LAND

Pound's criticism of *The Waste Land* was not of its meaning; he liked its despair and was indulgent of its neo-Christian hope. He dealt instead with its stylistic adequacy and freshness. For example, there was an extended, unsuccessful imitation of *The Rape of the Lock* at the beginning of "The Fire Sermon."

It described the lady Fresca (imported to the waste land from "Gerontion" and one day to be exported to the States for the soft drink trade). Instead of making her toilet like Pope's Belinda, Fresca is going to it, like Joyce's Bloom. Pound warned Eliot that since Pope had done the couplets better, and Joyce the defacation, there was no point in another round. To this shrewd advice we are indebted for the disappearance of such lines as:

The white-armed Fresca blinks, and yawns, and gapes,
Aroused from dreams of love and pleasant rapes.
Electric summons of the busy bell
Brings brisk Amanda to destroy the spell
Leaving the bubbling beverage to cool,
Fresca slips softly to the needful stool,
Where the pathetic tale of Richardson
Eases her labour till the deed is done...
This ended, to the steaming bath she moves,
Her tresses fanned by little flutt'ring Loves;
Odours, confected by the cunning French,
Disguise the good old hearty female stench.

The episode of the typist was originally much longer and more laborious:

A bright kimono wraps her as she sprawls
In nerveless torpor on the window seat;
A touch of art is given by the false
Japanese print, purchased in Oxford Street.

Pound found the décor difficult to believe: "Not in that

lodging house?" The stanza was removed. When he read the later stanza,

—Bestows one final patronising kiss,
And gropes his way, finding the stairs unlit;
And at the corner where the stable is,
Delays only to urinate, and spit,

he warned that the last two lines were "probably over the mark," and Eliot acquiesced by cancelling them.

Pound persuaded Eliot also to omit a number of poems that were for a time intended to be placed between the poem's sections, then at the end of it. One was a renewed thrust at poor Bleistein, drowned now but still haplessly Jewish and luxurious under water:

Full fathom five your Bleistein lies
Under the flatfish and the squids.
Graves' Disease in a dead jew's/man's eyes!
Where the crabs have eat the lids...
That is lace that was his nose
Roll him gently side to side,
See the lips unfold unfold
From the teeth, gold in gold....

Pound urged that this, and several other mortuary poems, did not add anything, either to *The Waste Land* or to Eliot's previous work. He had already written "the longest poem in the English langwidge. Don't try to bust all records by prolonging it three pages further." As a result of this resmithying by *il miglior fabbro,* the poem gained immensely in concentration. Yet Eliot, feeling too solemnized by it, thought of prefixing some humorous doggerel by Pound about its composition. Later, in a more resolute effort to escape the limits set by *The Waste Land,* he wrote *Fragment of an Agon,* and eventually, "somewhere the other side of despair," turned to drama.

So it would have been about mid-January 1922, in London, that *The Waste Land* received its final form, and likely its title too. The state of the manuscripts Eliot had unpacked after his return from the continent may be readily summarized. "The Burial of the Dead" had lost its Cambridge opening but was otherwise lightly annotated. "A Game of Chess" had had its opening heavily worked over by Pound, to tighten the meter, and Vivien Eliot had supplied a few suggestions for improving the pub dialogue. "The Fire Sermon" was a shambles; it needed much work. "Death by Water" had been cut back to ten lines. "What the Thunder Said" was "OK."

Pondering these materials, Eliot perceived where the poem's centre of gravity now lay. Its centre was no longer the urban panorama refracted through Augustan styles. That had gone with the dismemberment of Part III. Its centre had become the urban apocalypse, the great City dissolved into a desert where voices sang from exhausted wells, and the Journey that had been implicit from the moment he opened the poem in Cambridge and made its course swing via Munich to London had become journev through the Waste Land. Reworking Part III, and retyping the other parts with revisions of detail, he achieved the visionary unity that has fascinated two generations of readers. He then went to bed with the flu, "excessively depressed."

He was anxious. He thought of deleting Phlebas, and was told that the poem needed Phlebas "ABsolootly." "The card pack introduces him, the drowned phoen sailor." He thought of using "Gerontion" as a prelude, and was told not to. "One don't miss it *at* all as the thing now stands."

What seems to have bothered him was the loss of a schema. "Gerontion" would have made up for that lack by turning the whole thing into "thoughts of a dry brain in a dry season." Later the long note about Tiresias attempted the same strategy: "What Tiresias *sees*, in fact, is the substance of the poem."

The lost schema, if we have guessed about it correctly, had originated in a preoccupation with Dryden as the poem grew outward from "The Fire Sermon." If Vergil had once sponsored the protagonist's journey as Homer sponsors the wanderings of Leopold Bloom, Vergil was pertinent to a poem prompted by Vergil's major English translator, John Dryden. Ovid, who supplied Tiresias and Philomel, and told the story of the Sibyl's terribly longevity which may underlie the line about fear in a handful of dust, was a favourite of Dryden's, and (on Mark Van Doren's showing) pertinent to Dryden's London and Eliot's.

Wren's churches, notably Magnus martyr, were built after the fire *Annus Mirabilis* celebrates, which is one reason Eliot works Magnus Martyr into his Fire Sermon. And in disposing ornate diction across the grid of a very tame pentameter, Eliot's original draft of the opening of Part II had rewritten in the manner of French decadence a Shakespearean passage ("... like a burnished throne") that Dryden had rewritten before him in a diction schooled by his own time's French decorum. No classroom exercise is more ritualized than the comparison of *Antony and Cleopatra* and *All for Love.*

But the centre from which such details radiate had been removed from the poem. What survived was a form with no form, and a genre with no name. Years later, on the principle that a form is anything done twice, Eliot reproduced the structural contours of *The Waste Land* exactly, though more briefly, in *Burnt Norton,* and later still three more times, to make the *Quartets,* the title of which points to a decision that such a form might have analogies with music. That was *post facto.*

In 1922, deciding somewhat reluctantly that the poem called *The Waste Land* was finished, he was assenting to a critical judgment, Pound's and his own, concerning which parts were alive in a sheaf of pages he had written. Two years afterward, in "The Function of Criticism," he averted to "the capital importance of criticism in the work of creation itself," and suggested that "the larger part of the labour of an author in composing his work is critical labour; the labour of sifting, combining, constructing, expunging, correcting, testing."

He called it "this frightful toil," and distinguished it from obedience to the Inner Voice. "The critical activity finds its highest, its true fulfilment in a kind of union with creation in the labour of the artist."

For it does no discredit to *The Waste Land* to learn that it was not striving from the first to become the poem it became: that it was not conceived as we have it before it was written, but reconceived from the wreckage of a different conception. Eliot saw its possibilities in London, in January 1922, with the mangled drafts before him: that was a great feat of creative insight.

In Paris he and Pound had worked on the poem page by page, piecemeal, not trying to salvage a structure but to reclaim the authentic lines and passages from the contrived. Contrivance had been guided by various neoclassic formalities, which tended to dispose the verse in single lines whose sense could survive the deletion of their neighbors. When they had finished, and Eliot had rewritten the central section, the poem ran, in Pound's words, "from 'April...' to 'shantih' without a break."

This is true if your criterion for absence of breaks is Symbolist, not neoclassical. Working over the text as they did, shaking out ashes from amid the glowing coals, leaving the luminous bits to discover their own unexpected affinities, they nearly recapitulated the history of Symbolism, a poetic that systematized the mutual affinities of details neoclassic canons had guided.

During the final stages of *The Waste Land's* composition Eliot put himself, for what was to be the last time, under Pound's direction. On 18 November, on his way to Switzerland, Eliot passed through Paris and left his wife with the Pounds who were then living there. It seems likely that Eliot showed Pound what he had done in Margate. Pound called Eliot's Lausanne draft 'the 19 page version' which implies that he had previously seen another.

He marked certain sheets on two occasions: once in pencil, probably on 18 November, once in ink, on Eliot's return from Lausanne early in January. Pound undoubtedly improved particular passages: his excisions of the anti-Semitic portrait of Bleistein and the misogynist portrait of Fresca curtailed Eliot's excessive animus, and his feel for the right word improved odd lines throughout. Pound was proud of his hand in *The Waste Land* and wrote:

If you must needs enquire
Know diligent Reader

That on each Occasion
Ezra performed the caesarian Operation.

I think that Pound's influence went deeper than his comment during the winter of 1921-2, going back rather to 1918, 1919, and 1920 when he and Eliot were engaged in a common effort to improve their poetry. Pound's *Hugh Selwyn Mauberly* (1920) is a covert dialogue with Eliot, a composite biography of two great unappreciated poets whose flaws are frankly aired.

Pound criticizes a Prufrock-like poet too given to hesitation, drifting, 'maudlin confession', and aerial fantasy—the phantasmal seasurge and the precipitation of 'insubstantial manna' from heaven.

As though in answer, Eliot put aside his most confessional fragments, 'Saint Narcissus' and 'Elegy', and in 1921 overlaid private meditation with documentary sketches of contemporary characters—a pampered literary woman, Fresca (like Pound's Lady Valentine), Venus Anadyomene (another *Mauberly* character), Cockneys, a typist with dirty camisoles, and a scurfy clerk. The Pound colouring in these sketches did not quite suit Eliot.

Where Pound is exuberant in his disgust, Eliot becomes callow or vitriolic—and Pound himself recognized this in his comments on typist and clerk: 'too easy' and 'probably over the mark'. Eliot's characters are not as realistic as Pound's. They are projections of Eliot's haunted consciousness—they could be termed humours.

Unlike the satirist, Eliot does not criticize an actual world but creates a unique 'phantasmal' world of lust, cowardice, boredom, and malice on which he gazes in fascinated horror. *The Waste Land* is about a psychological hell in which someone is quite alone, 'the other figures in it / Merely projections'.

It is against this background that we must reconsider the Eliot-Pound collaboration on *The Waste Land*. For despite all the stylistic changes that Pound brought about in Eliot's long poem, changes that have recently been submitted to careful study—the thematic strains of the original *Waste Land* are not significantly altered in the final version.

Indeed, one might argue that Pound's excisions and revisions made Eliot's central themes and symbols more prominent than they would otherwise have been, buried as they were under the weight of such satirical intrusions as "He Do the Police in Different Voices" (Part 1) or the Popean couplets about Fresca at her toilet at the beginning of Part II 1.37

Consider what happens to "Death by Water," which Pound reduced from ninety-two lines to ten. The first section, written in quatrains rhyming abab, introduces a parodic version of Ulysses in the person of a foolish sailor on shore leave, regaling his cronies in the public bars, who are "Staggering, or limping with a comic gonorrhea," with stories of the "much seen and much endured."

In the margin of the manuscript, Pound wrote, "Bad—but cant attack until I get typescript." The second section, written in rather slack Tennysonian blank verse, is the dramatic monologue of the sailor, telling of a fishing expedition from the Dry Salvages north to the Outer Banks of Nova Scotia.

Even as the sailor meditates on the significance of a mysterious Sirens' song heard one night on watch (lines 65-72), a song that makes him question the relationship of reality to dream, the ship hits an iceberg and is destroyed. After this ending ("And if *Another* knows, I know I know not, / Who only knows that there is no more noise now"—) comes the "Phlebas the Phoenician" lyric, which is the only part of the original that remains in the finished poem.

Pound seems to have decided that the long account of the sailor's voyage was an unnecessary digression. But when Eliot wrote from London, "Perhaps better omit Phlebas also???" Pound replied, "I DO advise keeping Phlebas. In fact I more'n advise. Phlebas is an integral part of the poem; the card pack introduces him, the drowned phoen. sailor. And he is needed ABSOLOOTLY where he is. Must stay in." Pound understood, in other words, that "Death by Water" is the essential link between the Madame Sosostris passage and the following lines near the end of Part V:

Damyata: The boat responded

Gaily, to the hand expert with sail and oar
The sea was calm, your heart would have responded
Gaily, when invited, beating obedient
To controlling hands
I sat upon the shore
Fishing, with the arid plain behind me
Shall I at least set my lands in order?

Phlebas' "death by water" is the necessary prelude to the hints of rebirth contained in these lines, whereas the actual sea voyage, as described in the cancelled narrative portion, is irrelevant to the poem's life-in-death theme. Curiously, then, Pound seems to have understood Eliot's purpose better than did Eliot himself.

In discussing Pound's "operation upon *The Waste Land*," Eliot notes:

I have sometimes tried to perform the same sort of maieutic task; and I know that one of the temptations against which I have to be on guard, is trying to re-write somebody's poem in the way I should have written it myself if I had wanted to write that poem. Pound never did that: he tried first to understand what one was attempting to do, and then tried to help one do it in one's own way.

This is an important distinction. Pound did not try to transform *The Waste Land* into the sort of city poem he himself might have written. Rather, he helped Eliot to write it in his own way. "What the Thunder Said," for example, is left virtually untouched by Pound, for here Eliot discovered his quest theme and brought it to a swift and dramatic conclusion.

In assessing Pound's response to *The Waste Land,* critics invariably cite the famous letter to Eliot (24 December 1921) in which Pound says: "Complimenti, you bitch. I am wracked by the seven jealousies, and cogitating an excuse for always exuding my deformative secretions in my own stuff, and never getting an outline. I go into nacre and objets d'art." But the fact is that, despite these self-depreciating words, Pound knew well enough that *The Waste Land,* like "Gerontion," was not his sort of poem. As Eliot himself observes, after thanking Pound for "helping one to do it in one's own way," "There did come a point, of course, at which difference of outlook and belief became too wide."

And yet it was evident, even in 1936, that 'Burnt Norton' was adapting the five-part structure of *The Waste Land,* for that structure was signalled by the use of a short lyric as part IV of the sequence.

But what did it mean, what does it mean, to feel the five-part structure of *The Waste Land* working within so different a poem? To answer this question it may help to review the process by which *The Waste Land* gained its peculiar structure, emerging from the hands of Ezra Pound, as Eliot says, reduced to half manuscript length.

First of all, without Pound's editorial intervention, we would not have the short lyric, 'Phlebas the Phoenician', appearing by itself as part IV of *The Waste Land,* and thus, presumably, we would not have the short lyrics constituting the fourth sections of all the *Four Quartets* — the short movement that helps to create analogies with Beethoven's late quartets.

Indeed we might not have the Phlebas lyric at all, without Pound's advice, for Eliot, upset by Pound's slashing away at the eighty-two lines preceding this lyric in the manuscript, wrote to Pound, 'Perhaps better omit Phlebas also???' Pound was horrified:

Eliot seemed not to understand the central principle of the poem's operation. 'I DO advise keeping Phlebas,' Pound replied. 'In fact I more'n advise. Phlebas is an integral part of the poem; the card pack introduces him, the drowned phoen. sailor, and he is needed ABSoloootly where he is. Must stay in.'

What Pound describes in that vehement answer is the sort of organization that Eliot later called musical, in his lecture 'The Music of Poetry', delivered in 1942, just as he was completing *Four Quartets*: 'The use of recurrent themes is as natural to poetry as to music,' Eliot says:

There are possibilities for verse which bear some analogy to the development of a theme by different groups of instruments ['different voices', we might say]; there are possibilities of transitions in a poem comparable to the different movements of a symphony or a quartet; there are possibilities of contrapuntal arrangement of subject-matter.

So, in *The Waste Land,* after the embers of lust have smouldered in 'The Fire Sermon' — 'Burning burning burning burning'— the death of Phlebas by water provides a moment of serenity, quiet, poise, as Phlebas enters the whirlpool in whispers to a death not to be feared, but foreseen and accepted. The lyric acts as the lines about the still point act in the two poems of 'Coriolan', where, first, amid the turmoil of the crowd at the parade, the people think they find their answer in the military leader:

'O hidden under the dove's wing, hidden in the turtle's breast, / Under the palmtree at noon, under the running water / At the still point of the turning world. O hidden.' But then, ironically, it appears in the second poem that the difficulties of a statesman have led him also to seek the still point: 'O hidden under the...

Hidden under the... Where the dove's foot rested and locked for a moment, / A still moment, repose of noon.' The lyric of Phlebas acts as such a moment of repose, a nodal moment, tying together the strands of the poem, as Pound explained. And the fourth part, the short lyric, in all the *Four Quartets,* performs a similar function of poise and knotting, as the poem finds a temporary rest where themes and images and voices merge for a moment.

One voice of great importance speaks at the close of the Phlebas lyric, which is not simply a translation from Eliot's poem in French, *Dans le Restaurant,* for the closing lines are quite different. The French poem ends in an offhand, conversational tone: 'Figurez-vous donc, c'était un sort pénible; / Cependant, ce fut jadis un bel homme, de haut taille.' (Imagine then, it was a distressing fate; / Nevertheless, he was once a handsome man, of tall stature). In *The Waste Land* Eliot has changed the tone from conversational to prophetic by evoking the voice of St Paul addressing 'both Jew and Gentile' in his epistle to the Romans: 'Gentile or Jew / O you who turn the wheel and look to windward, / Consider Phlebas, who was once handsome and tall as you.' A similar effect is created by Pound's critical slashing away of all those weak and in part offensive Popeian couplets at the outset of part III of *The Waste Land* manuscript. 'Do something different,' Pound advised. So Eliot did: he pencilled on the back of the manuscript page a draft of the new opening passage, 'The river's tent is broken...' — lines that stress the eternal presence of the river within the waste land, culminating in the line that echoes the voice of the psalmist in exile: 'By the waters of Leman I sat down and wept', with its attendant question, 'How shall we sing the Lord's song in a strange land?'

A similar concentration upon the emergence of the prophetic voice is created by the removal of the monologue that opens *The Waste Land* manuscript, the monologue of the rowdy Irishman telling of a night on the town in Boston. This was excised by Eliot himself, perhaps under Pound's influence, perhaps because Eliot himself saw that the rowdy vitality of those singing, drinking men who stage a footrace in the dawn's early light does not accord with the voice that follows, the voice of one who is so reluctant to live that April becomes the cruelest month. That excision brings us quickly to the voice of a modern Ezekiel, speaking the famous lines:

What are the roots that clutch, what branches grow
Out of this stony rubbish? Son of man,
You cannot say, or guess, for you know only
A heap of broken images.

Then these lines of true prophecy play their contrapuntal music against the voice of the false prophet, Madame Sosostris.

But I need to explain what I mean by the prophetic voice. With William Blake, we should discard the notion that the prophet's main function is to foretell the future. If, like Blake, we think of the biblical prophets, we will recall at once that they spend a great deal of time in denouncing the evils of the present, evils that derive from the people's worship of false gods and the pursuit of wealth and worldly pleasures. Prophecies of the future appear, but these are often prophecies of the disasters that will fall upon the people if they do not mend their evil ways.

Denunciation of present evil is the primary message of the Hebrew prophet: he is a reformer, his mind is upon the present. But then he also offers the consolation of future good, if the people return to worship of the truth. Thus the voice of the prophet tends to oscillate between denunciation and consolation: he relates visions of evil and good, mingling within the immense range of his voice the most virulent excoriation and the most exalted lyrics. This, I think, is exactly the sort of oscillation that we find in Pound's *Cantos* and *The Waste Land*.

Eliot admitted that he "placed before [Pound] in Paris the manuscript of a scrawling, chaotic poem"; in his hesitation to claim those discontinuities as signs of power, he resembles Prufrock—unerect, indecisive, unable to come to the point. Pound treats the manuscript of *The Waste Land* as if it were an effeminate Prufrock he wishes to rouse: he cures the poem of its hysteria by suggesting that representations of the feminine be cut, and by urging Eliot to make his language less qualified. Pound, who wrote to Eliot,

"May your erection never grow less," approved of neither the poem's nor the man's sexual neurasthenia. Within a sequence of opposites, pairs that glide into each other and, in my hands, often blur (straight / gay, man / woman, active / passive, willful / indecisive), Pound urges his friend to inhabit the primary term; however, by metaphorically impregnating Eliot, Pound places him in a passive position that they must have considered unmanly.

Pound's gestures are paradoxical, he denounces instances of linguistic effeminacy, and yet the very act of intruding commentary is homosexually charged. In the "erection" letter to Eliot, Pound writes, "I merely queeried the dialect of 'thence', dare say it is o.k." The act of queerying—critiquing, editing, collaborating—has suspicious overtones of queerness, inferences which Pound highlights and denies. In discussing Pound's ambiguous "queeries," I will put aside questions of literary quality. Focusing only on whether or not Pound's suggestions were justified blinds us to other motives for his excisions. I would like to offer a different reading of Pound's

Caesarian performance. Because Pound sought to establish Eliot's primacy in literary history with *The Waste Land,* he disapproved of beginning the poem with an epigraph from Joseph Conrad, a living writer.

In the "obstetric" letter, Pound wrote to Eliot. "I doubt if Conrad is weighty enough to stand the citation." I suspect that Pound objected not merely to Conrad's lack of eminence, but to the epigraph's content: a passage from *Heart of Darkness* ("The horror! the horror!"), it records a man crying out in fear of the dark (and feminine) continent. Beginning the poem with a cry of emasculated terror would not help keep Eliot erect. However, in this letter to Eliot, Pound criticizes another portion of the poem by echoing the very language of horror he disliked in the epigraph. "It also, to your horror probably, reads aloud very well. Mouthing out his OOOOOOze."

Pound uses words that reflect *The Waste Land*'s fear of things that gape: he mentions "the body of the poem," and describes his Sage Homme verses as a "bloody impertinence" which should be placed "somewhere where they would be decently hidden and swamped by the bulk of accompanying matter."

Pound describes the poem's body in a language of mouths, horror, blood, and swamps—a vocabulary calculated to affect Eliot, who thought of his verse as a woman's "purulent offensive discharge."

Pound separated *The Waste Land* from dread female discharge by criticizing Eliot's portraits of women. Pound questioned the lines—"'You gave me hyacinths first a year ago, / 'They called me the hyacinth girl'"—with the marginal annotation, "Marianne," which, according to critic Barbara Everett, refers to the heroine of the Pierre Marivaux novel *La Vie de Marianne,* a work whose "Frenchness" attracted Eliot. Did Pound object to these lines because "hyacinth" signified homosexuality, and because Eliot—impersonating a hyacinth girl—was indulging in French tendencies? (Pound remembers the note as a possible reference to Tennyson's Mariana; perhaps he disapproved of Eliot's identification with this pining hysteric, an emblem of the kind of Victorian poetry that modernists condemned as effete.) Pound tersely indicts these lines as mere "photography":

"My nerves are bad tonight. Yes, bad. Stay with me.
"Speak to me. Why do you never speak. Speak.
"What are you thinking of? What thinking? What?
"I never know what you are thinking. Think."

Pound wrote "photo" beside the line, "Are you alive, or not? Is there nothing in your head?" Pound faulted these passages for their photographic style—cheaply realistic, insufficiently wrought by artistic muscle—and for their subject: these snapshots portray Eliot as neurasthenic, silent, unable to satisfy his wife, and portray Vivien as hysterically adamant.

Nothing fills the husband's head: he is the gaping "horror" of the cancelled epigraph. Vivien, the camera's subject, commented that these lines were "WONDERFUL," and added a further photographic line which Eliot kept "What you get married for if you dont want to have children". Lil may refuse to have children, but the "nothing" husband was guilty of a truly hysterical reluctance—the refusal to speak.

The portrait of a lady that Pound most wholeheartedly blotted out was a swathe of Pope-like couplets concerning Fresca. In the typescript, Pound dismissed the whole passage with the comment, "rhyme drags it out to diffuseness", but only crossed out the four lines which portrayed her as poet:

From such chaotic misch-masch potpourri
What are we to expect but poetry?
When restless nights distract her brain from sleep
She may as well write poetry, as count sheep.

Eliot had described his poem as "chaotic"; Pound called it a "masterpiece." Pound, as male collaborator and editor, divides Eliot's discourse from Fresca's, and ensures that readers do not confuse the chaotic *Waste Land* with Fresca's chaotic potpourri, Eliot's masterpiece with Fresca's hysteric fits, Eliot's Uranian muse with Fresca's forays into gay and lesbian writers:

"Fresca was baptised in a soapy sea / Of Symonds—Walter Pater—Vernon Lee". Pound's revisions intend to save Eliot from seeming like soapy Symonds. By crossing out Fresca,

Pound suggests that Eliot begin "The Fire Sermon" with the narrator, an "I," "Musing upon the king my brother's wreck / And on the king my father's death before him." Pound lets this depiction of a dead king and wrecked brother remain: male royalty, even when dismembered, seemed preferable to a woman reading lesbian literature in the bathtub.

Pound particularly objected to syntactic inversion—which suggests, in turn, sexual inversion. The word "inversion" mattered to Pound. He wrote, in a letter to Eliot, "I should leave it as it is, and NOT invert," and commented in the manuscript, "Inversions not warranted by any real exigence of metre". For Pound, inverted word order, a dated poetic affectation, implied the aesthete's "nacre" and "objets d'art." Pound wrote "1880" and "Why this Blot on Scutchen *between* 1922 & Lil" beside

And if it rains, the closed carriage at four.
And we shall play a game of chess:
The ivory men make company between us
Pressing lidless eyes and waiting for a knock upon the door.

These lines clashed with the nearby jazzy "O O O O that ShakespeherIan Rag" and "hurry up please it's time." But Pound disliked the passage for reasons other than its dated tonality; he found fault with the scene of sexual inaction between husband and wife, and accused Eliot of a sexual and stylistic listlessness. Modernism defined itself in opposition to that "1880" of literary and sexual ennui.

As hysterical discourse, *The Waste Land* remains as passive as Coleridge's wedding-guest: the poem invites a reader to master it. Uniwilling to explain itself, requiring a reader-as-collaborator ("mon semblable, —mon frère!") to unravel its disguises, it remains passive toward a "frère" whose attentions it solicits by this technique of direct presentation without transitions. Modernist ideograms refuse to soften the image's blow with commentary, and place the reader in the active though reluctant role of elucidator.

Between two men, passivity and activity have sexual valences that the poem bodies forth in its thematics of violation, and the hysterical discontinuities, aphasias, and amnesias that follow from the repressed moment of surrender. Eliot's abulia creates antitheses of itself in the "flushed and decided" young man carbuncular, or the sailor (in excised portions from "Death by Water") who aims his "concentrated will against the tempest and the tide".

Despite these representations of sexual will, the poem's heart is in its passivity toward interpretation, the moments of collage, potpourri, and fragmentation which place enormous faith in the reader as analyst.

In this sense, Eliot's manuscript reads like the premonition of Pound's arrival: the text implies a second man who might interpret its absences. Eliot's dismissal of his work as merely chaotic, and his passivity toward revision, correspond to the poem's own willingness to stay broken. Eliot could "connect nothing with nothing"; it remained for Pound to redefine disjunction, to convert female hysteria, through male collaboration, back into a powerful discourse.

Indeed, Pound's revisions changed *The Waste Land* from a series of *poems* into a unity which he trumpeted as "the longest *poem* in the English langwidge," nineteen pages "without a break." With its feigned seamlessness, the poem avoids the bodily breaks that Claude the Cabin Boy, Philomel, and Coriolanus must suffer. Though Pound himself penetrates the poem by editing it, Eliot owed him the illusion of unbroken textual hymen, and the accompanying sense of power.

By giving his text to Pound, Eliot set up the paradigm for the relationship that readers and critics have established with *The Waste Land*: man to man. The footnotes embody the implied male reader they invite him to enter and understand the poem. They demonstrate that the poem has absences which an external body must fill. The footnotes give value to the poem's hysteria, and transform it from meaningless chaos into allusiveness. Readers armed with the notes have approached *The Waste Land* not as if it were a fragment of hysterical discourse, but an artifact converted, by Pound's mediation, into something masculine.

Conrad Aiken, on the poem's publication wrote that it succeeds "by virtue of its incoherence, not of its plan"; if a woman had written a proudly incoherent text, how would its absences have been judged? *The Waste Land* has always been a scene of implicit collaboration between the male poet and his male reader, in which Eliot's hysterical discourse—by the act of collusive interpretation, by the reader's analytic listening—suffers a sea-change into masculinity.

Eliot used hysterical discourse to invoke the corrective affections of another man. Together, they performed an ambiguous act they engaged in a symbolic scene of homosexual intercourse while freeing themselves from imputations of inverted style.

Collaboration was particularly popular in the fin de siècle among men who wrote together to define their distance from homosexuality sometimes this distance was not more than a few inches, though they made it seem like miles. In the next section, by reading doubly authored works of the 1880s, 1890s, and early 1900s (texts contemporaneous with *Studies on Hysteria* and *Sexual Inversion*), I hope to reveal the roots of Pound's and Eliot's Uranian experiment. By 1922, when *The Waste Land* emerged, its double authorship concealed, male collaboration had already earned a reputation for perversity.

The peculiar "obstetrics" to which the manuscript of the poem was subjected has often been discussed. It is generally agreed that Pound's cuts transformed a chaotic mass of poetry into a precise, aggressively modern masterpiece.

Koestenbaum contends that the poem was "feminine" in its original form but transformed radically by Pound s assertive masculinity. We might indeed he tempted to see in this productive coediting of a great poem the shift away from a bisexuality that left open many potentialities to masculine values mistakenly identified with the essence of high modernism. Moreover, Eliot's prose poem "Hysteria" already points toward such a feminized pathologia. Koestenbaum writes "Eliot's poem—semiotic, negative, riddled with absences—is 'feminine' not because women always sound like *The Waste Land*, but because, in 1922, its style might have seemed more recognizable a hysterical woman's than a male poet's."

He adds curiously "Hysteria is a disturbance in language, and the very word 'hysteria' marks it as a woman's affliction"—which seems to imply that there is no male hysteria! Such an etymological fundamentalism is strange in a critic who wishes to reread modernism from the point of view of gay discourse.

Koestenbaum's predilection for the anus starts from an understandable rehabilitation but leads him into absurdities at times (as when he sees the fatefully repressed organ in Eliot's identification with a "broken Coriol-anus" or when he reads a double inscription of 'anus" in the way Pound dates a letter "24 Saturnus, An 1").

Whereas I am entirely ready to see the enigma of bisexuality as one of the most intriguing subplots of the *Waste Land,* I think that the attempt to queer Eloit and Pound's collaboration leads to a series of misreadings.

The most crucial case in point is Pound's rather bawdy letter written to celebrate the "birth" of the poem. This well-known piece of male bantering had been expurgated in D. D. Paige's edition of Pound's letters and was only published in full in the first volume of Eliot's *Letters of T.S. Eliot.* In the letter, Pound assumes the function of a midwife or rather 'sage homme," a masculinization of the French *sage-femme* (midwife):

"These are the Poems of Eliot / By the Uranian Muse begot, / A Man their mother was, / A Muse their Sire." The letter leaves no doubt as to the role Pound has chosen: he is only the midwife ("Ezra performed the caesarean operation") and not the impregnator of his friend. From the suppressed lines in which Pound speaks of his own masturbatory activity, Koestenbaum finds an argument for his having actually "fathered" the poem. In fact, Pound merely laments his own impotence, or the fact that his masturbatory writing has prevented him from producing really *modern* creations, such as *Ulysses* or the *Waste Land*:

E. P. hopeless and unhelped
Enthroned in the marmorean skies
His verse omits realities,
Angelic hands with mother of pearl

Retouch the
Balls and balls and balls again
Can not touch his fellow men.
His foaming and abundant cream
Has coated his world. The coat of a dream;
Or say that the upjut of sperm
Has rendered his sense pachyderm.

The ironic self-portrait is quite in the mode of Mauberly's derision. What is deprecated is Pound's too easy recourse to an ananistic "dangerous supplement"— which apparently takes "strapping servant girls" as libidinal objects rather than, say, Eliot's anus. This is why I cannot agree with Koestenbaum's conclusion: "Pound, Eliot's male muse, is the sire of *The Waste Land*."

Koestenbaum superimposes two scenes: the scene described in the June 1921 postscript to Pound's translation of *The Natural Philosopy of Love* by Remy de Gourmont, in which Pound sees himself as an overactive phallus fertilizing the passive vulva of London, and the many traces of femininity left in Eliot's *Wastle Land*.

But Koestenbaum forgets that one of the major consequences of Pound's excisions was to make it much more of a London poem than it had been originally. Pound has not deleted the "femininity" of the poem: he has "framed" it, as it were, within a mythical discourse that is less "male" or "phallocratic" than neutral.

Such is the effect of the famous beginning of the poem ("April is the cruelest month"), which leaves the voice anonymous, the "we" asexual and floating in the void, until we hear it modulate into Marie Larisch's familiar confidences.

In view of these complex issues, I would emphasize instead the disjunctive nature of Eliot and Pound's collaboration and stress that the blind spots in their joint parturition left what I again would like to call textual ghosts. It is true that Pound drastically modified the draft given to him. He reduced it by half, deleted the long opening describing a night out in Boston ("He Do the Police in Different Voices"), suppressed the hesitations, the autobiographical tone, and some of the pastiches of classical genres, and hence changed the polyphonic texture or tessitura of the poem.

Pound also tried to eliminate all the reminiscences of "Prufrock," as Koestenbaum aptly notes: "Eliot's wobbliness was made flesh in Prufrock, echoes of which Pound sought to cut," but while he was impatient with Tiresias as a central figure (Pound originally felt the same misguided distaste for Leopold Bloom who, according to him, unduly supplanted Stephen Dedalus), going so far as to write "make up / yr mind / you Tiresias / if you know / know damn well / or / else you / dont" [*sic*] in the margin, he never persuaded Eliot to change anything substantially in the characterization of the blind and bisexual seer.

Strangely enough, what annoys Pound also annoys Koestenbaum, who would prefer to see Eliot "come out," as it were, rather than hide in ambiguities and ambivalences. Yet it us precisely these hesitations (as later *Finnegans Wake* will be written in a systematically undecidable language) that make up the irreducible force of its modernist poetry. This corresponds to the fact that modernism as such, despite Hugh Kenner's insistence, cannot be reduced so easily and univocally to a phallocratic stance. In a way, this would lead us to admit that high modernism, too, is "softer" than we thought and also closer to Verlaine than to Rimbaud.

If Tiresias is the most important figure of the poem, as Eliot's central note clearly states, is it not because he embodies a hysterical bisexuality of which Eliot was dreaming at the time? This fantasy cannot be reduced to the clear-cut opposites suggested by Koestenbaum: "Through Tiresias, Eliot describes (from the inside) an epoch we might call The Age of Inversion, when heterosexuality was in the process of being undermined and traduced by its eerie opposite." If indeed the Tiresias paradigm provides Eliot with another "epoch," it us less a dream of inversion than of ecstatic fusion, a dream expressed in the deleted poem, "The Death of Saint Narcissus":

First he was sure that he had been a tree
Twisting its branches among each other
And tangling its roots among each other

Then he knew that he had been a fish
With slippery white belly held tight in his own fingers
Writhing in his own clutch, his ancient beauty
Caught fast in the pink tips of his new beauty.
Then he had been a young girl
Caught in the woods by a drunken old man
Knowing at the end the taste of her own whiteness
The horror of her own smoothness,
And he felt drunken and old.

Here, Eliot rewrites Nietzsche's praise of dancers in *Thus Spake Zarathustra* through a myth of metempsychosis that borrows from Empedocles' famous distych according to which the Greek philosopher had once been "a boy and a girl, a bush, a bird and a fish," and from Buddha's own transformations: these ascetic "rapes" were to lead him to the way of absolute compassion.

The rape of a passive girl by an old man whose taste lingers in bitterly in the speaker's memories, the Buddhist acquiescence to universal metamorphosis, the Keatsian rapture at selflessness – all this sums up what Pound intensely dislikes. This compendium of Eastern mysticism and Western "negative capability" has remained to this date a textual ghost (now and then added to Eliot's collected works as a curious appendix), outside of the canon constituted by Pound. This shows a different Eliot, closer to Flaubert when he could identify utterly with Emma Bovary and the setting of her love scenes.

The joint attempt by Pound and Eliot to provide a justification for the "modern movement" by publishing at last a modernist masterpiece derives from the very high claims they had made for themselves. All this looks a little like a wholesale takeover bid, a tender offer on European culture, seen as a whole from two conflicting and half-imaginary opposites: Eastern mysticism on the one hand (Pound rewrites Eliot's more metaphysical drift in his Chinese idiom) and the American pseudo-wilderness on the other.

In a letter to his British friend, Mary Hutchinson, Eliot makes a revealing admission, just as he announces his essay on "Tradition" as forthcoming. He concludes a discussion of the different meanings of "culture" and "civilization" on a more personal note:

"But remember that I am a *metic*—a foreigner, and that I *want* to understand you, and all the background and tradition of you. I shall try to be frank—because the attempt is so very much worthwhile with you — it is very difficult with me — both by inheritance and because of my suspicious and cowardly disposition. But I may simply prove to be a savage." In this wildly flirtatious tone, Eliot conflates images of barbarism and strong moral values inherited from his family, thus discovering the best word to introduce himself (in every sense): a *metic,* that is, an alien who has been admitted into the city (as in Athens), who has been granted certain rights and pays taxes but cannot have full citizenship or access to the most intimate mysteries.

The metic, both inside and outside, is thus defined from within the polis, which also accounts for the thematic centrality of the city as metropolis in the *Waste Land*: Oedipus's Thebes, Augustine's Carthage, and Baudelaire's Paris are superimposed upon a London where the city provides a fulcrum for international capitalism. Indeed, the suppressed passage beginning with "He Do the Police in Different Voices" looks back to Dickens's London with the subtle allusion to Betty Higden's praise of Sloppy in *Our Mutual Friend*: Sloppy manages to recreate different policemen's voices when he reads to her, thanks to his wonderful mimetic abilities. Here, "police" rhymes ironically with polis, while metic leads to a "mimetic" who remains well hidden in the "world's metropolis" (as Mr. Podsnap says). The ending of the *Waste Land* finally releases all the voices that had been kept more or less separate and creates a bewildering vortex of hysterical polyphony. This is also a dominant feature in Pound's *Cantos*: we keep hearing individual voices whose interaction creates an epic through counterpoint. However, this similarity should not blind us to a crucial divergence—which shall oblige me to examine a last "uncoupling."

If Pound and Eliot agree that "tradition" supposes an "historical sense" that sees the presence of the past as well as its pastness (since "It is dawn at Jerusalem while midnight hovers above the Pillars of Hercules. All ages are contemporaneous," as the preface to the *Spirit of Romance* momentously states), then they would not translate the Greek concept of polis in exactly the same way. T

hough both are indeed metics in the British Empire, they opt for different strategies of assimilation and adaptation. Pound always sees the polis in its original Greek meaning, as a religious and political context determined by local polytheism and the domination of a few brilliant minds. Eliot, on the other hand, follows the conclusions of his investigation into European roots and therefore revives linguistic energies dormant in Virgil, Augustine, and Dante.

He translates the polis into the "City" (of God or men), that is, into Augustine's *civitas.* As Emile Benveniste has shown, polis cannot be translated into civitas without some distortion. In the Greek mind, polis is a concept that predetermines the definition of the citizen as *polites.* One is a citizen because one partakes of the abstract concept of the polis, a linguistic radical divided between sameness and otherness, belonging and rejection.

In the Latin mentality, the adjective *civis* comes first, the radical is anterior to the derivation of civitas (meaning "city" in the sense of a group of people living together, and not *Urbs,* reserved for Rome, the "capital"). In the Latin model, actual people as citizens help derive the concept: thus, civitas refers to a community understood as a mutuality, a collection of mutual obligations.

Eliot's choice of a quote from *Our Mutual Friend* to highlight the polyphonic nature of urban discourse out of which contemporary civility must emerge is hardly accidental. Nor was Pound's erasure of the same motif random. Pound's historical point of departure is the American Revolution, seen as the birth of the modern idea of the just state and "volitionist" politics; Eliot consistently returns to the English Revolution as the main "catastrophe" of the modern world.

According to Eliot, the introduction of the new parliamentary democracy triggered all its attendant negative side effects: the loss of centralized values and the "dissociation of sensibility," which had weakened British culture since the seventeenth century. Thus, Pound is ready to acclaim the "Tovarishes" of the Soviet Revolution in his first cantos, while Eliot condemns the uprising as chaotic, atheistic and "drunken" (through a German quotation taken from Hesse) in the notes to the *Waste Land*.

Pound's specific mode of hysterization leads him to play the eccentric, to leave the confines of the Empire, and to embrace Mussolini as a symbolic father, out of sheer ignorance of his regime's true nature—all the while insisting that he was fighting against ignorance! Eliot, who knew better, and maybe knew too much, chose the opposite strategy, becoming more British than the British after 1927 and his conversion to Anglo-Catholicism and devising a new and quite personal game of hide-and-seek with high culture.

The literary "ghost" produced by such a disjunction must be found in the way Eliot's success in British and American culture served to acclimatize modernism as a purely intellectual adventure—a "betrayal" that was deeply lamented by William Carlos Williams.

The "monsters" Eliot was led to suppress indeed concerned sexuality as well as politics, as Koestenbaum suggests, but his attitude led to dissimilar enabling or disabling strategies if we compare him with Pound who, at least, never really tried to hide his peculiar monsters. These finally brought about the sublimation of modernism into academic enshrining, while at the same time Eliot himself had embraced the values of a revisited classicism. The real ghost generated by the coupling/uncoupling collaboration between Pound and Eliot was in fact just a word: the term "modernism," which could then be thrown as a sop to the academics of the entire world.

The Waste Land is a much more complex case—in part because the poem that Eliot wrote and the poem that was published differ considerably. *The Waste Land* would have openly established popular culture as a major intertext of modernist poetry if Pound had not edited out most of Eliot's popular references.

Though Pound, like Eliot, assailed the "very pernicious current idea that a good book must be of necessity a dull one," he did not consider contemporary popular culture seriously as a potential antidote to literary dullness. His work on *The Waste Land* simply made the poem more Poundian: he collapsed its levels of cultural appeal while leaving its internationalism and historicism intact, recasting the poem as the first major counteroffensive in high culture's last stand. To be sure, almost all Pound's emendations improve the poem, and Eliot acceded to the recommendations of "*il miglior fabbro*" in virtually every instance.

Still, part of Eliot's original impulse in composing *The Waste Land* was lost in this collaboration precisely because Pound's relation to the cultural divide differed from Eliot's own. Had Eliot improved rather than deleted the passages condemned by Pound, he might have given literary modernism a markedly different spin.

The manuscript of *The Waste Land* shows Eliot drawing on popular song to a greater extent than he uses the Grail myth in the final version. For the long idiomatic passage that was to have opened the poem he considered several lyrics from popular musicals. "I'm proud of all the Irish blood that's in me / There's not a man can say a word agin me," he quotes from a George M. Cohan show; from two songs in the minstrel tradition he constructs "Meet me in the shadow of the watermelon Vine / Eva Iva Uva Emmaline"; from *The Cubanola Glide* he takes "Tease, Squeeze lovin & wooin / Say Kid what're y' doin.'" The characters' nocturnal spree then takes them to a bar that Eliot frequented after attending melodramas in Boston:

Blew into the Opera Exchange,
Sopped up some gin, sat in to the cork game,
Mr. Fay was there, singing "The Maid of the Mill."

Pointing out that these lines are "the first examples in the draft of [Eliot's] famous techniques of quotation and juxtaposition," Michael North suggests a direct connection between the miscellaneous format of the minstrel show—or, one might add, the English music hall—and the very form of

The Waste Land. But the hints of popular song that survive in the published *Waste Land* are eclipsed by the more erudite allusions that dominate the poem.

Thanks to the deletion of the original opening section, for example, the first line places the poem squarely within the "great tradition" of English poetry. A long poem called *The Waste Land* that begins, "April is the cruellest month," largely shaped the course of literature and criticism for years to follow. One can only imagine the effect of a long poem called *He Do the Police in Different Voices* beginning, "First we had a couple of feelers down at Tom's place."

Chapter 2

"Prufrock" and Hamlet Revisited

No! I am not Prince Hamlet, nor was meant to be" (l. 111), asserts the narrator of Eliot's "Love Song of J. Alfred Prufrock." Let us explore the resemblances between "Prufrock" and *Hamlet* to which Eliot's narrator here obliquely calls our attention.

Begin by noting that "Prufrock"'s *Hamlet* subtext is present from the poem's beginning, in the epigraph spoken by the ghost of Dante's Guido da Montfeltro returned from Hell (just as the ghost of King Hamlet returned from Purgatory) to tell us the horrors which have been visited upon him.

Though the ghostly visitations have differing effects in their respective works, they colour the self-perceptions of both Hamlet and Prufrock. The ghost of Hamlet's father prompts Hamlet to action and self-reproach; the ghost of Guido, whose words are positioned so that they appear to be a response to a question posed by Prufrock himself, appears to be assuring Prufrock and his readers that he answers Prufrock's implied question only because he assumes he is speaking to a fellow denizen of hell.

Like Hamlet, Prufrock is perplexed by an "overwhelming question" (l. 10). Though that question is at no point explicitly articulated in Eliot's poem, several large questions are implied: Does life have meaning? Will the woman to whom Prufrock's love song is addressed accept his marriage proposal? Is the ghost who addresses Prufrock in the poem's epigraph a "true" ghost whose tale is to be believed (the question which perplexes Hamlet) or is it a false ghost attempting to lure him to damnation?

Like Hamlet, Prufrock inhabits a world in which something seems rotten and time seems out of joint. Prufrock's evening bears the lifeless aspect of a "patient etherised upon a table" (l. 3). The would be singer of a love song has "a bald spot in the middle" of his "hair" (l. 40). His "arms and legs are thin!" (l. 44), and he is "afraid" (l. 86). The streets he must travel "follow like a tedious argument / Of insidious intent" (ll. 8-9). The voices in the chamber which he visits are "dying with a dying fall" (l. 52).

The world itself seems to Prufrock, as it did to Hamlet, "stale," for he has "measured out [his] life with coffee spoons" (l. 51). Like Hamlet, he has "lost all [his] mirth, foregone all custom of exercises," and the earth itself "appeareth nothing to [him] but a foul and pestilent congregation of vapours" (II.ii.296-303). This last phrase seems to me to lie behind Prufrock's preoccupation with the soot-colored "fog" which has fallen "asleep" on the "October night" (ll. 21-22).

Like Hamlet, Prufrock has a troubled relationship with the women in his life, feels some awkwardness contemplating female sexuality – or so his brooding on the "light brown hair" which downs the ladies' arms (and doubtless other body parts) suggests. So too does the peevish response he imagines the woman offering in response to his "overwhelming question": "That is not what I meant at all / That is not it, at all" (ll. 97-98).

Although Prufrock (l. 44) is neither "fat" nor "scant of breath" as is Hamlet (V.ii.290), he experiences at one moment a situation analogous to Hamlet's in his duel with Laertes (V.ii), when he finds himself prospectively "sprawling on a pin, /...pinned and wriggling on the wall" (ll. 57-58). Like Hamlet (II.ii.322-323), Prufrock seems "delight[ed]" neither by man nor by woman. In Prufrock's case, as in Hamlet's, "the native hue of resolution /Is sicklied o'er with the pale cast of thought" (III.I.84-85). Like Hamlet as well, Prufrock must "prepare a face to meet the faces that you meet" (l. 27) The face Hamlet prepares is one of madness. The face that Prufrock prepares is one of feigned confidence – confidence that will permit him, for instance, to "dare" ascend the stair rather than "turn back" (ll. 38-39). In both instances the time that is given to "prepare a face to meet the faces that you meet" is granted for the purpose of giving its wearer "time to murder" (l. 28) – an action which the utterly passive Prufrock is incapable of carrying out but is obviously as capable of contemplating as is Hamlet.

Prufrock resembles Hamlet in his indecision, in his ineffectuality, in his incapacitation by overthought, in his sensitivity to the eyes of those others for whom he must "prepare a face," in his awareness that his auditor is prying him for information, examining his expression as her "hands... lift and drop a question on [his] plate" (ll. 29-30) Hamlet tells Guildenstern,

"You would play upon me; you would seem to know my stops; you would pluck out the heart of my mystery; you would sound me from my lowest note to the top of my compass" (III.ii.355-358), sounding very much as Prufrock does when he tells us he feels "as if a magic lantern threw the nerves in patterns on a screen".

Like Hamlet, Prufrock has "known the eyes already, known them all –/The eyes that fix you in a formulated phrase" (ll. 55-56) and seek to compel him, as Claudius, Gertrude, Polonius, Rosencrantz, and Guildenstern had sought to compel Hamlet, "To spit out all the butt-ends of my days and ways" (l. 60).

Prufrock is a less heroic character than Hamlet, of course — as witness the disparity between Prufrock's frail body and the bodies of Michelangelo's massively limbed and confidently muscled nude statutes of which the ladies in the room are evidently talking.

Prufrock is a smaller prince than Hamlet — more concerned about his dress, more tightly cravated, less fiercely armed. His tie is "asserted" not with a "bare bodkin" but by a "simple pin" (l. 43) directed perpetually toward his heart. It is not a king whom he wonders if he "dare[s]" dispatch but a "peach" (l. 122). Prufrock's "lovesong" is an ineffectual one, as ineffectual as Hamlet's efforts to communicate with the women in his life – with his mother and Ophelia in particular.

The conjectured response of the lady to whom Prufrock would "tell... all" (l. 95) sounds a bit like Hamlet's mother after observing her son's interaction with the invisible ghost of his father: "... you do bend your eye on vacancy/And with the incorporal air do hold discourse" (III.iv.117-118). Hamlet asks, "Do you see nothing there?" His mother responds, "nothing at all (III.iv.133), a phrase that echoes "Prufrock's "That is not it at all, /That is not what I meant, at all" (ll. 109-110).

But Prufrock is of course correct. He is "not Prince Hamlet, nor was meant to be." Rather, he is Polonius, "an attendant lord,"

one that will do
To swell a progress, start a scene or two,
Advise the prince; no doubt, an easy tool,
Deferential, glad to be of use,
Politic, cautious, and meticulous;
Full of high sentence, but a bit obtuse;
At times, indeed, almost ridiculous –
Almost, at times, the Fool.
(ll. 111-119)

Like Polonius, Prufrock is "politic" — aware that "In a minute there is time /For decisions and revisions which a minute will reverse" (ll. 47-48). Like Polonius, he "grow[s] old" (l. 120) and is prone to "digress" — "Full of high sentence," given to excess verbiage, for instance in his insistent deployment of such figures of repetition as epistrophe ("And I have known the eyes already, known them all"; l. 55) and anaphora ("And would it have been worth it, after all, / Would it have been worth while, /After the sunsets..., /After the novels, after the teacups, after the skirts..."; ll. 99-102).

As I have suggested, Prufrock, like Hamlet, must "prepare a face to meet the faces that you meet" (l. 27), in which respect he also resembles woman — and in particular Ophelia — as she is depicted by Hamlet: "God has given you one face and you make yourselves another" (III.i.144-146). And though Prufrock does not "jig and amble," "lisp," or "nick-name God's creatures" (III.i.146-147), he appears to share Ophelia's death wish when he tells us, at the end of the poem,

We have lingered in the chambers of the sea
By sea-girls wreathed with seaweed red and brown
Till human voices wake us, and we drown.
(ll. 128-130)

Why does Prufrock say "we drown"(l. 131) rather than "I drown"? To whom does "we" refer? Here, as in his use of "you" in the first line of the poem, Prufrock seems to be speaking to himself, addressing himself as the hapless other – as he does again when he speaks of having "seen my head... brought in upon a platter" (l. 82). Recall that Hamlet's mother Queen Gertrude reports that "mermaid-like, awhile they [Ophelia's clothes] bore her up..."

(IV,vii.175). Perhaps not incidentally, Prufrock too invokes "mermaids." He does so in the poem's final moments, as a prelude to his drowning: "I have heard the mermaids singing, each to each" (l. 124). It is not with Hamlet or with Polonius but with the scorned sweetheart Ophelia that Prufrock most closely identifies at the poem's conclusion.

Chapter 3

The Making of "Journey of the Magi"

T. S. Eliot was born on September 26, 1888, in St. Louis, Missouri, with a congenital hernia which kept him quiet as a child and out of school until he was seven or eight years old. Eliot remembers these years and the years that he attended Smith Academy and then Milton Academy in New England as happy times.

After this, Eliot concentrated on philosophy, especially Hindu and Buddhist philosophy, as a student at Harvard University in order to know the truth not only of the age but of life as a whole (Pinion 9-12). After his studies at Harvard were complete, Eliot transferred to Merton College in Oxford, England, where he met Vivienne Haigh-Wood, whom he married on June 26, 1915. But by the end of 1915, Vivienne took ill, an event that was the beginning of health problems for both of them (Pinion 15-26).

In the early years of his first marriage, Eliot would visit churches to admire their beauty; in later years, he visited them for the sake of peace, contemplation, and spiritual refreshment (Pinion 31). Ambition seemed to deepen his sense of marital guilt and, in 1926, while visiting Rome with his brother and sister-in-law, Eliot surprised everyone by kneeling before Michelango's "Pieta."

"Here was a spiritually humble, contrite man ritualizing his acceptance of a higher authority" (Pinion 34). According to Peter Ackroyd, Eliot had a sense of tradition and an instinct for order within himself and found the church and faith gave him this security within a life of frustrations and struggles (159-160). "He was aware of what he called 'the void' in all human affairs—the disorder, meaninglessness, and futility which he found in his own experience; it was inexplicable intellectually... and could only be understood or endured by means of a larger faith" (Ackroyd 160).

Eliot's faith continued to grow and on June 29, 1927, he was baptized in the Anglican-Catholic church. This great event in Eliot's life was done privately and behind closed doors. On the next day Eliot was confirmed by the Bishop (Ackroyd 162).

"Journey of the Magi," the first in a series of poems Eliot later grouped together as the Ariel Poems, was published in August of 1927 shortly after his baptism. Caroline Behr suggests that this poem reflects Eliot's state of mind in transition between his old and new faiths. As Lyndall Gordon suggests, "Journey of the Magi" is one part of Eliot's conversion story in that it tells about his being "ill-at-ease in the 'old dispensation' after his conversion".

It has been reported that Vivienne was against his conversion and this added to their marital problems (Sharpe 116). In 1933, Eliot separated from Vivienne and then, in 1949, while working for Faber and Faber, Eliot met Valerie Fletcher, whom he would later marry. After hearing a recording of "Journey of the Magi," Fletcher had been drawn to Eliot and knew she had to get to know him (Ackroyd 298). From 1957 to his death on January 4, 1965, Eliot's life with Valerie Fletcher was happy and peaceful.

According to Ackroyd, "Thomas Stearns Eliot, in his last years, declared that there had been only two periods of his life when he had been happy—during his childhood, and during his second marriage". Eliot's baptism and writing of "Journey of the Magi" come in between these periods of happiness during times of struggle and uncertainty.

'A cold coming we had of it,
Just the worst time of the year
For a journey, and such a long journey:
The ways deep and the weather sharp,
The very dead of winter.'

And the camels galled, sore-footed, refractory,
Lying down in the melting snow.
There were times we regretted
The summer palaces on slopes, the terraces,
And the silken girls bringing sherbet.
Then the camel men cursing and grumbling
And running away, and wanting their liquor and women,
And the night-fires going out, and the lack of shelters,
And the cities hostile and the towns unfriendly
And the villages dirty and charging high prices:
A hard time we had of it.
At the end we preferred to travel all night,
Sleeping in snatches,
With the voices singing in our ears, saying
That this was all folly.
Then at dawn we came down to a temperate valley,
Wet, below the snow line, smelling of vegetation;
With a running stream and a water-mill beating the darkness,
And three trees on the low sky,
And an old white horse galloped away in the meadow.
Then we came to a tavern with vine leaves over the lintel,
Six hands at an open door dicing for pieces of silver,
And feet kicking the empty wine-skins.
But there was no information, and so we continued
And arrived at evening, not a moment too soon
Finding the place; it was (you may say) satisfactory.
All this was a long time ago, I remember,
And I would do it again, but set down
This set down
This: were we led all that way for
Birth or Death? There was a Birth, certainly,
We had evidence and no doubt. I had seen birth and death,
But had thought they were different; this Birth was
Hard and bitter agony for us, like Death, our death.
We returned to our places, these Kingdoms,
But no longer at ease here, in the old dispensation,
With an alien people clutching their gods.
I should be glad of another death.

MAJOR IMAGES FOUND

First Five Lines: The first five lines were "lifted from Lancelot Andrewes's Nativity Sermon of 1622, and modified"; Eliot happened to be himself steeped in Andrewes at the time... but basically he used them because he needed a second voice to precipitate the poetic drama. They must be understood as being read by, or to, the magus and thereby occasioning his own flow of memory" (Barbour 190-91).

Cities Hostile: According to Dean, these are "all places which remind the travellers, by their violent contrast, of the place of contentment they have deserted" ("Confrontation with Christianity" 76). Traveling through these forboding places, "Eliot's Magus hastens to end an unpleasant journey; what he 'regretted' is the vanishing of 'the silken girls bringing sherbet'" (Harris 840).

Temperate valley: Dean points out that the early morning descent into a "temperate valley" evokes three significant Christian events: "The nativity and all the attendant ideas of the dawning of a new era... the empty tomb of Easter... as well the image of the Second Coming and the return of Christ from the East, dispelling darkness as the Sun of Righteousness" ("Confrontation with Christianity" 77). Wohlpart adds that the Magi's dawn arrival is "symbolic of the new life attained from their penance".

Beating the darkness: Dean notes Elizabeth Drew's view that "'beating the darkness' can refer to the triumph and victory of Christ, a conquering that could occur in the events of Christ's earthly life, or in His resurrection, or in His return in glory at the end of time" (Quoted in Dean, "Confrontation with Christianity" 77).

Three trees: To Dean, the image of the three trees "seems clearly to be a reference to the crosses of Calvary" ("Confrontation with Christianity" 78). Barbour writes, "It is appropriate that his [the Magus'] language... unwittingly evoke [sic] the Crucifixion".

White horse: Dean refers to Robert Kaplan and Richard Wall's suggestion that "the white horse is 'perhaps a reference to the militaristic and conquering Christ of Revelation...'"; "However," he continues, "there is nothing in the poem to indicate that the horse is being ridden; on the contrary, it seems more natural to assume that the horse is riderless..." ("Confrontation with Christianity" 78).

Dean also quotes Kaplan and Wall's speculation that the horse is symbolic of the "death of paganism under the onslaught of Christianity," and notes Nancy Hargrove's suggestion that "the horse's 'being old... perhaps represents the old dispensation that will fade away with Christ's birth'".

Satisfactory: R. D. Brown writes that "the obvious meaning [of the word "satisfactory"] is 'expiatory,' payment for a debt or sin". Barbour, however, sees a more complex connotation: "The parenthetical remark/gesture dramatizes a certain drawing back at the end into something between understatement and velleity.

The key word is the ambiguous 'satisfactory,' emphasized by rhythm and position, which for us, though not the magus, evokes the Thirty Nine Articles, expiation, and the Atonement". In addition, E. F. Burgess sees the word "satisfactory" as evidence that "every condition of prophecy was met, leaving the alienated magus... stranded, suspended between the realization and the consummation of God's plan".

Old dispensation: Dean quotes Geneviene Foster's comment that "The birth of the new era involves the destruction of the old" ("Confrontation with Christianity" 79). Barbour writes that "The Birth he [the magus] saw began the death of his old world, old life, but did not, with the same certainty, give him anything new"; the magus is therefore "alienated from everything 'in the old dispensation'".

NATURE AND CONVERSION IMAGERY

Criticism of T. S. Eliot's "Journey of the Magi" suggests that the images of nature and conversion are representative of the ambiguity of the world. The images of nature are at times beautiful—as in the "fertile valleys" and "running streams"—but are also ominous and dark in other portions of the poem. Images of conversion are also both positive and negative, as they are intended to convey a sense of hope and uncertainty—just as conversion had left an enigmatic feeling in Eliot's own life.

Sean Lucy, in *T. S. Eliot and the Idea of Tradition,* suggests that "Journey of the Magi" is a poem about the unclear nature of conversion. Reading the poem in the context of other religious poems, Lucy suggests that

"Journey of the Magi," "A Song for Simeon" and "Animula"... are all poems of the Christian perspective, they are all poems of acceptance and of resignation to a destiny which is the only possible answer, but which seems to the protagonists, as human beings, almost impossibly hard and painful. They are purgatorial poems.

Here, Lucy uses "acceptance" in the same sentence as "hard," "painful," and "resignation" to demonstrate the grayness of the world. Nothing is black and white; even the glory of the birth of Christ may have negative consequences to some people: "'The Magi' and 'A Song for Simeon' show little of that high joy which the birth of Our Lord can often inspire even in the most austere artists". The Magi don't feel any of that "high joy" because their comfortable place in the world has been changed and they no longer feel at peace.

Leonard Unger discusses "Journey of the Magi" in detail twice in his book *T. S. Eliot: Moments and Patterns,* both times in reference to the nature and conversion imagery. In the first instance, Unger compares both Eliot's and Conrad's use of the word "regret." Unger feels that their definition of the word is to "miss poignantly" and, in the case of Eliot, this would complement the theory of ambiguity in conversion.

The Magi miss the "old dispensation" in which they were at ease before the birth of Christ. Unger also points out that "Images of smell in Eliot's later poetry... are for the most part references to the smell of growing things and of earth and sea... [and are similar to] the 'valley... smelling of vegetation' in 'Journey of the Magi"'.

He concludes that the smells of nature are important in all of Eliot's work and represent "the deepest and most intense kind of awareness". In "Journey of the Magi" this awareness is of the vague nature of the world and the knowledge that conversion will be painful as well as rewarding.

Martin Scofield, in *T. S. Eliot: The Poems,* makes note of the fact that the three Ariel Poems, which includes "Journey of the Magi," should be read in the context of Eliot's baptism and confirmation. This poem is an attempt to describe, poetically, what this experience means:

Eliot clearly chose the magus as a *persona* because he represented the experience of being caught "between two worlds", of having had an intimation of faith but now being left "No longer at ease here, in the old dispensation"—the experience of conversion without the full benefit of assured faith.

In discussing the magi's reactions after the birth of Christ, Scofield suggests that the tone is deliberately anti-climactic and that the reason for the Magi's lack of animated reaction to Christ's birthplace is that the loss of the old ways has put them into a world that has lost its meaning.

According to Elizabeth Drew in *T. S. Eliot: The Design of His Poetry,* nature and conversion are the foundations of the "Journey of the Magi." Drew maintains that the dominant feeling in the poem about conversion is faith without revelation and that "The meaning of the new birth is obscure, full of doubt, accompanied by pain, not joy, and perplexing in the extreme". Her analysis of the conversion imagery is typified by statements like "a bewildering sense of paradox" and "great weariness and disillusionment".

These are not images of a joyous experience or conversion. They reflect the indefinite nature of a world in which positives and negatives often coalesce. Drew also discusses the inexactness of the nature imagery.

To her, the positive nature imagery—the fertile valley and the trees, the old white horse galloping away in the meadow, the vine-leaves over the door of the tavern—speak of "hope and freedom and fruitfulness". However, Drew also reflects on the grimmer images, noting "the hindrances of nature; the cold, the bad roads, the sore-footed camels 'lying down in the melting snow"' and "the implied vision of the three 'trees' on

Golgotha". Drew's juxtaposition shows the ambiguity of the images and the poem itself.

As many critics point out, the three trees foreshadow Christ's crucifixion—on the one hand, a negative image relating to Christ's death but, on the other, a positive image relating to Christ's sacrifice for humanity. Many critics have demonstrated that the ambiguity of the nature and conversion imagery in "Journey of the Magi" is reflective of the author's view of the world as an inexact place.

JOURNEYING TOWARDS AFFIRMATION OF FAITH

T.S. Eliot's poem "Journey of the Magi" describes the journey of the "Wise men from the East" towards Christ and thus, symbolically, towards Christianity. Many critics parallel the Magi's journey with Eliot's own journey in search of "satisfaction" in Christianity. Critics suggest that Eliot's "Journey of the Magi" focuses on the affirmation of Christ that comes from the Magi's journey towards faith through birth, death, and rebirth, a journey that parallels Eliot's own struggles with his faith.

Brian Barbour, in "Poetic Form in 'Journey of the Magi,'" approaches the events in T.S. Eliot's dramatic monologue as a journey of perplexity and spiritual anguish in search of "satisfactory" faith. Barbour suggests that Eliot's poem "presents two journeys related through paradox: it narrates the arduous physical journey and then dramatizes the even more difficult and uncomplete spiritual one".

The spiritual journey "leads us to the deepest perplexity and, indeed, alienation". At the physical journey's end the spiritual perplexity remains. Referring to the "old dispensation" of birth and rebirth, Brian Barbour writes "The Birth he saw began the death of his old world, old life, but did not, with the same certainty, give him anything new". The Magi are caught in the middle between birth and death, moving towards the centre of the Christian mystery where death is the way to birth through Christ.

Barbour's interpretation of the poem suggests that St. Matthew is "the audience that gives the poem its greatest richness and deepest meaning. His search for background information about Jesus is the poem's occasion, and speaker, audience, and occasion all cooperates to define the full poetic significance".

T.S. Eliot's journey to faith is like that of the magus, a purposeful struggle to attain faith in God's power to save sinners. Michael Dean, in "'T.S. Eliot's 'Journey of the Magi': Confrontation with Christianity" focuses on a confrontation that Eliot creates between the reader and the theme. Dean begins with the "Christian allusions in the poem and will conclude with an examination of the purpose behind Eliot's use of these allusions: the creation of a confrontation between the reader and Eliot's affirmation of the truth revealed in Jesus Christ".

The imagery suggests that a "difficulty arises from the mixing of the old and new dispensations, as the Magus, transformed by the revelation at the end of his journey, lives on uncomfortably as a man of the new dispensation among people of the old". T.S. Eliot, just like the old Magus, knows the difficult road one must travel in a spiritual pursuit of faith against those who scorn along the way.

In Eliot's poem the magus tells us "I would do it again" in the same way Eliot would make that same bold statement. Dean goes on to say that he believes Eliot "challenges others, in such ways as writing 'Journey of the Magi,' to join him in that affirmation".

In "The Sacrament of Penance in T.S. Eliot's 'Journey of the Magi,'" A. James Wohlpart focuses on a parallel between the three part structure of the poem and a reordering in the stages of the Sacrament of Penance to emphasize the idea of a continuing spiritual journey.

Wohlpart concludes: "Instead of beginning with contrition and ending with satisfaction, an order which might connote fulfillment of the sacrament and an end to the process of perfection, Eliot opened with contrition in stanza one, moved on to satisfaction in stanza two, and then concluded with confession in stanza three, suggesting that the soul, in its journey towards Christ and heavenly perfection, akin to the journey of the Magi, can never rest in the certainty of perfection but must be continually engaged in the process of becoming perfect".

According to Wohlpart, "The journey becomes, then, not only a physical movement towards Christ, but also the first step in the Magi's spiritual progress as they truly regret their previous spiritual stasis". This spiritual journey takes us in search of perfection, but in order to obtain perfection on a higher level, Christ's death is the only way that satisfaction can occur.

E. F. Burgess, in his *Explicator* article "T.S. Eliot's 'Journey of the Magi,'" bases the magi's "satisfactory" journey in conditions of a prophecy hundreds of years before. Burgess first notes that the Magi were not Kings but priests: "holy Zoroastrian astronomers who followed the signs of the heavens.

'Yonder Star' the Magi followed was a sign prophesied 600 years before by Zoroaster. The prophecy not only described the celestial occurrence, but also specifically named Bethlehem as the birthplace of the new prophet". Burgess then offers a reinterpretation of the "satisfaction" image in the poem: "it simply means that every condition of the prophecy was met, leaving the alienated magus, a priest no more, secure in his knowledge of Zoroaster's truth, and in that knowledge stranded, suspended between the realization and the consummation of God's plan". Burgess suggests that with the prophecy met, the old magus was satisfied in Zoroaster's truth.

At the end of Eliot's long and difficult journey he concludes his poem with "I should be glad of another death," thus bringing"satisfactory" to his search for a life of faith. The spiritual perplexity of the meaning of birth, death, and rebirth is the journey that the magi and Eliot himself underwent in their attempt to find a new faith. In the end, the magi moved to the centre of Christian faith and found that death is the way to rebirth.

THE MAGI'S HUMAN CONVERSION EXPERIENCE

T. S. Eliot's "Journey of the Magi" was first published in

1927, the same year that "Eliot was received by baptism into the Anglican Church" (Basu 15). Critics suggest that the significance of Eliot's religious conversion cannot be understated for an analysis of "Journey of the Magi," as it recounts Eliot's personal conversion experience. While analyzing different aspects of the poem, the critics agree that Eliot's "Journey of the Magi" is about his own personal and spiritual conversion experience.

In "The Infirm Glory of the Positive Hour: Re-Conversion in 'Ash Wednesday,'" Melissa Eiles considers Eliot's "Journey of the Magi" as a beginning to Eliot's exploration of the theme of religious conversion. Eiles writes "The essence of a religious conversion... in Eliot's poetry is change—almost torturous intellectual and spiritual growth that pushes the soul into a conflict between its old life of sin and its new life of grace".

This process of conversion produces a new "convert," while only suppressing the material interests of the "old life"; the struggle between physical and spiritual worlds still continues. Eiles goes on to explain her view of Eliot's poem as an examination of the better understood "type of conversion: a gradual and bitter death to oneself and a growth into Christ".

Eliot's Magus engages in "a physical and spiritual journey to the... Christ Child and experiences conversion in the form of a spiritual death and rebirth". Eliot's own journey to Christ and conversion was not without struggles between the physical world of life and the spiritual world of God. Eiles sees conversion as "vital" to Eliot's poem: "it is the difference between animals and men. Without conversion, man risks loss of passion and hollowness—both in life on earth and in life after death".

In *A Reader's Guide to T.S. Eliot: A Poem-by-Poem Analysis*, George Williamson analyzes Eliot's "Journey of the Magi" as a perpetual story of the process of conversion. In the poem, "one of the Magi recounts the journey to Christ," a journey that brought death to their "old life" and their "rebirth" to a new experience, the experience of conversion. Eliot uses symbols and images, significant to him, that "recur, charged with emotion," such as the "water-mill and the six ruffians," to bring connection and continuation to the journey. "The description of the journey—in nature from death to life—not only projects the inner struggle of the Magi, but foreshadows events to come in the life of Christ... " in the lives of the Magi and in Eliot's personal life as well. According to Williamson, Eliot has taken an old Bible story, added personal symbols and imagery, and changed it to reflect his personal "journey to Christ".

In *T.S. Eliot's Theory of Poetry: A Study of the Changing Critical Ideas in the Development of His Prose and Poetry,* Rajnath explores Eliot's "Journey of the Magi" in relation to the metaphysical poets, focusing on the theme of discord between the physical and spiritual worlds. Rajnath holds that the similarity between Eliot and the metaphysical poets extends beyond the common theme of struggle between two worlds to similar religious experiences and expression of conversion within their poetry. The contradictory division "of body and soul that one finds in the metaphysicals... is at the very centre of Eliot's poetry".

Eliot's "Journey of the Magi" displays this "conflict between two lives, one worldly and the other Divine," placing him "in line with the metaphysicals, particularly Herbert" in its descriptions of the discomforts endured and the pleasures left behind when undertaking a spiritual journey "to glimpse the infant Christ".

Eliot's "Magi are simply caught up between two worlds and cannot decide whether they were led all the way for Birth or Death". They realise their journey was to see "the birth of Christ," but not that it would cause a painful death to their old ways. "They fail to realise that Death which was so painful to them is the prerequisite of birth, the spiritual rebirth". Eliot's "Journey of the Magi" is an exploration of the spiritual battles fought while undergoing the religious experience of conversion.

In *T. S. Eliot: A Study in Character and Style,* Ronald Bush agrees with other critics on the meaning of the "Journey of the Magi," and goes on to examine the influences of Eliot's borrowing from St. J. Parse and Lancelot Andrewes and their effect upon the poem. According to Bush, Eliot's "Journey of the Magi" is a dramatization of "the period in Eliot's life that followed his official conversion, when his old ways of thinking and feeling seemed irrevocably alien and his new life as a Christian existed more in intention than fact". Eliot begins the poem by borrowing from a sermon by Andrewes and sets up a rhythm using elements from both Andrewes and Parse to lull the reader into a transcendence of reality.

Eliot's adoption of Perse's syntax and style enhances the poem's "incantatory power" and produces "a Persean world of Imagination". However, Eliot casts doubt upon the experience by mixing imagery from the "three realms of reference—the fictional frame, the correspondences of Christian typology, and his own deepest and most troublesome feelings" throughout the poem, thereby testing the significance of the experience. The poem "Journey of the Magi" is Eliot's testing of his conversion experience.

Regardless of the specific focus, critics agree that Eliot's "Journey of the Magi" is about the personal and spiritual aspects of his religious conversion experience. In "Journey of the Magi," Eliot displays the depth to which his journey affected his life by relating his own conflicts with conversion to the struggles of the original Magi on the first journey to Christ.

Chapter 4

T.S. Eliot's View

"There was one critic who apparently possessed all the virtues—fine taste, poetic sensitiveness, intellectuality, an experimental inclination. His literary scholarship was beyond dispute, his writing deft and memorable. He was, moreover, a poet of the first rank, which gave his criticism of the art an extraordinary authority.

He was universally respected: by Pound, by the later expatriates, by the impressionists of the Dial, by the Hound and Horn group. This critic was T. S. Eliot. His volume of essays, The Sacred Wood, published in 1920, is still considered to be one of the truly distinguished works of esthetic criticism produced in this century.... The reader will note that he is here described in the past tense.

His works are many now, but The Sacred Wood alone is a consideration of esthetic problems. In the rest the emphasis is on the esthetic effects of moral and social beliefs. His development is one of the 'consequences' touched upon in the following chapter.... (358-359).

"[T.S. Eliot wrote,] 'There are two and only two finally tenable hypotheses about life: the Catholic and the materialistic [i.e., Marxist]. It is quite possible, of course, that the future may bring neither a Christian nor a materialistic civilization. It is quite possible that the future may be nothing but chaos or torpor. In that event, I am not interested in the future; I am only interested in the two alternatives which seem to me worthier of interest....'

"Eliot chose not only the Catholic hypothesis, but also its political corollaries. His literary opinions were thus given a firm philosophical base to rest upon, and from that fact he drew the reasonable conclusions...[that] 'Literary criticism should be completed by criticism from a definite ethical and theological standpoint. In so far as in any age there is common agreement on ethical and theological matters, so far can literary criticism be substantive.

In ages like our own, in which there is no such common agreement, it is then more necessary for Christian readers to scrutinize their reading, especially of works of imagination, with explicit ethical and theological standards. The 'greatness' of literature cannot be determined solely by literary standards; though we must remember that whether it is literature or not can be determined only by literary standards.'

"To this has esthetic criticism at last come—to a realization that non-esthetic criteria are the ultimate tests of value. Whether they be called philosophical, moral, or social criteria, they are still the ideas that men have about the way human beings live together and the way they ought to live. The quest of beauty had become the quest of reality. It had become, in essence, literary criticism as socially conscious and as polemical as the criticism of the Marxists....

"Eliot spoke of alternatives, not of choices.... He believes that one of the alternatives has greater value, is nobler, is in a sense more real, than the other. The question is therefore not simply one of personal taste. It is a question of evidence and reason. But the alternative he favors admits of no evidence and derogates from reason. His philosophy is, in the last analysis, wholly mystical. It is not capable of being tested and verified and improved. The alternative he rejects is, on the other hand, the one that is favored by those who are determined to be as scientific as one can be in a non-physical field.

"The literary criticism of the neo-classicists is a criticism composed of obiter dicta inspired by intangible emotions. The literary criticism of the materialists stands or falls by the findings of the social scientists, psychologists, and historians. Eliot's alternative involves a revulsion against democracy; the materialists are partisans of democracy. The literary criticism of his school tends to create a literature that will express the sensibilities and experiences of a few fortunate men. The criticism of the opposing school tends to create a literature that will express the ideals and sympathies of those who look forward to the conquest of poverty, ignorance, and inequality—to the material and intellectual elevation of the mass of mankind...." (384-387).

"To whom does the future belong? In January 1939 Eliot announced that the Criterion, the literary journal he had edited since 1922, would no longer be published. His Europe had crumbled; the culture in which he had put his faith was dying. The Criterion had served its purpose. Eliot had arrived at a mood of detachment. There was nothing he could hopefully fight for now. But those who believe in scientific methods, in realism, in social equality and democracy, are hopeful and are fighting."

MORE, RELATED, FROM BERNARD SMITH, FORCES IN AMERICAN CRITICISM (1939)

"Socialist criticism in America may conveniently be dated from the founding of the Comrade—'An Illustrated Socialist Monthly'—in 1901.... The Comrade appeared at the beginning of the muckrake era. It was superior to the muckrakers in the clarity of its vision as to the basic cause of social evils and the way to cure them....

"The aims of socialist critics were propagandistic, and it was inevitable that they should be paramount in a time when American critical systems were divided between art for art's sake, art for morality's sake, and various compromises between those two exhausted theories of esthetic purpose.1 Consider the essays and lectures on the contemporary theatre by the anarchist Emma Goldman. Miss Goldman made no bones about her intentions. Her essay on 'The Modern Drama' in Anarchism and Other Essays (1911) was frankly a salute to its subject as an instrument for the dissemination of radical thought."

(1"'propaganda' is not used here as an invidious term. It is used to describe works consciously written to have an immediate and direct effect upon their readers' opinions and actions, as distinguished from works that are not consciously written for that purpose or which are written to have a remote and indirect effect. It is possible that conventional critics have learned by now that to call a literary work 'propaganda' is to say nothing about its quality as literature. By now enough critics have pointed out that some of the world's classics were originally 'propaganda' for something").

"The socialist's affinity with realism was stated forcefully in the leading editorial of the Masses in February 1911—the second issue of a magazine...which was a successor, on a more mature and 'politicalized' level, to the Comrade. It said: 'It is natural that Socialists should favour the novel with a purpose, more especially, the novel that points a Socialist moral. As a reaction against the great bulk of vapid, meaningless, too-clever American fiction, with its artificial plots and characters remote from actual life, such an attitude is a healthy sign ...'".

"Its militancy is the most obvious characteristic of American criticism since the war. In the whole of nineteenth century there was only one critic, Poe, who was deliberately and consistently disputatious. No one else made polemics the basis of a critical method. Whitman was a maverick, but he was exclamatory rather than argumentative. Now, however, it is customary for critics to be bellicose, and there are few who have let politeness stand in the way of controversy. The reason is not hard to find. Criticism in our time has been largely a war of traditions—a struggle between irreconcilable ideologies...".

"The academy was growing up. It was beginning to share the emotions of serious adults who were trying to adjust themselves to an America become rich and imperialistic. In its own special field, literary history, it was beginning to achieve mature and realistic interpretations. In 1927 it came of age: V. L. Parrington, professor of English at the University of Washington, published the two completed volumes of his Main Currents in American Thought. With that work the academy was at last brought face to face with the ideas, sentiments, and historical methods of today....

"Parrington's Main Currents arrived to supply the most

needed things: an account of our literary history which squared with recent works on the history of our people and a realistic technique for analyzing the relationship of a writer to his time and place—in addition to a militantly progressive spirit. Professorial and literary circles had consciously been waiting for such a work, and if the one that did come forth was far more radical than some people cared for, it simply could not be rejected.

The author was a professor too; his scholarship defied scrutiny; and his ideas were couched in terms that were Native American, most of them having come over shortly after the Mayflower. One must emphasize Parrington's radicalism because it is probably the most significant aspect of his work. He sharpened, gave point to the economic interpretation of literary movements because of his desire to reveal the motivating interests and real direction of specific works of literature...".

Chapter 5

On "The Love Song of J. Alfred Prufrock"

Prufrock's paralysis follows naturally from this subjectivizing of everything. If each consciousness is an opaque sphere, then Prufrock has no hope of being understood by others. "No experience," says Bradley in a phrase Eliot quotes, "can lie open to inspection from outside" (KE, 203). Prufrock's vision is incommunicable, and whatever he says to the lady will be answered by, "That is not what I meant at all./That is not it, at all". The lady is also imprisoned in her own sphere, and the two spheres can never, like soap bubbles, become one. Each is impenetrable to the other.

If other consciousnesses exist only as opaque objects for Prufrock, he has an equally unhappy relation to time and space. One of the puzzles of the poem is the question as to whether Prufrock ever leaves his room. It appears that he does not, so infirm is his will, so ready "for a hundred indecisions,/ And for a hundred visions and revisions,/Before the taking of a toast and tea".

In another sense Prufrock would be unable to go anywhere, however hard he tried. If all space has been assimilated into his mind, then spatial movement would really be movement in the same place, like a man running in a dream. There is no way to distinguish between actual movement and imaginary movement.

However far Prufrock goes, he remains imprisoned in his own subjective space, and all his experience is imaginary. It seems to be some perception of this which keeps him in his room, content to imagine himself going through the streets, ascending the lady's stair, and telling her "all," like Lazarus back from the dead. There is no resurrection from the death which has undone him, and this is one meaning of the epigraph from Dante.

Time disappears in the same way. Space must be exterior to the self if movement through it is to be more than the following of a tedious argument in the mind. In the same way only an objective time can be other than the self, so that the flow of time can mean change for that self. But time, like space, has only a subjective existence for Prufrock. As a result, past, present, and future are equally immediate, and Prufrock is paralyzed.

Like one of Bradley's finite centers, he "is not in time," and "contains [his] own past and future" (KE, 205). Memories, ironic echoes of earlier poetry, present sensations, anticipations of what he might do in the future ("I grow old... I grow old... / I shall wear the bottoms of my trousers rolled" [CP, 71)—these are equally present.

There is a systematic confusion of tenses and times in the poem, so that it is difficult to tell if certain images exist in past, present, future. Prufrock begins by talking of his visit to the lady as something yet to be done, and later talks of his failure to make the visit as something long past ("And would it have been worth it, after all,/Would it have been worth while" (CP, 61).

Like the women talking of Michelangelo, he exists in an eternal present, a frozen time in which everything that might possibly happen to him is as if it had already happened: "For I have known them all already, known them all" (CP, 4). In this time of endless repetition Prufrock cannot disturb the universe even if he should presume to try to do so. Everything that might happen is foreknown, and in a world where only one mind exists the foreknown has in effect already happened and no action is possible. Prufrock's infirmity of will is not so much a moral deficiency as a consequence of his subjectivism.

This five-line interlude ending on "the floors of silent seas" forms an encapsulated version of the remainder of the poem, in which the frustrated effort to establish purposive discourse leads once again to withdrawal downward and inward to a silent world of instinctual being. A return to images of distension and distracting sensuality provokes a final impulse toward violent imposition of the will—"to force the moment to its crisis"—which ends, like previous thoughts of disturbing the universe, in ruthless self-mockery. The image of decapitation parodies the theme of disconnected being and provides for at least a negative definition of the self: "I am no prophet."

By this point the tense has quietly shifted from present to past, and the speaker offers a series of prolonged interrogatives on the consequences of action not taken. While its grammatical context ("And would it have been worth it") reduces it to the contemplation of "what might have been"; the language and imagery of this passage enact with renewed intensity the recurring drama of mental conflict:

Would it have been worth while,
To have bitten off the matter with a smile,
To have squeezed the universe into a ball
To roll it towards some overwhelming question,
To say: "I am Lazarus, come from the dead,
Come back to tell you all, I shall tell you all."

The infinitives in this passage—*to have bitten, to have squeezed, to roll*—conform to the poem's widespread use of transitive verbs of direct action in expressing the speaker's violent impulse to combat the forces of disorder: *to murder and create, to disturb the universe, to spit out all the butt-ends, to force the moment.*

The poem's linguistic and thematic strategy consistently opposes active verbs to the passive voice which causes things to be spread out, etherized, smoothed, and stretched. It sets these infinitives against present participles, which are constantly muttering, sprawling, rubbing, scuttling, and settling. Finally, it opposes these transitive verbs to intransitive verbs which lie, linger, malinger, lean, curl, trail, wrap, slip, and sleep. A relative lack of modifiers and the absence of plural forms further distinguishes the passage cited above. By contrast the language of disordered experience, of imprecision and aimlessness, abounds in modifiers and plurals: restless nights, one-night cheap hotels, visions and revisions, the sunsets and the dooryards, and the sprinkled streets.

The structure of the imagery at this point in the poem corresponds to the thematic role played by linguistic form. To have "bitten off" the matter, in addition to its hint of blunt force, would constitute a positive reaction against endlessly idle talk; squeezing the universe into a ball would counteract the world's tendency to fall apart and to spread itself out like yellow fog; finally, the act of rolling it toward some overwhelming question at least imparts direction to the movement of the universe, even if the actual destination, like the question, remains unclear.

The idea of proclaiming oneself a prophet "come back to tell you all" implies a power of linguistic discourse equal in magnitude to the physical act of squeezing the universe into a ball. Once more the idea of language joins with images of purpose, only this time in such hyperbolic fashion that the ultimate failure of discourse strikes one as inevitable: "That is not what I meant at all."

The speaker's failure to master language—"It is impossible to say just what I mean!"—leads in this case not to a statement on the inadequacy of words themselves, but rather reflects upon the speaker's own impotence. In a poem so obsessed with problems of speech and definition, to have failed with words is to have lost the war on the inarticulate: the speaker as heroic Lazarus or Prince Hamlet is suddenly reduced to the stature of an attendant lord, "Full of high sentence, but a bit obtuse." The old man with rolled-up trouser bottoms has shrunk from his former size. Paradoxically, this diminution of the outer self—the part of the mind concerned with imposing order on experience—brings about a corresponding expansion of the inner self.

In the same essay where Eliot locates the beginnings of a poem in an unknown, dark "psychic material" that is put into form by the conscious mind, he allows for a secondary resurgence of the unconscious that arises from the very process of poetic composition: "the frame, once chosen, within which the author has elected to work, may itself evoke other psychic material; and then, lines of poetry may come into being, not from the original impulse, but from a secondary stimulation of the unconscious mind."

The mental forces at work in Eliot's description of the poetic process serve as an analogy to the conflicts besetting the speaker in Prufrock. The speaker is a failed poet in terms of his inability to "murder" existing structures in order to "create" anew; be finds it impossible to say what be wants to say. In the "secondary stimulation of the unconscious mind" that occurs at this point, he partly abandons and partly resolves the struggle of form and matter; the integration of the psyche remains at best incomplete.

It is a striking fact that three of the principal modernist poets—Eliot, Pound, and Williams—each wrote a poem entitled "Portrait of a Lady" within a few years of 1910. The title, of course, alludes to James's novel and, for Eliot and Pound, refers to the Jamesian project of some of their early verse. Pound asserted that *Hugh Selwyn Mauberley* was an attempt to condense the James novel, and Eliot told Virginia Woolf that his early inclination was to develop in the manner of Henry James.

Behind the model of Henry James, however (indeed, behind James's *Portrait of a Lady*), is a nineteenth-century poetic mode of female portraiture. Tennyson, Browning, Rossetti, and Swinburne wrote portrait poems – "Mariana," "'The Gardener's Daughter," "Andrea del Sarto," "The Blessed Damozel," "The Portrait," and "Before the Mirror," to name just a few — that identify poetic style with the portrait of a lady. These poems engage not just the subject of woman but the gender of the poetical.

For Eliot, poetic representation of a powerful female presence created difficulty in embodying the male. In order to do so, Eliot avoids envisioning the female, indeed, avoids attaching gender to bodies.

We can see this process clearly in "The Love Song of J. Prufrock." The poem circles around not only an unarticulated question, as all readers agree, but also an unenvisioned centre, the "one" whom Prufrock addresses.

The poem never visualizes the woman with whom Prufrock imagines an encounter except in fragments and in plurals — eyes, arms, skirts - synecdoches we might well imagine as fetishistic replacements. But even these synecdochic replacements are not clearly engendered. The braceleted arms and the skirts are specifically feminine, but the faces, the hands, the voices, the eyes are not.

As if to displace the central human object it does not visualize, the poem projects images of the body onto the landscape (the sky, the streets, the fog), but these images, for all their marked intimation of sexuality, also avoid the designation of gender (the muttering retreats of restless nights, the fog that rubs, licks, and lingers). The most visually precise images in the poem are those of Prufrock himself, a Prufrock carefully composed – "My morning coat, my collar mounting firmly to the chin, / My necktie rich and modest, but asserted by a simple pin" — only to be decomposed by the watching eyes of another into thin arms and legs, a balding head brought in upon a platter.

Moreover, the images associated with Prufrock are themselves, as Pinkney observes, terrifyingly unstable, attributes constituting the identity of the subject at one moment only to be wielded by the objective the next, like the pin that centers his necktie and then pinions him to the wall or the arms that metamorphose into Prufrock's claws. The poem, in these various ways, decomposes the body, making ambiguous its sexual identification.

These scattered body parts at once imply and evade a central encounter the speaker cannot bring himself to confront, but in the pattern of their scattering they constitute the voice that Prufrock feels cannot exist in the gaze of the other.

The physical and psychological enervation of Eliot's early personae may be read in part as correlatives of his literary situation; this is the way Prufrock, for example, states his problem:

And I have known the eyes already, known them all—

The eyes that fix you in a formulated phrase,
And when I am formulated, sprawling on a pin,
When I am pinned and wriggling on the wall,
Then how should I begin
To spit out all the butt-ends of my days and ways?
And how should I presume?

Prufrock does not know how to presume to begin to speak, both because he knows "all already"—this is the burden of his lament—and because he is already known, formulated. His consciousness of the other's eye—I haunts his language at its source: "Let us go then, you and I." An "I" who addresses a "you" becomes subject to the laws of communication, and his voice is subsumed by expression. In his critical replay of the poetic process, Eliot remarks that the poet expresses not a personality but a particular medium.

The particular medium expressed in "Prufrock" is a confession or a dramatic monologue. The you-I split being the formal ground of his medium, Prufrock's problem is in fact the problem the expressive medium introduces, and this identification of the formal and rhetorical dimensions of the medium with the emotion or psychic burden of the speaker makes for the airless closure of the poem. As in Poe's "Raven," the speaker's relationship to the form within which his adventure transpires constitutes the nature of his adventure: his form determines the content of his story.

And if Prufrock's problem coincides with the dynamics of Eliot's particular medium of dramatic monologue, Eliot's problem coincides with the dynamics of the poetic medium itself; just as Prufrock is paralyzed by his consciousness of the other, his author is paralyzed by his consciousness of the tradition.

In the line "It is impossible to say just what I mean!" the dramatic character and his author meet, "uttering the words in unison, though perhaps with somewhat different meaning," and displaying the rhetorical advantage a dramatic poet holds. And Eliot's imprisoning his speaker in the very medium of expressive or even confessional speech may register his own intertextual interment in a medium inscribed with prototypes of original or central speech—whether prophetic, like John the Baptist's, or epic, like Dante's, or dramatic, like Shakespeare's—which are codified in and reinforced by conventions precluding the possibility of saying "just what I mean." Eliot's ironic use of rhyme and meter in "Prufrock" acknowledges the complicity of the poet's conventions with his persona's "de-meaning" language.

On the one hand, the "comic" meter of lines like "In the room the women come and go / Talking of Michelangelo" equates poetic forms that channel force and the social forms of keeping conversation light. On the other hand, dreams of escape from the pre-formulating formulae are them- selves recounted in formulaic lines, for the solution to Prufrock's problem would be a "solution" for Eliot as well-forgetting the present and the separate self, surrendering to the oblivion of an unconscious nature and the "natural" meter of English poetry:

I should have been a pair of ragged claws
Scuttling across the floors of silent seas.

The epigraph to "Prufrock" formally subsumes its hero's problem with expressive language to the poet's problem with textuality. The poem is a dramatic monologue, a mimesis of speech, yet it opens with an epigraph that identifies it as writing and diminishes its urgency by absorbing it within the prototype of another confession, so that the beginning "let us go" is already the "end of something." At the same time that the epigraph consigns the persona to the company of his "semblables"—all those confined in the deadly circle of their solipsistic-confessional speech-likenesses—it seals the poet in the prison of literary "truth," which cancels out his life and tells someone else's "lie."

Supernatural vision and natural blindness—issuing in prophetic or lyric utterances—would alike deliver Prufrock from himself; but such ascents and descents are not possible within writing, a historically coded and prescribed medium where vision drowns in revision and human voices drown out natural and supernatural music. And if Prufrock—too decorous and conventional to be a prophet or to dally with mermaids—is incarcerated in the echo chamber of his and others' chatter, Eliot finds himself locked in the "room" of literary "talk," too late to "tell all" *or* to "sing."

The poem's epigraph at once opens and closes this discourse of a poet-hero generically old before his time. Eliot's early work is unusual in its dependence on epigraphs that mediate between the poet and the poem, preformulating the poem before it can begin, and his epigraphs often explicitly concern belatedness, exhaustion, and endings.

Indeed, the epigraph to *Prufrock and Other Observations* locates Eliot's beginning as a poet by placing him in the company of Jean Verdenal and other "shadows"—Statius, Virgil, and Dante.

In "Prufrock," the literary epigraph, bespeaking "not only... the pastness of the past, but... its presence" (*SW*, 49), casts such a shadow over the poem that nature itself disappears, for a "sky" that recalls "ether" is, in fact, "etherized" for the present speaker. Thus, social paralysis resulting from knowing all and being known or seen through parallels a literary anesthesia—knowing all predecessors and being preformulated and "epigraphed" by them. Both kinds of anesthesia subject the individual voice to anterior fon11ulas, forms, and styles.

Prufrock's acute consciousness of his age is thus the classic symptom of Eliot's philosophical and literary problem. Prufrock's body is presented as a text, for he literally carries the burden of the past on his body—in the lines, the thinning hair and arms and legs, and other signs of age that record time's passage.

In the same way, his monologue is a "polylogue," superscribed with quotations, allusions, and echoes that document the presence of the past. Since existential experience is subsumed by textual experience in early Eliot, bodily and natural forms correlate with literary forms. The labyrinthine cities and "corridors" of history, the sepulchral drawing rooms with their "atmosphere of Juliet's tomb", the body aging "on its own," and the formulas of discourse are all experienced as suffocating incarcerations. They are all modeled as texts, as stages set and scripts written before the speaker enters to recite his lines. And attempts to free the individual voice by breaking out of forms register, as in "Prufrock," only as impulses to dismemberment and suicide.

The complications of "Prufrock" involve from the poem's beginning a more direct transformation of the dramatic monologue than does "Gerontion" when the pronouns that "I" uses suggest the presence of an unspecified listener. In many dramatic monologues the listener is also not specified, and the reader is invited to take over the role of listener in a one-sided conversation.

In "Prufrock," however, it is not clear whether a real conversation is being dramatically presented, whether the "I" is having an internal colloquy with himself, or whether the reader is being addressed directly. The "you" that is "I"'s counterpart stands in two places at once, both inside and outside Prufrock's mind and inside and outside scenes that can with difficulty be imagined based on the minimal details provided.

The reader's situation resembles the position of the viewer of Velásquez's "Las Meninas," in which a mirror invites an identification with the observers of the scene depicted in the painting while the painting's geometry indicates that the illusion of that identification can be sustained only by ignoring obvious details. Reader and viewer stand both inside and outside the frame of an illusion that cannot be sustained.

Two epigraphs from Dante precede and follow the poem's title, one for the entire volume that takes its name from "Prufrock," the other for the poem itself, which stands first in the volume. Together they suggest the oscillation and indeterminacy of Prufrock's position and the reader's. In the first epigraph, Statius mistakes Virgil's shade for a "solid thing" and forgets momentarily what he himself is and can do.

In the second, Guido da Montefeltro predicates his address to Dante on the opposite mistake, that Dante is not human and cannot carry his words further. Like Statius and Guido, the reader who tries to pin down the indeterminate identities and locations of "you and I" in the poem will always be mistaken. What is taken for a shade or a figment may be flesh and blood, and what is taken for living flesh may be only a figment in a perpetual instability that marks "Prufrock," like "Rhapsody," as the transforming end of a sequence of poems to which it can be said to belong but some of whose implications it subverts.

The subversion occurs largely through the removal of those referential, seemingly stable elements of scene and character that contribute to making the illusion of hearing a personal voice in poetry possible.

Eliot's particular transformation of the dramatic monologue in "Prufrock" depends on the character of the pronouns "you" and "I," which linguists call "shifters" because they are mutually defining and depend for their meanings on the pragmatic context of the discourses in which they occur. Instead of naming something unchanging, these pronouns indicate positions that can be variously occupied.

The general fragmentation of "The Love Song of J. Alfred Prufrock" is obvious and notorious. The poem seems a perfect example of what Terry Eagleton calls the modern "transition from metaphor to metonymy: unable any longer to totalize his experience in some heroic figure, the bourgeois is forced to let it trickle away into objects related to him by sheer contiguity."

Everything in "Prufrock" trickles away into parts related to one another only by contiguity. Spatial progress in the poem is diffident or deferred, a "scuttling" accomplished by a pair of claws disembodied so violently they remain "ragged." In the famous opening, "the evening is spread out against the sky / Like a patient etherised upon a table," and the simile makes an equation between being spread out and being etherised that continues elsewhere in the poem when the evening, now a bad patient, "malingers, / Stretched on the floor, here beside you and me."

There it "sleeps so peacefully! / Smoothed by long fingers...." This suspension is a rhetorical as well as a spatial and emotional condition.

The "streets that follow like a tedious argument / Of insidious intent" lead not to a conclusion but to a question, a question too "overwhelming" even to ask. Phrases like the "muttering retreats / Of restless nights" combine physical blockage, emotional unrest, and rhetorical maundering in an equation that seems to make the human being a combination not of angel and beast but of road-map and Roberts' Rules of Order.

In certain lines, metaphor dissolves into metonymy before the reader's eyes. "The yellow fog that rubs its back upon the window-panes" appears clearly to every reader as a cat, but the cat itself is absent, represented explicitly only in parts — back, muzzle, tongue — and by its actions — licking, slipping, leaping, curling.

The metaphor has in a sense been hollowed out to be replaced by a series of metonyms, and thus it stands as a rhetorical introduction to what follows. The people in the poem also appear as disembodied parts or ghostly actions. They are "the faces that you meet," the "hands / That lift and drop a question on your plate," the "Arms that are braceleted and white and bare," the "eyes that fix you in a formulated phrase."

Prufrock himself fears such a reduction, to use Kenneth Burke's term for the effect of metonymy. The dread questions "How his hair is growing thin!" and "But how his arms and legs are thin" reduce Prufrock to certain body parts, the thinness of which stands in for the diminution caused by the rhetorical figures. What Prufrock fears has already been accomplished by his own rhetoric.

In this poem the horror of sex seems to come in part from its power to metonymize. Like Augustine, Eliot sees sex as the tyranny of one part of the body over the whole. Though Eliot is far too circumspect to name this part, he figures its power in his poetry by the rebelliousness of mere members: hands, arms, eyes. Sexual desire pulls the body apart, so that to give in to it is to suffer permanent dismemberment. This may account for the odd combination in Eliot's work of sexual ennui and libidinous violence. The tyranny of one part scatters all the others, reducing the whole to impotence. In this way, the violence of sex robs the individual of the integrity necessary to action.

An oddly similar relationship of part to whole governs Prufrock's conception of time. In a burst of confidence he asserts, "In a minute there is time / For decisions and revisions which a minute will reverse." Yet he seems to quail before the very amplitude of possibility contained in time, so that all these decisions and revisions are foreclosed before they can be made.

Thus Prufrock's prospective confidence in the fullness of time becomes a retrospective conviction that "I have known them an already, known them all: — / Have known the evenings, mornings, afternoons...." To know "all" already is to be paralyzed, disabled, because "all" is not full of possibility but paradoxically empty, constituted as it is by pure repetition, part on part on part.

In a figure that exactly parallels the bodily metonymies, time becomes a collection of individual parts, just as the poem's human denizens had been little more than parts: "And I have known the eyes already, known them all"; "And I have known the arms already known them all." The instantaneous movement from part to whole, from eyes, arms, evenings, mornings, to "all," expresses the emptiness between, the gap between dispersed parts and an oppressive whole made of purely serial repetition.

The very reduction of human beings to parts of themselves and of time to episodes makes it impossible to conceive of any whole different from this empty, repetitious "an." As Burke says, metonymy substitutes quantity for quality, so that instead of living life Prufrock feels "I have measured out my life with coffee spoons.

J. Alfred Prufrock is not just the speaker of one of Eliot's poems. He is the Representative Man of early Modernism. Shy, cultivated, oversensitive, sexually retarded (many have said impotent), ruminative, isolated, self-aware to the point of solipsism, as he says, "Am an attendant lord, one that will do / To swell a progress, start a scene or two." Nothing revealed the Victorian upper classes in Western society more accurately, unless it was a novel by Henry James, and nothing better exposed the dreamy, insubstantial centre of that consciousness than a half-dozen poems in Eliot's first book.

The speakers of all these early poems are trapped inside their own excessive alertness. They look out on the world from deep inside some private cave of feeling, and though they see the world and themselves with unflattering exactness, they cannot or will not do anything about their dilemma and finally fall back on self-serving explanation.

They quake before the world, and their only revenge is to be alert. After *Prufrock and Other Observations*, poetry started coming from the city and from the intellect. It could no longer stand comfortably on its old post-Romantic ground, ecstatic before the natural world.

The practice of allusion, justified in "Burbank" by the need to characterize the tourist, performs in "Gerontion" the function of condensing into decent compass a whole panorama of the past. If any notion remained that in the poems of 1919 Eliot was sentimentally contrasting a resplendent past with a dismal present, "Gerontion" should have helped to dispel it.

What are contrasted in this poem are the secular history of Europe, which the life of Gerontion parallels, and the unregarded promise of salvation through Christ. Gerontion symbolizes civilization gone rotten. The mysterious foreign figures who rise shadow-like in his thoughts—Mr. Silvero, Hakagawa, Madame de Tornquist, Fräulein von Kulp—are the inheritors of desolation.

Against them is set the "word within a word, unable to speak a word"—the innocent Redeemer, swaddled now in the darkness of the world. But Christ came not to send peace, but a sword; the Panther of the bestiaries, luring the gentler beasts with His sweet breath of doctrine, is also the Tiger of destruction. For the "juvescence of the year," in which He came, marked the beginning of our dispensation, the "depraved May" ever returning with the "flowering judas" of man's answer to the Incarnation.

And so "The tiger springs in the new year," devouring us who have devoured Him. Furthermore, the tiger becomes now a symbol not only of divine wrath but of the power of life within man, the springs of sex which "murder and create." "Depraved May," the season of denial or crucifixion, returns whenever, in whatever age, apostolic or modern, the life of sense stirs without love.

Eliot's The *Family Reunion* repeats the horror: "Is the spring not an evil time, that excites us with lying voices?" So now it returns and excites the memories of Gerontion. The source of his grief—the passionate Cross, the poison tree, "the wrath-bearing tree"—is both the crucifixion yew tree and the death tree of the hanged traitor, a token of Christ and Iscariot, redemption and the universal fall in Eden.

The futility of a world where men blunder down the blind corridors of history, guided by vanity and gulled by success, asserting no power of choice between good and evil but forced into alternatives they cannot predict—this is the futility of a labyrinth without an end. Someone has remarked that Eliot's obsessive image is the abyss.

It is not: it is the corridor, the blind street, the enclosure; the "circular desert" and "the stone passages / Of an immense and empty hospital," imprisoning the inconsolable heart. At the centre is the physician, the Word, enveloped in obscurity. But without is the abyss also, yawning for those who in their twisted course have never found their centre.

"Gerontion" points no way inward; it shows the outward, the *eccentric* propulsion of the damned, who, as Chaucer says, echoing the *Somnium Scipionis,* "Shul whirle aboute th'erthe alwey in peyne." Alone in his corner, having rested, unlike Ulysses, from travel (and indeed having never taken the highways of the earth), the old man sits while the wind sweeps his world "Beyond the circuit of the shuddering Bear / In fractured atoms."

The opposite movement, which discloses "a door that opens at the end of a corridor," opening, as one reads in "Burnt Norton," "Into the rose garden" and "Into our first world," leads to "the still point of the turning world," where, as Eliot put it in *Ash Wednesday,* "the unstilled world still whirled / About the centre of the silent Word." "Gerontion" describes only "the unstilled world," the turning wheel, the hollow passages—not "the Garden / Where all love ends," the ending of lust and the goal of love.

The point at which time ends and eternity begins, at which history disappears in unity and the winding spiral vanished in the Word, is lost to the world of the poem. Yet the Word exists; it is only history which cannot find Him, history with a positivistic conception of the universe, a deterministic view of causation, a pragmatic notion of morals.

As Chesterton's Father Brown remarks, "What we all dread most... is a maze with no centre. That is why atheism is only a nightmare." Eliot's symbol of the mazelike passages, or the clocklike wheel of time, or the whirlwind of death, the gaping whirlpool, is the antithesis of the single, unmoving, immutable point within. History is the whirlwind, for history is of the world, and history like the world destroys all that dares the test of matter and time.

From his draughty windows Gerontion looks up a barren hill: once again the eye ascends in order to descend into an abyss, reversing the motion of Dante and the Christian saints who followed St. Augustine's "Descend that ye may ascend." Gerontion's mind wanders backward, however, not upward—as far back as 480 B.C. and the battle of Thermopylae (which translates as "hot gates"), then forward through a series of wars that Gerontion feels would have compensated him if he had been there to fight.

He thinks of history as a system of corridors ingeniously contrived to confuse and finally to corrupt the human race. History is a "she"—like his old housekeeper, poking a clogged drain; also like Fräulein von Kulp (for *culpa?)* who turned seductively in the hallway; or the mystical Madame de Tornquist (a tourniquet, or screw for stopping blood?). Like these women, history leads nowhere but to corruption. She "gives too late or too soon," like a frustrating woman, and she leaves her lover not only ill-at-ease but frightened. Heroic efforts to satisfy the unclear demands of history have led to nothing but cruelty and hate. And into this history "Came Christ the tiger."

Gerontion thinks of the coming of Christ in two ways, first

as a useless infant and then as a hunted tiger. This part of the poem is usually misread because no one notes that Eliot pointedly left the phrase borrowed from Lancelot Andrewes with "the Word" uncapitalized. Thus in "Gerontion" we read only of "The word within a word, unable to speak a word." Eliot knew what he was about when he restored the capital in "A Song for Simeon" and "Ash-Wednesday" (1930): "The Word within [the biblical] word, unable to speak a word."

As Gerontion reflects, the answer to the Philistines' cry for a "sign" was disappointingly a speechless child, who passed from winter darkness and swaddling clothes into a "depraved" spring, when he was transformed into a ravening tiger—a sacrificial beast which in contemporary life is hunted and eaten by bloodless transients like the boarders Silvero, Hakagawa, Fräulein von Kulp, and Madame de Tornquist.

"The tiger springs in the new year" makes "springs" a syllepsis, or pun, meaning both "arises like a rejuvenating spring" and "pounces like a murderous animal."

In John 6:52-58, Jesus says that those who take his body and blood to become one with him in communion will live eternally, while those who reject him will die. Gerontion concludes that this death-dealing doctrine came to devour those who do not devour "the tiger," as do Gerontion's fellow boarders. To them the ritual meal is no "communion" but a cannibal "dividing." "After such knowledge," indeed, "what forgiveness?"

Hugh Kenner has noticed that Eliot's characterization of Senecan drama provides a fair description of "Gerontion." In the Greek drama, says Eliot, "we are always conscious of a concrete visual actuality," while in the plays of Seneca "the drama is all in the word, and the word has no further reality behind it." Part of the reason for the extraordinary difficulty of "Gerontion" is its conspicuous lack of the concrete visual images that illuminate even the most obscure passages of *The Waste Land*. "Gerontion" is all talk.

Signs are taken for wonders. "We would see a sign!"
The word within a word, unable to speak a word,
Swaddled with darkness.

Here Gerontion has quoted St. Matthew's report of the pharisees' challenge to Christ ("We would see a sign!") and has followed it with a line from Lancelot Andrewes's Nativity Sermon on that text ("The word within a word, unable to speak a word").

In his 1926 essay on Andrewes, Eliot remarks that Andrewes is "extracting all the spiritual meaning of a text" in this passage. That is precisely what Gerontion cannot do. Andrewes is talking about the logos, the Word within the word. Gerontion's words have no metaphysical buttressing, and his language is studded with puns, words within words. The passage on history is a series of metaphors that dissolve into incomprehensibility:

History has many cunning passages, contrived corridors
And issues, deceives with whispering ambitions,
Guides us by vanities.

Gerontion has already described himself as "an old man in a draughty house," and his "house" of history has its corridors and passages and issues. Written histories also have "cunning passages," and historians write about "Issues." Gerontion's history is also a woman:

She gives when our attention is distracted
And what she gives, gives with such supple confusions
That the giving famishes the craving. Gives too late
What's not believed in, or if still believed,
In memory only, reconsidered passion.

From Eliot's point of view, this is merely self-deception. Given the idealist historicism that Eliot inherited from Bradley, history cannot possibly be an "other," separated from the self who conceives it. By presenting history as something other than an "ideal construction," a product of his own mind, Gerontion shifts the blame for his own situation from himself onto history:

Gives too soon
Into weak hands, what's thought can be dispensed with
Till the refusal propagates a fear. Think
Neither fear nor courage saves us. Unnatural vices
Are fathered by our heroism. Virtues

Are forced upon us by our impudent crimes.

Neither passive fear not active courage will save us, says Gerontion, because history has duped us, perverting our heroic intentions. Gerontion's understanding of history is a rationalization of his own inability to act or feel. It is to his advantage to be what Bradley calls an "uncritical historian" or what Eliot calls an "imperfect critic."

Unlike Eliot, the speaker of "Gerontion" does not understand that his knowledge of history is his own "ideal construction," and that a vision of historical chaos is a product of the mind that cannot unify the present and the past. As I mentioned in the introduction, Eliot's drafts for "Gerontion" show that the passage on history was finished in all but one crucial point before other sections of the poem were given their final forms.

In his last revision, Eliot altered only one word: he substituted "history" for "nature." Had the change not been made, our sense of the entire poem would be drastically different; on a much smaller scale, I want to point out that Eliot's substitution of "history" for "nature" confirms the fact that the word "history" is to be understood in "Gerontion" not as a sequence of events in the "real" past but as an "ideal construction" of those events: history is not the same thing as nature, the real world outside us.

Even nature is an "ideal construction" for Eliot, a fabrication of the mind: in his essay on Tennyson's *In Memoriam* (1936) he writes of "that strange abstraction, 'Nature.'" Eliot's substitution of the word "history" emphasizes what his persona in "Gerontion" does not understand: that history is not something separate from the life of the individual in the present.

Many lines of "Gerontion,", including the opening ones, are conversational in character: "Here I am, an old man in a dry month, / Being read to by a boy, waiting for rain" (*CPP* 21). But the poem provides no continuing determinate scene or narrative within which such lines can confidently be placed, though there are sporadic indications of possible scenes and narratives.

The relatively disjointed quality of both "Prufrock" and "Gerontion," especially the lack of good continuity between the verse paragraphs, makes it hard to ascribe the language to a speaker, even one who is in the kind of extreme situation mentally or physically that is sometimes portrayed in dramatic monologues.

Instead of being located, grounded in a referential way, the language, which is full of dislocations, tends to float; it refuses to be tied to a limiting scene or to a limited meaning. The conversational language is not sustained, for instance, in the lines that follow the opening ones in "Gerontion":

I was neither at the hot gates
Nor fought in the warm rain
Nor knee deep in the salt marsh, heaving a cutlass,
Bitten by flies, fought.

We find out where this "I" was not and what it did not do, not where or what it is in any positive sense. The passage gives rise to questions that it does not answer and that are not answered elsewhere in "Gerontion." Stylistically, both the sequence of negatives and the repetition of "fought" at the end of the sentence indicate the composed, written character of the lines rather than the spontaneous utterance of an "I" with a personal voice.

The difficulty of maintaining the illusion of an "I" who speaks becomes greater as "Gerontion" proceeds, for example, in the fifth stanza with its sequence of sentences beginning with the verb "Think," which continues into the next stanza. The sentences may be in the imperative mood.

Or the subject of an indicative verb may have been omitted. The grammatical indeterminacy disturbs the statements' coherence in ways that resist resolution. The language pertains not to a character whose name indicates that he is a person but to one who is named artificially. Like a figure in a medieval allegory whose name points to a concept that is abstract and general rather than personal and individual, Gerontion is not a person but one among many possible incarnations of the meaning of his name in Greek, "little old man."

graph,

The psychological coherence of the first verse principle instrumental in clarifying both the main structf the house of superimposed contexts and the main imes to his second within the house, is abandoned as Eliotóns that critics have stanza. The tenuous psychological comese two stanzas are pointed to as transitions betwe
inventions, not discoveries. elled by a desire for order. The

They are fabrications za "follows" the first only in its fact is that the second ge; logically and psychologically, the arrangement on the w at all. It does not properly begin, and second does not t simply starts, and then, without a period or it does not en a, in the middle of a sentence, in the middle of a even a co
line, it ops.

his stanza relocates readers, giving them a far more clusive vantage point. All of those ruined houses in windy spaces—from Gerontion's withered brain to Europe's war-shattered civilization—are suddenly placed in the context of the rejection of Christ. Although the second stanza lacks the internal coherence of the first, it is unified by the fact that all these fragments are related to the Christian religion and, as will become evident, to a special relation between knowledge and unbelief.

As far as the overall structure of the poem is concerned, this stanza takes the most teratical image of the previous stanza—the Jew lying in wait for his prey—and superimposes one of history's greatest houses, the house of David. The principal tenants in this vision of the house of Israel are the Pharisees, Christ, and pulling together nineteen hundred years of history, the landlord squatting on the window sill of Europe.

But these sons of David are not the only tenants of this antique house. Joining the natural brothers are many half brothers, audacious upstarts who irreversibly alter Abraham's line. The rejection of Christ by his brothers in blood led to an expansion of the house of Israel. Anyone of any race whatsoever who would accept Christ in faith was adopted into what the Bible calls the new Israel, the Christian Church. The tenants in Jacob's greater house include, then, Christ's adopted

brothers
seventeenth-joint heirs, including in this stanza the of Israel, like thry preacher, Lancelot Andrewes. The house sieged. se of Gerontion, is decayed, dry, wind-

Eliot's main allusio a sermon preached by Lanthis second verse paragraph is to I on Christmas Day, 1618: Andrewes before King James

> *Verbum infans, the Word witho word; the eternal*
> *Word not able to speak a word; a wo sure and...*
> *swaddled; and that a wonder too. He th kes the sea*
> *"and rolls it about the swaddled bands of da ess," to*
> *come thus into clouts, Himself.*

This sermon deals with the particular theme of Christmas—the Incarnation. The mystery of the Incarnation, of course, is the mystery of God being immured in a house of flesh. The ancient image of the body as a house, central in the previous stanza of this poem, has a special meaning here.

In the case of Jesus of Nazareth, the tenant of the body is a god; the house, therefore, is much more than a house—it is a temple. The Bible frequently describes the body of Christ as a temple. The book of Hebrews, for example, contains a detailed analogy between the Jewish house of God, the tabernacle, and the incarnate Christ, "a greater and more perfect tabernacle, not made with hands".

And Christ referred to his own body in just these terms in a text alluded to by both Andrewes and Eliot. The temple of the Christ, then, is superimposed upon the Jewish temple which it transformed.

The greater temple was swaddled in darkness, the darkness of infancy's powerlessness, the darkness of corrupted Judaism, the darkness of history. The body of Christ is a house apart in "Gerontion"; it also stood in a dry and windy land, but instead of decaying in the general aridity, it was arrested in full strength and destroyed. The ruin in all of the houses in in the poem is related to the destruction of this temple.

The text for Andrewes's sermon (and for Eliot's poem) is the demand by the Pharisees that Christ give them proofs of his divinity—"We would see a sign!" This text focuses attention on another house within the house of Israel. The mind of the Pharisees is this new house, and it is in certain ways analogous to the mind of Gerontion.

Then certain of the scribes and of the Pharisees answered, saying, Master, we would see a sign from thee. But he answered and said unto them, An evil and adulterous generation seeketh after a sign; and there shall no sign be given to it, but the sign of the prophet Jonas.

This passage is crucial to understand "Gerontion," for it identifies the curse that has brought all these houses (Greek, Jewish, Christian) to ruin; this curse is a mentality that isolates intelligence from passion and from belief. Separated from its context, the above passage seems to say that Christ refused to give the Pharisees a sign, demanding that they accept him by faith alone. In context, the passage says almost the opposite. Most of Christ's career was devoted to giving signs to these professors of law and religion; but whenever a sign was given, the proud but unperceiving scholars took it for a wonder and, ironically, resumed their campaign for a sign.

In the incident quoted above, Christ gave two signs of his divinity. First, he restored a paralyzed hand, and then he cast out a demon which was making its victim blind. The Pharisees witnessing these signs responded with their usual request, "We would see a sign!" They accepted the authenticity of the miracles, but they refused to accept their validity as signs. They would soon see the supreme sign, but their unbelief, inseparable from their learning, would prevent them from recognizing it. This rejection by the Pharisees, quoted by Andrewes and by Eliot, was a turning point in the life of Christ and in history, because it led to an expansion of the house of Jacob. In his immediate response to these Pharisees, Christ oversteps the racial definition of Israel by asking "Who is my mother? And who are my brethren?" and by answering "Whosoever shall do the will of my Father, who is in heaven, the same is my brother, and sister, and mother".

In the second stanza of "Gerontion," Eliot's use of Andrewes's sermon superimposes this more inclusive house of Israel, the Christian Church. It may be supposed that Eliot, who became an admirer of Andrewes's theology, is contrasting the rejection of Christ by the Jews to the acceptance of Christ by the Church, or that he is contrasting the Pharisees' blindness to Andrewes's insight. But Eliot's opening fragment, "Signs are taken for wonders," is as applicable to Andrewes as it is to the Pharisees, as applicable to the Christian Church as to Israel.

In the specific part of the sermon to which Eliot alludes in his poem, Andrewes repeatedly declares that the Incarnation is a "wonder too," a "wonder sure." The seventeenth-century divines loved to preach about the supreme wonder of infinity incarcerated in a finite prison, of the one who swaddled the sea being swaddled in baby clouts. Seduced by paradox, they were enthralled by the wonder of omnipotence dependent upon a young woman for diaper changes, of omnipresence locked up in infant flesh. By transforming the Incarnation into an abstraction, by treating it as an occasion for rhetorical play, the Church had also taken the sign for a wonder.

The Church is another of this poem's decaying, crumbling houses in dry and windy lands. The Church, furthermore, is occupied by desiccated and dying tenants housing dull and shriveled thoughts; the churchyard is parched and, literally as well as figuratively, packed with dry bones, dry stones, dry excreta. The third stanza, which describes a corrupt eucharist ceremony, elaborates and complicates the houses already introduced in the poem. Attention is focused on the house of the twentieth-century Church as contemporary participants in the Mass are superimposed upon the Pharisees and upon the seventeenth-century Church as accomplices in the ongoing rejection of Christ.

The motif of the body as a house is extended in this stanza. In the Church Age, i.e., after Pentecost, the bodies of Christians constitute the house of God. "Ye are the temple of the living god," Paul tells the weak Christians in Corinth (II Corinthians 6:16).

Mr. Silvero, Hakagawa, Madame de Tornquist, and Fraulein von Kulp, then, are decayed temples, windswept, wind-sieged, wind-abandoned, wind-destroyed.

Chapter 6

On The Waste Land

The bundle of quotations with which the poem ends has a very definite relation to the general theme of the poem and to several of the major symbols used in the poem. Before Arnaut leaps back into the refining fire of Purgatory with joy he says: "I am Arnaut who weep and go singing; contrite I see my past folly, and joyful I see before me the day I hope for. Now I pray you by that virtue which guides you to the summit of the stair, at times be mindful of my pain."

This theme is carried forward by the quotation from *Pervigilium Veneris:* "When shall I be like the swallow." The allusion is also connected with the Philomela symbol. (Eliot's note on the passage indicates this clearly.) The sister of Philomela was changed into a swallow as Philomela was changed into a nightingale.

The protagonist is asking therefore when shall the spring, the time of love, return, but also when will he be reborn out of his sufferings, and—with the special meaning which the symbol takes on from the preceding Dante quotation and from the earlier contexts already discussed—he is asking what is asked at the end of one of the minor poems: "When will Time flow away."

The quotation from "El Desdichado," as Edmund Wilson has pointed out, indicates that the protagonist of the poem has been disinherited, robbed of his tradition. The ruined tower is perhaps also the Perilous Chapel, "only the wind's home," and it is also the whole tradition in decay. The protagonist resolves to claim his tradition and rehabilitate it.

The quotation from *The Spanish Tragedy*—"Why then Ile

fit you. Hieronymo's mad againe"—is perhaps the most puzzling of all these quotations.

It means, I believe, this: The protagonist's acceptance of what is in reality the deepest truth will seem to the present world mere madness. ("And still she cried... 'Jug jug' to dirty ears.") Hieronymo in the play, like Hamlet, was "mad" for a purpose. The protagonist is conscious of the interpretation which will be placed on the words which follow—words which will seem to many apparently meaningless babble, but which contain the oldest and most permanent truth of the race:

Datta. Dayadhvam. Damyata.

Quotation of the whole context from which the line is taken confirms this interpretation. Hieronymo, asked to write a play for the court's entertainment, replies:

Why then, I'll fit you; say no more.
When I was young, I gave my mind
And plied myself to fruitless poetry;
Which though it profit the professor naught
Yet it is passing pleasing to the world.

He sees that the play will give him the opportunity he has been seeking to avenge his son's murder. Like Hieronymo, the protagonist in the poem has found his theme; what he is about to perform is not "fruitless."

After this repetition of what the thunder said comes the benediction:

Shantih Shantih Shantih

The foregoing account of *The Waste Land* is, of course, not to be substituted for the poem itself. Moreover, it certainly is not to be considered as represent*ing the method by which the poem was composed.* Much which the prose expositor must represent as though it had been consciously contrived obviously was arrived at unconsciously and concretely.

The account given above is a statement merely of the "prose meaning," and bears the same relation to the poem as does the "prose meaning" of any other poem. But one need not perhaps apologize for setting forth such a statement explicitly, for *The Waste Land* has been almost consistently misinterpreted since its first publication. Even a critic so acute as Edmund Wilson has seen the poem as essentially a statement of despair and disillusionment, and his account sums up the stock interpretation of the poem. Indeed, the phrase, "the poetry of drouth," has become a cliché of left-wing criticism.

It is such a misrepresentation of *The Waste Land* as this which allows Eda Lou Walton to entitle an essay on contemporary poetry, "Death in the Desert"; or which causes Waldo Frank to misconceive of Eliot's whole position and personality. But more than the meaning of one poem is at stake.

If *The Waste Land* is not a world-weary cry of despair or a sighing after the vanished glories of the past, then not only the popular interpretation of the poem will have to be altered but also the general interpretations of post-War poetry which begin with such a misinterpretation as a premise.

Such misinterpretations involve also misconceptions of Ellot's technique. Eliot's basic method may be said to have passed relatively unnoticed. The popular view of the method used in *The Waste Land* may be described as follows: Eliot makes use of ironic contrasts between the glorious past and the sordid present—the crashing irony of

But at my back from time to time I hear
The sound of horns and motors, which shall bring
Sweeney to Mrs. Porter in the spring.

But this is to take the irony of the poem at the most superficial level, and to neglect the other dimensions in which it operates. And it is to neglect what are essentially more important aspects of his method. Moreover, it is to overemphasize the difference between the method employed by Eliot in this poem and that employed by him in later poems.

The basic method used in *The Waste Land* may be described as the application of the principle of complexity. The poet works in terms of surface parallelisms which in reality make ironical contrasts, and in terms of surface contrasts which in reality constitute parallelisms. (The second group sets up effects which may be described as the obverse of irony.) The two aspects taken together give the effect of chaotic experience ordered into a new whole, though the realistic surface of experience is faithfully retained. The complexity of the experience is not violated by the apparent forcing upon it of a predetermined scheme.

The fortune-telling of "The Burial of the Dead" will illustrate the general method very satisfactorily. On the surface of the poem the poet reproduces the patter of the charlatan, Madame Sosostris, and there is the surface irony: the contrast between the original use of the Tarot cards and the use made by Madame Sosostris.

But each of the details (justified realistically in the palaver of the fortune-teller) assumes a new meaning in the general context of the poem. There is then, in addition to the surface irony, something of a Sophoclean irony too, and the "fortune-telling," which is taken ironically by a twentieth-century audience, becomes *true* as the poem develops—true in a sense in which Madame Sosostris herself does not think it true.

The surface irony is thus reversed and becomes an irony on a deeper level. The items of her speech have only one reference in terms of the context of her speech: the "man with three staves," the "one-eyed merchant," the "crowds of people, walking round in a ring," etc.

But transferred to other contexts they become loaded with special meanings. To sum up, all the central symbols of the poem head up here; but here, in the only section in which they are explicitly bound together, the binding is slight and accidental. The deeper lines of association only emerge in terms of the total context as the poem develops—and this is, of course, exactly the effect which the poet intends.

[....]

The poem would undoubtedly be "clearer" if every symbol had a single, unequivocal meaning; but the poem would be thinner, and less honest. For the poet has not been content to develop a didactic allegory in which the symbols are two-dimensional items adding up directly to the sum of the general scheme. They represent dramatized instances of the theme, embodying in their own nature the fundamental paradox of the theme.

We shall better understand why the form of the poem is

right and inevitable if we compare Eliot's theme to Dante's and to Spenser's. Eliot's theme is not the statement of a faith held and agreed upon (Dante's *Divine Comedy)* nor is it the projection of a "new" system of beliefs (Spenser's *Faerie Queene*). Eliot's theme is the rehabilitation of a system of beliefs, known but now discredited.

Dante did not have to "prove" his statement; he could assume it and move within it about a poet's business. Eliot does not care, like Spenser,. to force the didacticism. He prefers to stick to the poet's business.

But, unlike Dante, he cannot assume acceptance of the statement. A direct approach is calculated to elicit powerful "stock responses" which will prevent the poem's being read at all. Consequently, the only method is to work by indirection.

The Christian material is at the centre, but the poet never deals with it directly. The theme of resurrection is made on the surface in terms of the fertility rites; the words which the thunder speaks are Sanscrit words.

We have been speaking as if the poet were a strategist trying to win acceptance from a hostile audience. But of course this is true only in a sense. The poet himself is audience as well as speaker; we state the problem more exactly if we state it in terms of the poet's integrity rather than in terms of his strategy.

He is so much a man of his own age that he can indicate his attitude toward the Christian tradition without falsity only in terms of the difficulties of a rehabilitation; and he is so much a poet and so little a propagandist that he can be sincere only as he presents his theme concretely and dramatically.

To put the matter in still other terms: the Christian terminology is for the poet a mass of clichés. However "true" he may feel the terms to be, he is still sensitive to the fact that they operate superficially as clichés, and his method of necessity must be a process of bringing them to life again. The method adopted in *The Waste Land* is thus violent and radical, but thoroughly necessary.

For the renewing and vitalizing of symbols which have been crusted over with a distorting familiarity demands the type of organization which we have already commented on in discussing particular passages: the statement of surface similarities which are ironically revealed to be dissimilarities, and the association of apparently obvious dissimilarities which culminates in a later realization that the dissimilarities are only superficial—that the chains of likeness are in reality fundamental.

In this way the statement of beliefs emerges *through* confusion and cynicism—not in spite of them.

In the *Cantos* and *The Waste Land,* however, it should have been clear that a radical transformation was taking place in aesthetic structure; but this transformation has been touched on only peripherally by modern critics. R. P. Blackmur comes closest to the central problem while analyzing what he calls Pound's "anecdotal" method.

The special form of the *Cantos,* Blackmur explains, "is that of the anecdote begun in one place, taken up in one or more other places, and finished, if at all, in still another. This deliberate disconnectedness, this art of a thing continually alluding to itself, continually breaking off short, is the method by which the *Cantos* tie themselves together. So soon as the reader's mind is concerted with the material of the poem, Mr. Pound deliberately disconcerts it, either by introducing fresh and disjunct material or by reverting to old and, apparently, equally disjunct material."

Blackmur's remarks apply equally well to *The Waste Land,* where syntactical sequence is given up for a structure depending on the perception of relationships between disconnected word-groups. To be properly understood, these word-groups must be juxtaposed with one another and perceived simultaneously.

Only when this is done can they be adequately grasped; for, while they follow one another in time, their meaning does not depend on this temporal relationship. The one difficulty of these poems, which no amount of textual exegesis can wholly overcome, is the internal conflict between the time-logic of language and the space-logic implicit in the modern conception of the nature of poetry.

Aesthetic form in modern poetry, then, is based on a space-logic that demands a complete reorientation in the reader's attitude toward language. Since the primary reference of any word-group is to something inside the poem itself, language in modern poetry is really reflexive. The meaning-relationship is completed only by the simultaneous perception in space of word-groups that have no comprehensible relation to each other when read consecutively in time.

Instead of the instinctive and immediate reference of words and word-groups to the objects or events they symbolize and the construction of meaning from the sequence of these references, modern poetry asks its readers to suspend the process of individual reference temporarily until the entire pattern of internal references can be apprehended as a unity.

It would not be difficult to trace this conception of poetic form back to Mallarmé's ambition to create a language of "absence" rather than of presence—a language in which words negated their objects instead of designating them; nor should one overlook the evident formal analogies between *The Waste Land* and the *Cantos* and Mallarmé's *Un Coup de dés.*

Mallarmé, indeed, dislocated the temporality of language far more radically than either Eliot or Pound has ever done; and his experience with *Un Coup de dés* showed that this ambition of modern poetry has a necessary limit. If pursued with Mallarmé's relentlessness, it culminates in the self-negation of language and the creation of a hybrid pictographic "poem" that can only be considered a fascinating historical curiosity.

Nonetheless, this conception of aesthetic form, which may be formulated as the principle of reflexive reference, has left its traces on all of modem poetry. And the principle of reflexive reference is the link connecting the aesthetic development of modern poetry with similar experiments in the modern novel.

The Waste Land summarizes the Grail legend, not precisely in the usual order, but retaining the principal incidents and adapting them to a modern setting. Eliot's indebtedness both to Sir James Frazer and to Jessie L. Weston's *From Ritual to Romance* (in which book he failed to cut pages 138-39 and 142-

43 of his copy) is acknowledged in his notes. Jessie L. Weston's thesis is that the Grail legend was the surviving record of an initiation ritual. Later writers have reaffirmed the psychological validity of the link between such ritual, phallic religion, and the spiritual content of the Greek Mysteries.

Identification of the Grail story with the common myth of the hero assailing a devil-dragon underground or in the depths of the sea completes the unifying idea behind *The Waste Land.* The Grail legend corresponds to the great hero epics, it dramatizes initiation into maturity, and it bespeaks a quest for sexual, cultural, and spiritual healing. Through all these attributed functions, it influenced Eliot's symbolism.

Parallels with yet other myths and with literary treatments of the "quest" theme reinforce Eliot's pattern of death and rebirth. Though *The Tempest,* one of Eliot's minor sources, scarcely depicts an initiation "mystery," Colin Still, in a book of which Eliot has since written favorably *(Shakespeare's Mystery Play),* had already advanced the theory in 1921 that it implies such a subject."

And Tiresias is not simply the Grail knight and the Fisher King but Ferdinand and Prospero, as well as Tristan and Mark, Siegfried and Wotan. In his feminine role he is not simply the Grail-maiden and the wise Kundry but the sibyl, Dido, Miranda, Brünnhilde.

Each of these represents one of the three main characters in the Grail legend and in the mystery cults—the wounded god, the sage woman (transformed in some versions of the Grail legend into a beautiful maiden), and the resurrected god, successful quester, or initiate. Counterparts to them figure elsewhere; Eliot must have been conscious that the "Ancient Mariner" and "Childe Roland" had analogues to his own symbolism.

In adopting fertility symbolism, Eliot was probably influenced by Stravinsky's ballet *Le Sacre du printemps.* The summer before writing *The Waste Land* he saw the London production, and on reviewing it in September he criticized the disparity between Massine's choreography and the music. He might almost have been sketching his own plans for a work applying a primitive idea to contemporary life: In art there should be interpenetration and metamorphosis. Even the Golden Bough can be read in two ways: as a collection of entertaining myths, or as a revelation of that vanished mind of which our mind is a continuation. In everything in the Sacre du Printemps, except in the music, one missed the sense of the present.

Whether Stravinsky's music be permanent or ephemeral I do not know; but it did seem to transform the rhythm of the steppes into the scream of the motor horn, the rattle of machinery, the grind of wheels, the beating of iron and steel, the roar of the underground railway, and the other barbaric cries of modern life; and to transform these despairing noises into music. In *The Waste Land* he imposed the fertility myth upon the world about him.

Eliot's waste land suffers from a dearth of love and faith. It is impossible to demarcate precisely at every point between the physical and the spiritual symbolism of the poem; as in "Gerontion" the speaker associates the failure of love with his spiritual dejection.

It is clear enough, however, that the contemporary waste land is not, like that of the romances, a realm of sexless sterility. The argument emerges that in a world that makes too much of the physical and too little of the spiritual relations between the sexes, Tiresias, for whom love and sex must form a unity, has been ruined by his inability to unify them. The action of the poem, as Tiresias recounts it, turns thus on two crucial incidents: the garden scene in Part I and the approach to the Chapel Perilous in Part V.

The one is the traditional initiation in the presence of the Grail; the other is the mystical initiation, as described by Jessie L. Weston, into spiritual knowledge. The first, if successful, would constitute rebirth through love and sex; the second, rebirth without either. Since both fail, the quest fails, and the poem ends with a formula for purgatorial suffering, through which Tiresias may achieve the second alternative after patience and self-denial—perhaps after physical death. The counsel to give, sympathize, and control befits one whom direct ways to beatitude cannot release from suffering. Conrad's *Heart of Darkness* is of course one of the "influences" in *TheWaste Land*. It seems to me, though, much more than this.

Conrad's story is of the primitive world of cannibalism and dark magic penetrated by the materialist, supposedly civilized world of exploitation and gain; and of the corruption of the mind of a man of civilized consciousness by the knowledge of the evil of the primitive (or the primitive which becomes evil through the unholy union of European trade and Congolese barbarism). The country of them as described by Conrid is a country of pure horror.

Eliot is usually thought of as a sophisticated writer, an "intellectual." For this reason, the felling of primitive horror which rises from depths of his poetry is overlooked. Yet it is there in the rhythms, often crystallizing in some phrase which suggests the drums beating through the jungle darkness, the scuttling, clawing, shadowy forms of life in the depths of the sea, the spears of savages shaking across the immense width of the river, the rough-hewn images of prehistoric sculptures found in the depths of the primeval forest, the huge cactus forms in deserts, the whispering of ghosts at the edge of darkness. Probably this is the most Southern (in the American sense) characteristic of Eliot, reminding one that he was a compatriot of Edgar Allan Poe and William Faulkner. And Conrad's *Heart of Darkness* is a landscape with which Eliot is deeply, disquietedly, guiltily almost, familiar, and with which he contrasts effects of sunlight, lips trembling in prayer, eyes gazing into the heart of light or hauntingly into the eyes, a ship answering to the hand on a tiller as a symbol of achieved love and civilization.

The Waste Land, Eliot's first long philosophical poem, can now be read simply as it was written, as a poem of radical doubt and negation, urging that every human desire be stilled except the desire for self-surrender, for restraint, and for peace. Compared with the longing expressed in later poems for the "eyes" and the "birth," the "coming" and "the Lady" (in "The Hollow Men," the Ariel poems, and "Ash-Wednesday"), the hope held out in *The Waste Land* is a negative one.

Following Hugh Kenner's recommendation, we should lay to rest the persistent error of reading *The Waste Land* as a poem in which five motifs predominate: the nightmare journey, the Chapel, the Quester, the Grail Legend, and the Fisher King.

The motifs are indeed introduced, as Eliot's preliminary note to his text informs us, but if (as this note says) "the plan and a good deal of the incidental symbolism of the poem were suggested by Miss Jessie L. Weston's book on the Grail legend," the plan can only have been to question, and even to propose a life without hope for, a quest, or Chapel, or Grail in the modern waste land.

The themes of interior prison and nightmare city—or the "urban apocalypse" elucidated by Kenner and Eleanor Cook—make much better sense when seen as furnishing the centripetal "plan" and "symbolism," especially when one follows Cook's discussion of the disintegration of all European cities after the First World War and the poem's culminating vision of a new Carthaginian collapse, imagined from the vantage point of India's holy men.

A passage canceled in the manuscript momentarily suggested that the ideal city, forever unrealizable on earth, might be found (as Plato thought) "in another world," but the reference was purely sardonic. Nowhere in the poem can one find convincing allusions to *any* existence in another world, much less to St.

Augustine's vision of interpenetration between the City of God and the City of Man in *this* world. How, then, can one take seriously attempts to find in the poem any such quest for eternal life as the Grail legend would have to provide if it were a continuous motif—even a sardonic one?

It seems that only since Eliot's death is it possible to read his life forward—understanding *The Waste Land* as it was written, without being deflected by our knowledge of the writer's later years. Before Eliot's death the tendency was to read the poem proleptically—as if reflecting the poems of the later period.

This is how Cleanth Brooks, writing the first fully

elucidative essay on *The Waste Land,* read it, stressing the Grail legends, the longing for new life, rather than the purely negative aspects of the theme. Thus Brooks interpreted the Sibyl's appeal for death at the beginning of the poem as exactly parallel to the Magus's appetite for death in the Ariel poems (the Magus's, of course, filled with the pain of knowing that Christ had subjected himself to weak mortality and not knowing yet the Resurrection).

To make the Sibyl and the Magus parallel was to read Eliot's development backward—perhaps an irresistible temptation when the pattern in his life was so little known and when (as then in 1939) Brooks was acquainted with the man at work on *Four Quartets,* who had recently produced the celebrated *Murder in the Cathedral.*

It was also irresistible, in a culture still nominally Christian, to hope that *The Waste Land* was about a world in which God was not dead. But the poem was not about such a world.

Within ten years after finishing *The Waste Land,* Eliot recognized that the poem had made him into the leader of a new "way." His own words of 1931, however, require us to read the poem as having pushed this roadway through to its end—for him.

It was no Grail quest. Those who followed him into it, and stayed on it, he said in "Thoughts After Lambeth," "are now pious pilgrims, cheerfully plodding the road from nowhere to nowhere." There could be no more decisive reference to the negative way he had followed till 1922, and also to the impasse where it ended.

A good reading of *The Waste Land* must begin, then, with recognition that while it expressed Eliot's own "way" at the time, it was not intended to lay down a way for others to follow. He did not expect that his prisonhouse would have corridors connecting with everyone else's.

"I dislike the word 'generation' [he said in "Thoughts After Lambeth"), which has been a talisman for the last ten years; when I wrote a poem called *The Waste Land* some of the more approving critics said that I had expressed the 'disillusionment of a generation,' which is nonsense. I may have expressed for them their own illusion of being disillusioned, but that did not form part of my intention."

Dismay at finding his personal, interior journey (which he later called "rhythmic grumbling") converted into a superhighway seems to have been one of the main impulses toward his discovery of a new way after 1922.

If we listen attentively to the negations of *The Waste Land,* they tell us much about the poem that was missed when it was read from the affirmative point of view brought to it by its early defenders and admirers. Ironically, it was only its detractors—among them Eliot's friend Conrad Aiken—who acknowledged its deliberate vacuity and incoherence and the life-questioning theme of this first venture into "philosophical" poetry on Eliot's part.

Aiken considered its incoherence a virtue because its subject was incoherence, but this was cool comfort either to himself or to Eliot, who was outraged by Aiken's opinion that the poem was "melancholy." It was far from being a *sad* poem—like the nineteenth-century poems that Eliot had criticized precisely because of their wan melancholias, based as he said on their excesses of desire over the possibilities that life can afford.

Neither Aiken, who found the poem disappointing, nor I. A. Richards, who was exhilarated by its rejection of all "belief, " spotted the poem's focus on negation as a philosophically meditated position.

[Levenson quotes the opening four lines]

Who speaks these lines? – presumably whoever speaks these next lines:

since the subject-matter (the life of the seasons) persists, as does the distinctive syntactic pattern (the series of present participles) and the almost obsessive noun-adjective pairings ("dead land," "spring rain," "little life," "dried tubers"). The second sentence, of course, introduces a new element, a narrating personal consciousness.

But surely this need not signal a new speaker; it suggests rather that there is and *has been* a speaker, the unspecified "us," who will receive greater specification in the next several lines. Certainly we want to identify the "us" that winter kept warm with the "us" that summer surprised, and with the "we" who stop, go on, drink coffee and talk. That is how we expect pronouns to behave: same referents unless new antecedents.

But if the pronouns suggest a stable identity for the speaker, much else has already become unstable. Landscape has given way to cityscape. General speculation (April as the "cruellest month") resolves into a particular memory: the day in the Hofgarten. And the stylistic pattern shifts. The series of participles disappears, replaced by a series of verbs in conjunction: "And went... And drank... And talked." The adjective-noun pattern is broken.

What can we conclude so far? — that a strain exists between the presumed identity of the poem's speaker and the instability of the speaker's world. If this is the speech of one person, it has the range of many personalities and many voices — a point that will gain clarity if we consider the remaining lines of the sequence: The line of German aggravates the strain, challenging the fragile continuity that has been established. Here is a new voice with a new subject-matter, speaking in another language, resisting assimilation. Is the line spoken, overheard, remembered? Among the poem's readers no consensus has emerged. Nor is consensus to be expected. In the absence of contextual clues, and Eliot suppresses such clues, the line exists as a stark, unassimilable poetic datum.

And yet, after that line a certain continuity is restored. The first-person plural returns; the pattern of conjunction reappears: "And when... And I... And down." Even that startling line of German, let us notice, had been anticipated in the "Hofgarten" and "Starnbergersee" of the previous lines. Discontinuity, in other words, is no more firmly established than continuity. The opening lines of the poem offer an elaborate system of similarities and oppositions, which might be represented in the following manner:

April is the cruellest month, breeding
Lilacs out of the dead land, mixing
Memory and desire, stirring

Dull roots with spring rain.
Winter kept us warm, covering
Earth in forgetful snow, feeding
A little life with dried tubers.
Summer surprised us, coming over the Starnbergersee
With a shower of rain; we stopped in the colonnade,
And drank coffee, and talked for an hour.
Btn gar kc inc Russin, stamm' aus Litauen, echt deutsche
And when we were children, staying at the arch-duke's,
My causin's he took me out on a sled,
And I was mountains, there you feel free.
I read, much of the night, and go south in the winter.

The diagram should indicate the difficulty. Lines 1-6 are linked by the use of present participles, lines 5-18 by personal pronouns, lines 8-12 by the use of German, lines 10-16 by the reiteration of the conjunction "and." The consequence is that in any given line we may find a stylistic feature which will bind it to a subsequent or previous line, in this way suggesting a continuous speaker, or at least making such a speaker plausible.

But we have no single common feature connecting all the lines: one principle of continuity gives way to the next. And these overlapping principles of similarity undermine the attempt to draw boundaries around distinct speaking subjects. The poetic voice is changing; that we all hear. Certainly we hear it when we compare one of the opening lines to those at the end of the passage. But the changes are incremental, frustrating the attempt to make strict demarcations.

How many speak in these opening lines? "One," "two" and "three" have been answers, but my point is that any attempt to resolve that issue provokes a collision of interpretive conventions.

On the one hand, the sequence of first-person pronouns — an "us" that becomes a "we," a "me" an "I," and then "Marie" — would encourage us to read these lines as marking the steady emergence of an individual human subject. But if the march of pronouns would imply that Marie has been the speaker throughout, that suggestion is threatened in the several ways we have considered: the shift from general reflection to personal reminiscence, from landscape to cityscape, from participial connectives to conjunctions, the disappearance of the noun-adjective pattern, the use of German.

Attitudes, moreover, have undergone a delicate, though steady, evolution. Can the person who was "kept... warm... in forgetful snow... " be that Marie, who prefers to "go south in winter?" Can the voice which solemnly intones the opening and explosive paradox: April is cruel, utter such conversational banalities as: "In the mountains, there you feel free"?

Perhaps – but if we insist on Marie as the consistent speaker, if we ask her to lay hold of this complexity, we can expect only an unsteady grasp. The heterogeneity of attitude, the variety of tone, do not resolve into the attitudes and tones of an individual personality.

In short, the boundaries of the self begin to waver: if we can no longer trust our pronouns, what can we trust? Furthermore, though we find it difficult to posit one speaker, it is scarcely easier to posit many, since we can say with no certainty where one concludes and another begins. Though the poem's opening lines do not hang together, neither do they fall cleanly apart. Here, as elsewhere, the poem plays between bridges and chasms, repetitions and aggressive novelties, echoes and new voices.

In the opening movement of *The Waste Land,* the individual subject possesses none of the formal dominance it once enjoyed in Conrad and James. No single consciousness presides; no single voice dominates. A character appears, looming suddenly into prominence, breaks into speech, and then recedes, having bestowed momentary conscious perception on the fragmentary scene. Marie will provide neither coherence nor continuity for the poem: having been named, she will disappear; her part is brief. Our part is larger, for the question we now face is the problem of boundaries in *The Waste Land.*

Eliot, as we have already seen, rejects the need for any such integrating Absolute as a way of guaranteeing order. His theory of points of view means to obviate that need. Points of view, though distinct, can be combined.

Order can emerge from beneath; it need not descend from above. And thus in the *Monist* he says of Leibniz' theory of the dominant monad: "I contend that if one recognizes two points of view which are quite irreconcilable and yet *melt into* each other, this theory is quite superfluous." And in the dissertation he writes that "the pre-established harmony is unnecessary if we recognize that the monads are *not wholly distinct*."

My italics are tendentious, dramatizing the repetitions in phrase. But the repetition is more than a chance echo; it identifies a problem which both the philosophy and the poetry address. How can one finite experience be related to any other? Put otherwise, how can difference be compatible with unity? Moreover, the poetic solution is continuous with the philosophic solution: individual experiences, individual personalities are not impenetrable. They are distinct, but not wholly so. Like the points of view described in the dissertation, the fragments in *The Waste Land* merge with one another, pass into one another.

Madame Sosostris, for instance, identifies the protagonist with the drowned sailor ("Here, said she/Is your card, the drowned Phoenician Sailor"). But the sailor, Phlebas, is also identified with Mr Eugenides: recall Eliot's phrase, "the one-eyed merchant, seller of currants, melts into the Phoenician Sailor." But, as Langbaum has shown, if the protagonist is identified with Phlebas and Phlebas with Eugenides, then it is difficult to escape the conclusion that the protagonist and the Smyrna merchant are, themselves, "not wholly distinct." What, then, do we make of these lines?

[Levenson quotes lines from "Under the brown fog of a winter noon" to "Followed by a weekend at the Metropole."

The protagonist, as Langbaum points out, "stands on both sides of the proposition," and such a conclusion will unnerve us only if we hold fast to traditional concepts of self, personal identity, personal continuity and the barriers between selves.

But in *The Waste Land* no consistent identity persists; the "shifting references" alter our notions of the self. The characters are little more than aspects of selves or, in the jargon of Eliot's dissertation, "finite centres," "points of view."

Here are the concluding lines of "The Fire Sermon":

Lines from Augustine alternate with lines from the Buddha, and, as Eliot tell us in the footnote: "the collocation of these two representatives of eastern and western asceticism, as the culmination of this part of the poem, is not an accident." Of course it is not.

It is the way the poem works: it collocates in order to culminate. It offers us fragments of consciousness, "various presentations to various viewpoints," which overlap, interlock, "melting into" one another to form emergent wholes.

The poems is not, as it is common to say, built upon the *juxtaposition* of fragments: it is built out of their *interpenetration.* Fragments of the Buddha and Augustine combine to make a new literary reality which is neither the Buddha nor Augustine but which includes them both.

But at my back from time to time I hear
The sound of horns and motors, which shall bring
Sweeney to Mrs. Porter in the spring.

The echo from Marvell passes into an echo from Day: the poetic effect depends on amalgamating these distinct sources, on recognizing them as not wholly distinct. For we know, argues Eliot, "that we are able to pass from one point of view to another, that we are compelled to do so, and that the different aspects more or less hang together." The movement of *The Waste Land* is just such a movement among points of view: Marvell and Day, the Buddha and St Augustine, Ovid and Virgil.

We find ourselves in a position to confront a problem, which, though distant, is not forgotten: the problem of the poem's unity, or what comes to the same thing, the problem of Tiresias. We may begin to see how Tiresias can serve the function of "uniting all the rest," without that obliging us to conclude that all speech and all consciousness are the speech and consciousness of Tiresias.

For, if we rush too quickly to Tiresias as a presiding

consciousness, along the lines established by Conrad or James, then we lose what the text clearly asks us to retain: the plurality of voices that sound in no easy harmony. What Eliot says of the Absolute can be said of Tiresias, who, also, "dissolves at a touch into... constituents."

But this does not leave us with a heap of broken fragments; we have seen how the fragments are constructed into new wholes. If Tiresias dissolves into constituents, let us remember the moments when those constituents resolve into Tiresias. Tiresias is, in this sense, an intermittent phenomenon in the poem, a *subsequent* phenomenon, emerging out of other characters, other aspects. The two sexes may, as Eliot suggests, meet in Tiresias, but they do not begin there.

"The life of a soul," writes Eliot in the dissertation, "does not consist in the contemplation of one consistent world but in the painful task of unifying (to a greater and less extent) jarring and incompatible ones, and passing, when possible, from two or more discordant viewpoints to a higher which shall somehow include and transmute them." Tiresias functions in the poem in just this way: not as a consistent harmonizing consciousness but as the struggled-for emergence of a more encompassing point of view.

The world, Eliot argues, only sporadically accessible to the knowing mind; it is a "felt whole in which there are moments of knowledge." And so, indeed, is *The Waste Land* such a felt whole with moments of knowledge. Tiresias provides not permanent wisdom but instants of lucidity during which the poem's angle of vision is temporarily raised, the expanse of knowledge temporarily widened.

The poem concludes with a rapid series of allusive literary fragments: seven of the last eight lines are quotations. But in the midst of these quotations is a line to which we must attach great importance: "These fragments I have shored against my ruins."

In the space of that line the poem becomes conscious of itself. What had been a series of fragments of consciousness has become a consciousness of fragmentation: that may not be salvation, but it is a difference, for as Eliot writes, "To realise that a point of view is a point of view is already to have transcended it."

And to recognize fragments *as* fragments, to name them as fragments, is already to have transcended them not to an harmonious or final unity but to a somewhat higher, somewhat more inclusive, somewhat more conscious point of view.

Considered in this way, the poem does not achieve a resolved coherence, but neither does it remain in a chaos of fragmentation. Rather it displays a series of more or less stable patterns, regions of coherence, temporary principles of order the poem not as a stable unity but engaged in what Eliot calls the "painful task of unifying."

Within this perspective any unity will be provisional; we may always expect new poetic elements, demanding new assimilation. Thus the voice of Tiresias, having provided a moment of authoritative consciousness at the centre of the poem, falls silent, letting events speak for themselves. And the voice in the last several lines, having become conscious of fragmentation, suddenly gives way to more fragments.

The polyphony of *The Waste Land* allows for intermittent harmonies, but these harmonies are not sustained; the consistencies are not permanent. Eliot's method must be carefully distinguished from the methods of his modernist predecessors. If we attempt to make *The Waste Land* conform to Imagism or Impressionism, we miss its strategy and miss its accomplishment. Eliot wrenched his poetry from the self-sufficiency of the single image and the single narrating consciousness. The principle of order in *The Waste Land* depends on a plurality of consciousnesses, an ever-increasing series of points of view, which struggle towards an emergent unity and then continue to struggle past that unity.

This might be as fair a place as any to take the pulse of the notion of a single and unifying protagonist in *The Waste Land*. Again, the argument is that this notion has not been sufficiently entertained and tested in earlier commentary on Eliot. Stanley Sultan's few pages on the subject in *Ulysses, The Waste Land, and Modernism* form—as will be more fully noted—the one substantial, and neglected, exception.

As has perhaps been demonstrated, part I presents no obstacles to reading the poem in this light. On the contrary, the hypothesis of a single speaker and performer adds shadow, depth, drama, and direction to everything in the movement. It discovers a poem of far more seriousness, profundity, and complexity than Edward Said (among others) regards it as being: namely, "a collection of voices repeating and varying and mimicking one another and literature generally."

Certainly the original working title, "He Do the Police in Different Voices," implies the presence of a single speaker in the poem who is gifted at "taking off" the voices of others—just as the foundling named Sloppy in Dickens's *Our Mutual Friend* is, according to the doubtless biased and doting Betty Higden, "a beautiful reader of a newspaper. He do the police in different voices."

This speaker has a flair for tones of criminality, sensationalism, and outrage—the whole gamut of abjection and judgment; or so the title implies. He shows a relish for such tones, he is virtuosic at rendering them. The working title was thus itself a harsh judgment on the protagonist (whom it travesties).

All speech is abjection? The very impulse to perform voice is suspect? A complicity in the fascination of crime—say, murder? To create and to murder are near akin? These severe intimations are of a piece with the *contemptus mundi* of the poem.

The hypothesis of an all-centering, autobiographical protagonist-narrator is not only consistent with the working title; it explains the confident surfacing, in the latter part of the poem, of an unmistakable religious pilgrim.

Unless this pilgrim can be shown to develop (to inch, scramble, flee) out of a waste land that is, or was, himself, the poem splits apart into two unequal sections, a long one constituted by what Lyndall Gordon calls "the Voices of Society" and a shorter one on a lone pilgrim to elsewhere. Neither Gordon nor A. D. Moody—each so admirable on *The Waste Land*—connects what they concur in regarding as a pilgrim with what they might agree to call the Voices of

Society. But there is no difficulty in the way of positing the former as the "doer" of the latter—as one of the social voices, yet *he who surpasses them* in being able to do and place them in an ironic relation to other voices, including his own.

Gordon's valuable suggestion that the poem belongs in the religio-literary category of "the exemplary life" is in fact better served by this more unifying reading. "In the lives Eliot invokes," Gordon comments, "—Dante, Christ, Augustine, the grail knight, Ezekiel—there is always a dark period of trial, whether in a desert, a slough of despond, or a hell, followed by initiation, conversion, or the divine light itself."

The protagonist is not merely one among others in hell (and the "conversation" between him and Stetson, who were alive and comparatively heroic together so long ago, only makes sense in a dimension of hell); hell is not merely others; the protagonist is hell, and it is out of this hell, at once his own and collective, that, through conversion, he must climb toward the divine light.

If he does the voices of others, it is because in the first instance his ears are whores to them; he dramatizes, thus, his own abjection. He is not merely one of the denizens of the waste land; he is their sum, he is sin upon sin, even sinner upon sinner—or so his self-multiplying and self-shading ventriloquism suggests.

Not that he does the voices altogether helplessly; on the contrary, he gathers them in his fist like a rattlesnake's severed coils and shakes them so as to disturb his own and his readers' war-dulled, jazz-dulled, machine-dulled ears. But, in any case, he demonstrates thus—he confesses—his own hellish entanglements with secularism and the flesh. The first three parts of the poem present the equation *the others = me,* if in a way that proves the equation a little false (it involves a sick self-belittlement). The rest of the poem clarifies the actual opposition of others/me that endows the first three parts with insidious drama.

The protagonist both suffers from and exploits this essential theatricality of voice. His nature is a poet's nature, at once powerfully secretive and helplessly "open"—empathetic, susceptible, yours for the asking. The protagonist is, in a phrase Delmore Schwartz applies to Eliot himself, a "sibylline listener."

He listens in on others with the mercilessness of one who fails to hear "the silence" in their speech yet with the full dramatic sympathy of his empathic nature, too—with a tenth of that capacity for sympathy which also, at its fullest and subtlest stretch, enables him to detect the ethereal presence of an attendant "hooded" figure (part 5), or look into the heart of light.

Eliot's prose poem "Hysteria" was about just such a protohysterical, protosalvational empathy. "As she laughed, I was aware of becoming involved in her laughter and being part of it... I was drawn in by short gasps, inhaled by each momentary recovery, lost finally in the dark caverns of her throat, bruised by the ripple of unseen muscles."

Laughter is hysteria, empathy with voice is hysteria-in-the-making, acting is controlled hysteria. The protagonist "acts" the voices of others as if he had little choice in the matter, and even his "own" voice is, to him, theater, the voice of Hieronymo as he plots a Babel of other voices, plots the crash of Babel itself.

Almost helplessly many, almost incapacitated by his capacity for openness, the protagonist will nonetheless find in this susceptibility to otherness and outsidedness (a susceptibility that, largely "sympathy," makes them inward, his) his *virtú* and virtue, his identification with what is pure and utter: so Other that sympathy with it minimalizes his abjection, which becomes no more than a clot of sound that he must cough up, a phlegm of speech.

By imbuing his protagonist with his own auditory and vocal genius of participation in the abjectness of his times and in approaches to the Absolute (for "the silence" must be heard, and speech must edge it), Eliot made his poem a barometer sensitive both to the foggy immediate air and to the atmospheric pressure high and far off, the "thunder of spring over distant mountains" (part 5).

A group or medley of voices cannot attend to a charged,

remote silence; for that a single protagonist was necessary, one who could both "do" the group and find in himself the anguish and strength to leave it, repressing the fatal impulse (as Moody puts it) "towards a renewal of human love" and seeking, instead, the Love Omnipotent.

The Waste Land does not merely reflect the breakdown of an historical, social, and cultural order battered by violent forces operating under the name of modernity. For Eliot the disaster that characterized modernity was not an overturning, but the unavoidable, and ironic, culmination of that very order so lovingly celebrated in Victoria's last decade on the throne.

Unlike the older generation, who saw in events like the Great War the passing of a golden age, Eliot saw only that the golden age was itself a heap of absurd sociopolitical axioms and perverse misreadings of the cultural past that had proved in the last instance to be made of the meanest alloy. The poem's enactment of the contemporary social scene in "The Burial of the Dead," "A Game of Chess," and "The Fire Sermon" exhibits the "negative liberal society" in which such events and people are typical.

Eliot's choice of these events and people—Madame Sosostris, the cast of characters in "A Game of Chess," and the typist—as *representative* of a particular society is susceptible, of course, to a political analysis, which is to say, their representativeness is not self-evident, though they are presented as if it is. The "one bold stare" of the house-agent's clerk, put back in the bourgeois context where staring is one of the major lapses in manners, does not hold up the mirror to a simple gesture, but illuminates the underlying conditions that make a mere clerk's swagger possible.

What is exposed is the "fact" that clerks in general no longer know their place. What we are to make of this fact is pointedly signaled by the disgust that the specifics of the rendering provoke and the social distance generated by the Tiresian foresufferance....

As its social critique was aimed negatively at the liberal ethos which Eliot felt had culminated in the War and its disorderly aftermath, *The Waste Land* could not visibly adopt some preliberal code of values. In the same way, the poem could not propose a postliberal, historicist or materialist ethic without an historicizing epistemology.

The poem's authority rested instead on other bases that provided, not a system of ideas as the primary form of legitimation, but a new lyric synthesis as a kind of experiential authenticity in a world in which the sacred cosmologies, on the one hand, had fallen prey to astrologers and charlatans, while, on the other, the cosmology of everyday life, i.e. the financial system (the "City" in the poem), had fallen into the soiled hands of racially indeterminate and shady importers of currants and the like, among them, of course, the pushing Jews of the plunderbund....

The poem attempts to penetrate below the level of rationalist consciousness, where the conceptual currencies of the liberal ethos have no formative and directive power. Below that level lay the real story about human nature, which "liberal thought" perversely worked to obscure, by obscuring the intersection of the human and the divine at the deepest levels of consciousness.

That stratum did not respond to the small-scale and portable logics of Enlightenment scientism, but to the special "rationality" of mythic thought. Its "logic" and narrative forms furnish the idiom of subrationalist, conscious life. To repeat: if not on the conventional rationalist basis, where does Eliot locate the authority of *The Waste Land*, and authority that can save the poem from mere eccentric sputter and give it a more commanding aspect? I think it was important for Eliot himself to feel the poem's command, and not simply to make it convincing to skeptical readers; Lyndall Gordon's biography makes this inner need for strength in his own convictions a central theme in Eliot's early life. But to answer our question: the authority the poem claims has two dimensions.

The first is based on the aesthetics of French *symbolisme* and its extension into the Wagnerian music-drama. Indeed the theoretical affinites of Baudelaire et al. and Wagner, which Eliot obviously intuited in the making of *The Waste Land*, can be seen now as nothing short of brilliant.

Only in our own time are these important aesthetic and cultural connections being seriously explored. From *symbolisme* Eliot adopted the notion of the epistemological self-sufficiency of aesthetic consciousness, its independence from rationalist instrumentality, and thus its more efficacious contact with experience and, at the deeper levels, contact with the divine through its earthly language in myth.

From his French and German forebears, Eliot formulated a new discourse of experience which in the 1920s was still very much the voice of the contemporary avant-garde in Britain and, in that sense, a voice on the margins, without institutional authority.

But here the ironic, even sneering, dismissal of the liberal stewardship of culture and society reverses the semiotics of authority-claims by giving to the voice on the margins an authority the institutional voices can no longer assume since the world they are meant to sustain has finally been seen through in all those concrete ways the poem mercilessly enacts. *The Waste Land* is quite clear on that point.

We are meant to see in "The Fire Sermon," for example, the "loitering heirs of City directors" weakly giving way to the hated *métèques,* so that the City, one of the "holy" places of mercantilism, has fallen to profane hands, The biting humour in this is inescapable....

The second dimension of the authority on which *The Waste Land* rests involves the new discourse on myth that comes from the revolutionary advances in anthropology in Eliot's time associated with the names of Émile Durkheim, Marcel Mauss, and the Cambridge School led by Sir James Frazer and Jane Harrison.

We know that Eliot was well acquainted with these developments at least as early as 1913-14. The importance of these new ideas involved rethinking the study of ancient and primitive societies.

The impact of these renovations was swift and profound and corresponds, though much less publicly, to the impact of *On the Origin of Species* on the educated public of midcentury Victorian life. Modernist interest in primitive forms of art

(Picasso, Lawrence, and many others), and, therefore, the idioms and structures of thought and feeling in primitive cultures, makes sense in several ways.

Clearly the artistic practices of primitive peoples are interesting technically to other artists of any era. Interest in the affective world or the collective mentality of a primitive society is another question altogether. That interest, neutral, perhaps, in scholarship, becomes very easy to formulate as a critique of practices and structures in the present that one wants to represent as distortions and caricatures of some original state of nature from which modernity has catastrophically departed.

Eliot's interest in the mythic thought of primitive cultures, beginning at Harvard, perhaps in the spirit of scientific inquiry, takes a different form in the argument of *The Waste Land*. There it functions pointedly as a negative critique of the liberal account of the origins of society in the institutions of contract, abstract political and civil rights, and mechanistic psychology.

The anthropologists rescued the major cultural production of primitive societies—myth—from the view that saw these ancient narratives either as the quaint decorative brio of simple folk or, if they were Greek, as the narrative mirrors of heroic society. Instead myth, and not just the myths of the Greeks, was reconceived as the narrative thematics of prerationalist cosmologies that provided an account of the relationship between the human and the divine. Myth was also interpreted psychologically, and Nietzsche is crucial in this development, as making visible the deeper strata of the mind. If the concept is the notional idiom of reason, myth is the language of unconscious life.

What Eliot intuited from this new understanding was that myth provided a totalizing structure that could make sense, equally, of the state of a whole culture and of the whole structure of an individual mind. In this intuition he found the idiom of an elaborated, universalizing code which was not entirely the product of rationalist thought.

In addition, this totalizing structure preserved the sacred dimension of life by seeing it inextricably entwined with the profane. For the expression of this intuition in the context of an environment with a heavy stake in the elaborated codes of a rationalist and materialist world view which had subordinated the sacred to the profane, Eliot adapted for his own use the poetics of juxtaposition.

The textual discontinuity *of The Waste Land* has usually been read as the technical advance of a new aesthetic. The poetics of juxtaposition are often taken as providing the enabling rationale for the accomplishment of new aesthetic effects based on shock and surprise.

And this view is easy enough to adopt when the poem is read in the narrow context of a purely literary history of mutated lyric forms. However, when the context is widened and the poem read as a motivated operation on an already always existing structure of significations, this technical advance is itself significant as a critique of settled forms of coherence.

Discontinuity, from this perspective, is a symbolic form of "blasting and bombardiering." In the design of the whole poem, especially in its use of contemporary anthropology, the broken textual surface must be read as the sign of the eruptive power of subrational forces reasserting, seismically, the element totalities at the origins of culture and mind. The poem's finale is an orgy of social and elemental violence. The "Falling towers," lightning and thunder, unveil what Eliot, at that time, took to be the base where individual mind and culture are united in the redemptive ethical imperatives spoken by the thunder.

What the poem attempts here, by ascribing these ethical principles to the voice of nature and by drawing on the epistemological autonomy posited by *symbolisme,* is the construction of an elaborated code in which an authoritative universalizing vision can be achieved using a "notional" (mythic) idiom uncontaminated by Enlightenment forms of rationalism.

Powerful as it is in the affective and tonal programme of the poem, functioning as the conclusion to the poem's "argument," this closural construction is, at best, precarious when seen beyond the shaping force of the immediate social and cultural context.

This construction, achieved rhetorically, in fact is neither acceptable anthropology, nor sound theology, nor incontestable history, but draws on all these areas in order to make the necessary point in a particular affective climate. he extent to which the poem still carries unsurpassable imaginative power indicates the extent to which our own time has not broken entirely with the common intuitive life that the poem addressed 60 years ago.

All the difficulties with the late-nineteenth-century idea of style seem to be summed up in *The Waste Land*. It is, to begin with, a poem that includes an interpretation—and one "probably not in accordance with the facts of its origin"—*as part of the poem,* and it is therefore a poem that makes a problem of its meaning precisely by virtue of its apparent (and apparently inadequate) effort to explain itself.

We cannot understand the poem without knowing what it meant to its author, but we must also assume that what the poem meant to its author will not be its meaning. The notes to *The Waste Land* are, by the logic of Eliot's philosophical critique of interpretation, simply another riddle—and not a separate one to be solved. They are, we might say, the poem's way of treating itself as a reflex, a "something not intended as a sign," a gesture whose full significance it is impossible, by virtue of the nature of gestures, for the gesturer to explain."

And the structure of the poem—a text followed by an explanation—is a reproduction of a pattern that, as the notes themselves emphasize, is repeated in miniature many times inside the poem itself, where cultural expressions are transformed, by the mechanics of allusion, into cultural gestures. For each time a literary phrase or a cultural motif is transposed into a new context—and the borrowed motifs in *The Waste Land* are shown to have themselves been borrowed by a succession of cultures—it is reinterpreted, its previous meaning becoming incorporated by distortion into a new meaning suitable to a new use.

So that the work of Frazer and Weston is relevant both

because it presents the history of religion as a series of appropriations and reinscriptions of cultural motifs, and because it is itself an unreliable reinterpretation of the phenomena it attempts to describe. The poem (as A. Walton Litz argued some time ago) is, in other words, not *about* spiritual dryness so much as it is about the ways in which spiritual dryness has been *perceived.*

And the relation of the notes to the poem proper seems further emblematic of the relation of the work as a whole to the cultural tradition it is a commentary on. *The Waste Land* is presented as a contemporary reading of the Western tradition, which (unlike the "ideal order" of "Tradition and the Individual Talent") is treated as a sequence of gestures whose original meaning is unknown, but which every new text that is added to it makes a bad guess at.

The author of the notes seems to class himself with the cultural anthropologists whose work he cites. He reads the poem as a coherent expression of the spiritual condition of the social group in which it was produced. But the author of the *poem,* we might say, does not enjoy this luxury of detachment. He seems, in fact, determined to confound, even at the cost of his own sense of coherence, the kind of interpretive knowingness displayed by the author of the notes. The author of the poem classes himself with the diseased characters of his own work—the clairvoyants with a cold, the woman whose nerves are bad, the king whose insanity may or may not be feigned. He cannot distinguish what he intends to reveal about himself from what he cannot help revealing: he would like to believe that his poem is expressive of some general reality, but he fears that it is only the symptom of a private disorder.

For when he looks to the culture around him, everything appears only as a reflection of his own breakdown: characters and objects metamorphose up and down the evolutionary scale; races and religions lose their purity ("Bin gar keine Russin, stamm' aus Litauen, echt deutsch"); an adulterated "To His Coy Mistress" describes the tryst between Sweeney and Mrs. Porter, and a fragmented Tempest frames the liaison of the typist and the young man carbuncular; "London bridge is falling down." The poem itself, as a literary object, seems an imitation of this vision of degeneration: nothing in it can be said to point to the poet, since none of its stylistic features is continuous, and it has no phrases or images that cannot be suspected of—where they are not in fact identified as—belonging to someone else.

The Waste Land appears to be a poem designed to make trouble for the conceptual mechanics not just of ordinary reading (for what poem does not try to disrupt those mechanics?) but of literary reading. For insofar as reading a piece of writing as literature is understood to mean reading it for its style, Eliot's poem eludes a literary grasp.

In *The Waste Land* Eliot, with a desperate virtuosity, presents various ways of constituting the male and female, as if in search of a poetic figuration and voice that place him beyond the conflicts that characterize his earlier poetic stances. The early sections of the poem, up to the entry of Tiresias, develop the strategy of "Portrait of a Lady." They juxtapose the meditations of a male voice with a number of female portraits: Mme. Sosostris, the wealthy woman and the working-class woman in "A Game of Chess," Marie, the hyacinth girl, and, in Eliot's rough draft of the poem, Fresca. In this collage Eliot gives the women of the poem the attributes of traditional literary character.

They inhabit settings, they exist in dramatic situations, they have individual histories, and they have voices. They constitute most of the identified speakers in the first three sections of the poem, and they contain among them a number of figures for the poet: the sibyl of Cumae; Mme.

Sosostris with her Tarot deck; Fresca, who "scribbles verse of such a gloomy tone / That cautious critics say, her style is quite her own"; and La Pia, who can connect "nothing with nothing." One might appropriately object that these are for the most part satiric portraits (indeed, some of them savagely satiric), but they are nonetheless the ways in which the poem locates both verbal fluency and prophetic authority.

In contrast, the male voice through which Eliot presents these women has none of the definitional attributes of conventionally centered identity. It resists location in time and space, it conveys emotion through literary quotation, and it portrays experience only through metaphoric figuration: the cruel April at the poem's beginning, the desert landscape, the rat's alley, where "dead men lost their bones."

Eliot thus turns the shifting figuration that appears as unsurety in "Portrait of a Lady" to a poetic strength. The very lack of location and attribute seems to place the speaker beyond the dilemmas of personality, as if Eliot had succeeded in creating the objective voice of male tradition.

But for all this voice seems to offer, the early parts of the poem imagine men as dead or dismembered: the drowned Phoenician sailor, whose eyes have been replaced by pearls, the one-eyed merchant, the fisher king, the hanged man, the corpse planted in the garden.

Thus Eliot allows us to read the sublimation of body and personality that mark the poem's voice as a repression of them as well, an escape from dismemberment by removing the male body from the text.

The one place where Eliot attaches a specific historical experience to the speaking voice of the poem — the episode of the hyacinth girl — supports such a reading. The episode begins with the speaker's quoting a woman who addressed him, recalling a gift he gave her: "You gave me hyacinths first a year ago." The speaker then describes his own consciousness of that moment in their relationship.

When they came back from the Hyacinth garden, her arms full and her hair wet, he could not speak and his eyes failed, he was neither living nor dead, and he knew nothing, "looking into the heart of light, the silence." Perhaps in recognition of the special status that this episode has by virtue of its attachment to the poet's "I," many critics have found in it the emotional centre of the poem.

The moment offers some revelation of spiritual and erotic fullness ("the heart of light"), but the speaker portrays himself as unequal to it. Speech and vision fail him, and he ends the passage by borrowing the articulation of another poem (*'Oed' und leer das Meer'*), a ventriloquized voice that is not his own, that reveals him at a loss for words. We have here a Tiresias who, at the moment of sexual illumination, loses not only his sight but his voice as well, a seer who does not gain prophetic power from sexual knowledge. As in his early poetry, Eliot represents the moment of looking at a woman as one that decomposes his voice.

Eliot's use of visual imagery in "A Game of Chess" sustains this sense of a moment of vision evaded. For all the elaborate description of the woman's dressing table and chamber, the passage avoids picturing the woman herself, unlike its source in *Antony and Cleopatra,* The long opening sentence of the description — seventeen lines long — carefully directs the eye around what is presumably the woman sitting in the chair, but she only appears at the end of the passage, in the fiery points of her hair, which are instantly transformed into words.

The passage thus finally gives the reader only a fetishistic replacement of the woman it never visualizes, a replacement for which he immediately substitutes a voice. A number of the images in "A Game of Chess" reinforce this concern with the desire to look and its repression the golden Cupidon that peeps out while another hides his eyes behind his wing, the staring forms leaning out from the wall, the pearls that were eyes, the closed car, the Pressing of lidless eyes, and in the second section, Albert's swearing he can't bear to look at Lil.

All of the eyes that do not look in this section of the poem are juxtaposed to images of a deconstituted body, imagined alternately as male and as female: the change of Philomel, withered stumps of time, the rat's alley where dead men lost their bones, and the teeth and baby Lil must lose. As the men in the section resist looking, so they do not speak. Albert is gone, and the speaker cannot or will not answer the hysterical questions of the lady.

The poem changes its figuration of gender with the introduction of Tiresias. Eliot states in a note to the passage that "the two sexes meet in Tiresias. What Tiresias *sees,* in fact, is the substance of the poem" — a declaration that critics have tended to view rather skeptically. But what Tiresias sees is the sight that the poem has heretofore evaded: the meeting of the sexes, a meeting that Tiresias experiences by identifying with the female. As the typist awaits her visitor, Tiresias asserts, "I too awaited the expected guest," and at the moment when the house agent's clerk "assaults" her, he states, "And I Tiresias, have foresuffered all," a position assumed again in the lines spoken by La Pia. Paradoxically, when the poem assumes the position of the female, male character becomes far more prominent: in the satiric portrait of the house agent's clerk, which is the first extended satiric male portrait in the poem, in the image of the fishermen, and in the extended fisherman's narrative that originally began Part IV and concludes with the death of Phlebas?

As if repeating the doubleness of identification that Tiresias represents, that death affords at once the definitive separation of male identity and a fantasy of its separation of male identity and a fantasy of its dissolution as "He passed the stages of his age and youth / Entering the whirlpool."

In the final section of the poem, Eliot changes its representation of gender dramatically. He drops the strategy of character that had been the principal way in which the poem had up to this point centered its emotion and develops a voice and figuration for the speaker that remains separate from categories of gender.

He accomplishes this by using both specifically religious allusions and natural images that for the most part avoid anthropomorphization. He seeks to evoke a poise from natural elements, as in the water-dripping song, which he gives a religious rather than a sexual resonance.

Through the song Eliot moves the power of articulation in the poem from character to nature. The hermit-thrush sings in the pine trees, and the sound of the water for which he yearns is finally realized in the last line of the section: "Drip drop drip drop drop drop drop." As if in recognition of its separation from gender, this temporary poise immediately issues in the appearance of the third figure, "who walks always beside you[,]... /... hooded / I do not know whether a man or woman...."

When the sexual concerns of the poem return, in the next passage, they assume a very different form than they have heretofore. Eliot does not locate them in relation to particular female characters or voices, although the image of the woman who "drew her long black hair out tight" does recall the woman in "A Game of Chess"; he evokes them through a sexual fantasy that represents the collapse of civilization as an engulfment within an exhausted and blackened vagina, suggested in the images of empty cisterns, exhausted wells, and bats "with baby faces" crawling "head downward down a blackened wall."

This passage develops the technique of "Prufrock" in displacing images of sexual anxiety onto elements of the poem's landscape, such that the world itself rather than the characters within it locates its sexual malaise. These feminized images now possess the power of music and song that had been given to the water and the thrush; the woman fiddles "whisper music" on the strings of her hair, the bats whistle, and voices sing out of the cisterns and wells. Despite what would seem the movement of the power of articulation to the feminine, Eliot's figurative technique here opens the way both for the poem's resolution and for the transfer, through nature, of the power of music and song to the male poet.

By shifting to a poetic mode that expresses emotion through landscape rather than through character, Eliot can achieve sexual potency in purely symbolic terms, as, in the decayed hole, the cock crows, and the damp gust comes, bringing rain.

The very way in which these images resist, because of their natural simplicity and the literary allusions with which Eliot surrounds them, what would seem to be their obvious sexual symbolism is precisely their virtue, for they enable the poem to resolve its sexual conflict at the same time that it arrives at a figuration that places the poet beyond it. At the moment when the cock crows, Eliot transfers the power of articulation to the landscape, as the thunder speaks, giving the power of translation to the poet.

When the poet interprets the commands of the thunder,

he once again describes human situations, but he articulates them in abstract and ungendered terms, as if only a language free from the categories of gender allows him to imagine human fulfillment.

The typist who appears next in the passage is a worker named metonymically for the machine she tends, so merged with it, in fact, that she is called a "typist" even at home. In *The Education,* Henry Adams proclaims his astonishment at the denizens of the new American cities: "new types, — or type-writers, — telephone and telegraph-girls, shop-clerks, factory hands, running into millions on millions.... " Eliot's point here seems very close to Adams's.

Eliot's woman is also a "type," identified with her type-writer so thoroughly she becomes it. She *is* a machine, acting as she does with "automatic hand."

The typist is horrifying both because she is reduced by the conditions of labour to a mere part and because she is infinitely multiple. In fact, her very status as a "type" is dependent on a prior reduction from whole to part. She can become one member of Adams's faceless crowd only by being first reduced to a "hand."

The typist is the very type of metonymy, of the social system that accumulates its members by mere aggregation. Yet this "type" is linked syntactically to Tiresias as well. In fact, the sentence surrenders its nominal subject, Tiresias, in favour of her.

The evening hour "strives / Homeward, and brings the sailor home from sea, / The typist home at teatime, clears her breakfast, lights / Her stove, and lays out food in tins." The typist shifts in mid-line from object to subject, from passive to active. Does the evening hour clear her breakfast, or should the reader search even farther back for an appropriate subject, to Tiresias himself.

Though this would hardly clarify the syntax, Tiresias could function logically as both subject and object, seen and seer, because, as the notes tell us, he *is* the typist: "All the women are one woman, and the two sexes meet in Tiresias." The confused syntax represents this process of identification, erasing ordinary boundaries between active and passive, subject and object.

On what basis can the typist merge with all other men and women to become part of Tiresias? In other words, what is the figurative relationship between the whole he represents and the part acted by the typist? The process of figurative identification seems similar to that in "Prufrock," where women are also represented as mere "arms" and where all women are also one woman.

As in "Prufrock," the expansion to "all" depends on a prior reduction of individual human beings to standardized parts, just as Prufrock has "known them all already, known them all," Tiresias has "foresuffered all." His gift of prophecy, however, depends on the supposition that human behaviour is repetitive, that "all" is in fact the mere repetition of a single act into infinity, enacted "on this same divan or bed." What, therefore, is the real difference between the industrial system, in which "all the women are one woman" and the identification represented by Tiresias? In which case is the typist less of a type?

The poem itself suggests that there may be no difference because Tiresias and the "human engine" are one and the same:

[North quotes from the line beginning "When the human engine" to the line ending "throbbing between two lives."]

By means of this intricate chiasmus, Eliot links the human engine that waits to Tiresias who throbs through the middle term of the taxi, which both waits and throbs. In so doing, Eliot suggests a link between the reduced conditions of the modern worker and the mythical hermaphrodite who includes all experience.

The passage contains within itself a representation of this link in Tiresias's throbbing "between two lives." Tiresias appears here almost as a metaphor for metaphor, throbbing between two lives as the common term that joins them. But the activity of joining, the throbbing that seems to evoke human longing, is in fact the noise of the taxi engine, the drumming of its pistons a travesty of human sexual activity.

In this way, the passage mocks its own insertion of Tiresias between two lives by positioning the taxi as the true medium between individual and race, present and eternity.

Even stylistically, the passage undermines its own assertion of metaphorical identification by merely juxtaposing the two elements that both terms share: There is no "between" between throbbing and waiting, no comma or other punctuation, and yet this is where the all important connection between Tiresias and the modern worker is accomplished.

Read in this, way, the passage suggests that the process by which Tiresias represents all men and women is no different from the process by which the modern industrial machine conglomerates them into one mass, that what looks like metaphorical representation is but the additive accumulation typical of industrialism.

The typist, that is to say, is just as much a type within the "inclusive human consciousness" represented by Tiresias as she is within the routines of her office. The same thing is true of the typist's lover. Tiresias is able to understand the young man carbuncular, "one of the low," because he has "walked among the lowest of the dead." He is able to understand human beings, in other words, only insofar as they are types.

The uniformity of modern industrialized life is therefore but one instance of the uniformity of all human life. Adorno makes this point when he says of Kafka, "The absence of choice and of memory which characterizes the life of white collar workers in the huge cities of the twentieth century becomes, as later in Eliot's 'Waste Land', the image of an archaic past." That archaic past is not the one the Victorians fondly identified with Athens but one in which human beings are "driven together like animals."

Adorno may well be thinking of Tiresias, in whom a sterile conglomeration of male and female represents an ancient situation still repeated in the modern city, inside, in the loveless sex of the typist and her young man, and outside, in the inorganic relationships of the crowd.

Tiresias was certainly at one point to have served the very function Eliot assigned to modern literature in his early essays.

As an observing eye that is both of the crowd and outside it, he is to reconcile individual and community, part and whole, freedom and necessity.

The directions Eliot included in his notes to the poem suggest that Eliot hoped even after the poem was written that Tiresias could fill this role. But the Tiresias he has actually portrayed in the poem itself is instead the incarnation of the failure of reconciliation, a mere juxtaposition of part and whole that dramatizes the gulf between them.

As a dramatic figure, Tiresias demonstrates two equal but opposite fears that both gripped Eliot, a fear of fragmentation and loneliness and a fear of featureless uniformity. In the modern world, it seems, freedom cannot be had without fragmentation and loneliness, and community cannot be had without coercion and conformity.

[Wyndham] Lewis' Nietzschean derision of "the crowd" in *Blast* was widely echoed in modernist representations of patriotic enthusiasm, as in Yeats's elegy for Major Robert Gregory, and the blind obedience of massed armies and the mass casualties they produced, as in Eliot's "A crowd flowed over London Bridge, so many / I had not thought death had undone so many." But in *Blast* Lewis doubly politicizes the crowd by naming its desire as suffrage, echoing Nietzsche's excoriation in *Ecce Homo* of women's democratic movements as bids for cattle voting rights: "Their attitude is as though these universal crowds wanted some new vague Suffrage" (*B2*, 94).

Of Cantleman, his alter ego in *Blasting and Bombardiering* running with the crowds at the Olympiad, Lewis writes, "he was very stupid. He was a suffragette." In "The Code of a Herdsman" Lewis writes, "As to women: wherever you can, substitute the society of men.

Treat them kindly, for they suffer from the herd" (*BB*, 70). This feminization of the crowd brings modernism's contradictory discourse of population control into sharper focus, and exposes the logical strategy that lodges control with art. The 1915 war issue of *Blast* blasts "Birth-Control" and blesses "War Babies" (*B2*, 92-93).

The logic of the etymological play—the blighting of birth control as enabling the breaking out of the embryo—is clearer than the political logic of a polemic that simultaneously despises the crowd produced by overpopulation and inveighs against the contraception that would reduce its size and proliferation.

The issue is clearly the investiture of control: the indiscriminate population control by war preferred to the discriminate population control by democratic female suffrage, because the violence of the war at least releases energy and creates a vortex while feminism empowers the herd. Modernism ultimately enacted, in its own textual strategies, the function of the war as an imperfectly self-correcting machine that disciplined the masses and thereby institutionalized itself as the war's cultural counterpart.

The modernist text that becomes most conspicuously identified with the contradictory effects of this project is, of course, Eliot's *The Waste Land.* Canonized as the premier address to "the unprecedented death toll of the First World War," its historical reference encloses the illogical nexus of maritial and feminist discourses of population control in order to sublate them wholly to the mythology of sacral fertility.

Upon the editorial pruning by Pound, the poem's opening introduces a montage of displaced historical codes for the outbreak and aftermath of World War I: the post-war haunting of watering places by the dislocated German aristocrats from eastern Europe, the ethnic chauvinisms and tensions of the Hapsburg Empire displaced from the Balkans to the Baltic, and the figure of the arch-duke careening downhill on a sled nearly out of control:

"Bin gar keine Russin, stamm' aus Litauen, echt deutsch. / And when we were children, staying at the arch-duke's / My cousin's, he took me out on a sled, / And I was frightened." The challenge of the poem may be sited in the insomniac reading of the baroness: "I read, much of the night, and go south in the winter."

What does one read after the catastrophe of a war that murders sleep, and what a writing replaces the peace foreclosed by historical nightmare? "Falling towers / Jerusalem Athens Alexandria / Vienna London." The fall and dispersal of the Austro-Hungarian Empire (Vienna) opens the text, and the deferred twilight of the British Empire (London), ingesting the religion of its colonies along with India's tea and spices, closes it in a cacophony of indigested and untranslated quotations that textually foreclose geopolitical peace.

The poem's tacit attempt to reconstitute a third empire of polyglot and polymath a culture—what Eagleton describes as "an alternative text which is nothing less than the closed, coherent, authoritative discourse of the mythologies a which frame it"—becomes no more than another haunting, another invasion of the poem by the dead. "Eliot celebrates the voices of the dead," Maud Ellmann writes, "but he comes to dread their verbal ambush in *The Waste Land*."

Ellmann's elegant rhetorical summation of the poem's compulsive attempt to remember and resurrect the dead through a doomed prosopopoeia—"*The Waste Land* strives to give a face to death"—endows the impossibility of representing the mass death and destruction of World War I with a compelling figure of poetic performativity.

But one might argue that there are two kinds of dead trying to appear in the poem, and that they are not equal: the poetic dead voices of the literary tradition, whose eloquence is the louder for the fragmentariness of their utterance, and the voiceless war dead.

Indeed, even the figure of the spared, the demobbed of returning soldier who gives the poem its most direct and specific historical reference, is not detachable from the repulsiveness of the mob. His wife, in fact, is given a face, or gives herself a face ("pulling a long face"), and it is the face of an anti-Helen; the face that launched a thousand ships becomes the young version of Pound's "old bitch gone in the teeth." Lil is a young bitch gone in the teeth, whose toothless face creates universal aversion:

"He said, I swear, I can't bear to look at you. / And no more can't I, I said." In fattaching Lil's supreme ugliness to the unwholesomeness of her class, Eliot tracks highly specific causalities—the toothlessness of calcium deficiency from the multiparity of six pregnancies before the age of thirty-one ["You ought to be ashamed, I said, to look so antique. / (And her only thirty-one)"]—back to the pullulating breeding of the masses.

The poem reverses the flow of the war dead to return them, by way of London Bridge, to the teeming slums from which they came. Eliot, like Lewis, tropes the war as a bridge between home and front, between living and dead—"The bridge, you see, is the war" (*BB,* 2)—and this bridge crosses, too, the discourses of population control that have cast their contradictory shadows upon other modernistic war writing. Reversing Gaudier's "good mouth,"

Lil's toothless head is carved into the barren landscape like a giant dead skull: "Dead mountain mouth of carious teeth that cannot spit" [I. 339] to be traversed by "the hooded hordes swarming / Over endless plain, stumbling in the cracked earth." But in spite of the industrial and urban pollution ("The river sweats oil and tar") they produce along with the "White bodies naked on the low damp ground / And bones cast in a little low dry garret," the poem blasts Birth-Control for the masses as surely as did *Blast.* "You are a proper fool," says Lil's interlocutor of her botched abortion, and Lil replies, "The chemist said it would be all right, but I've never been the same."

As a form of population control, the war too was a botched abortion—of the sort that reduced her progeny, but left Lil ill, disfigured, and prematurely aged. World War I may have reduced some of Europe's unwanted masses, but at the price of leaving her countries weak, disfigured, and spiritually dessicated.

The conversation in the pub that retells the conversation with Lil is Eliot's Arnoldian demonstration that the discourse of the Populace is impervious to poetry because it lacks the porosity of other parts of the poem that let quotation leak in. For discourse to become art like sculpture requires the scission of metaphoric teeth. "I didn't mince my words," the speaker says, and her narrative is conspicuous in its seamless wholeness, unchopped by the parataxes that segment the poem's other speech.

The masses produce a nearly perfect redundancy of citation, the episode suggests; culture and tradition are replaced by verbatim or unmasticated reproduction of earlier verbatim reproductions. This pullulation or regurgitation of trivial discourse—the speaker telling us what she told Lil Albert had said before he left—reproduces endless Heideggerean *Gerede* or idle talk deprived of teeth,

"You have them all out, Lil, and get a nice set, / He said." The conversation's twice-told and triangular structure, whose parenthetical asides make a confidante of the poem's addressee, restores the implied reader herself to the masses. It is among the poem's projects to break up this mindless abulia of the masses by using the text's erudition to babelize its readership, carving its homeogeneous philistinism into polyglottal segments and cultural elites. By refusing to translate or reference many of its citations, the poem's cultivation creates borderlines of incommunication and minefields of incomprehension that recreate the conditions of geopolitical war and class revolution. The unified empire of culture the poem conjures up in its referenced appeal to the cosmopolitanism of Cambridge anthropology and the archetypalism of comparative religion becomes no more than a bogus sublation of the poem's politics into a myth of universal order that its own textual babelization ritually destroys.

My account of impersonality shifts the critical debate away from closet logic toward a different way of conceptualizing sexuality's impact on Eliot's poetry. Sexuality in Eliot involves hiddenness not as a mode of concealment, but as an occult mode of access with erotic implications. His impersonalist theory of poetry compels Eliot—even in the face of his own conscious intentions—to embrace a passivity and openness that renders him vulnerable to what feels like bodily violation. Hence his propensity for embodying these qualities in women and sexually ambiguous youths, such as Saint Sebastian and Narcissus.

Eliot imagines figures for the ideal impersonalist poet as eminently rapable, and he conceives this violation as the paradoxical precondition for that "inviolable voice," which, in *The Waste Land*, he attempts not merely to represent but actually to approximate.

The raped and wounded figures in his poetry represent not abject bodies that Eliot repudiates as a means of shoring up his precarious masculine heterosexual identity, as recent critics have claimed. On the contrary, these violated figures represent Eliot's poetic ideal. Rejecting the terms of revelation and concealment that have dominated Eliot criticism, I shall argue that from his impersonalist practice something fundamental remains to be learned about the relation between transhistorical conceptions of poetic utterance and modern forms of sexuality.

A rather different way of reading Eliot's gestures of renunciation stems from recognizing in the modernist use of masks a technique of self-dispossession that entails a structural rather than a psychological form of masochism. By this I mean that impersonal masking—the speaking in a voice other than one's own—involves the poet in a suspension or diminuition of self that tends to accompany the poetic medium itself, irrespective of his or her own preferences.

While modernist impersonality is readily grasped as entailing the use of personae, we need not understand masking as solely or even primarily a technique of concealment. *Persona* originally referred to the mask worn by actors in Greek drama, but the word etymologically derives from the Latin phrase *per sonare,* meaning "to sound through."

Rather than designating the visual form hiding the actor's face, *persona* initially denoted the mask's mouthpiece or a reed device inserted into it for amplifying the actor's voice. Thus in the first place a persona was less a means of visual concealment than of vocal channeling; it entailed a form of speaking through rather than of speaking falsely.

More than a mode of camouflage, impersonation may represent a way to inhabit other existençes—a way to transform oneself by becoming possessed by others. This distinction furnishes us with a rationale for approaching modernist impersonality as a strategy not of dissimulation but of access to regions of voice beyond the self's.

Eliot's ideas about occult transmission are dramatized in *The Waste Land*. While Madame Sosostris stands as the poem's best known medium, she is not the only figure associated with clairvoyance. Both the Sibyl, whose words compose the poem's epigraph, and Tiresias, who supposedly unites the poem, are second-sighted.

Given that Eliot derived Madame Sosostris's name from a fortune-teller called Sesostris in Aldous Huxley's *Crome Yellow* (a novel published only in November 1921), biographer Lyndall Gordon is justified in claiming that the Sosostris scene must have been a significant late addition to the poem; her pack of cards "is a unifying device," Gordon suggests, "a late attempt to draw the fragments together with a parade of the poem's characters." Madame Sosostris is thus in one respect a modern incarnation of Tiresias, himself "the most important personage in the poem, uniting all the rest," according to Eliot's note. It is not only as mediums but also as ostensibly unifying consciousnesses that Tiresias and Sosostris represent surrogates for the impersonalist poet.

Although associated with femininity and so-called passive homosexuality, the experience of self-dispossession cannot be understood as the prerogative of any psychological identity because it represents the loss of identity as such. Self-dispossession is rendered intelligible by psychoanalytic theories of masochism—or by cultural stereotypes about heterosexual women and effeminate homosexuals—but may in fact be a structural entailment of the poetic medium as much as a psychological impulse.

"[T]he poet has... no identity... he has no self," argued Keats, in a formulation suggesting that the poet's identity consists in the loss of identity or, as he put it in the same letter, in self-annihilation.

In this transhistorical conception of poetic utterance, which stretches back to Plato's *Ion*, the suspension of individual identity, by whatever means, is deemed necessary for poetic making. With Bersani's account in mind, we could say that the "appeal of powerlessness" concerns aesthetic pleasure as much as it does erotic *Jouissance,* because the medium requires a self-shattering or impersonalization that is synonymous with poetic practice itself.

Pound's criticism of *The Waste Land* was not of its meaning; he liked its despair and was indulgent of its neo-Christian hope. He dealt instead with its stylistic adequacy and freshness.

For example, there was an extended, unsuccessful imitation of *The Rape of the Lock* at the beginning of "The Fire Sermon." It described the lady Fresca (imported to the waste land from "Gerontion" and one day to be exported to the States for the soft drink trade). Instead of making her toilet like Pope's Belinda, Fresca is going to it, like Joyce's Bloom. Pound warned Eliot that since Pope had done the couplets better, and Joyce the defacation, there was no point in another round. To this shrewd advice we are indebted for the disappearance of such lines as:

The white-armed Fresca blinks, and yawns, and gapes,
Aroused from dreams of love and pleasant rapes.
Electric summons of the busy bell
Brings brisk Amanda to destroy the spell
Leaving the bubbling beverage to cool,
Fresca slips softly to the needful stool,
Where the pathetic tale of Richardson
Eases her labour till the deed is done...
This ended, to the steaming bath she moves,
Her tresses fanned by little flutt'ring Loves;
Odours, confected by the cunning French,
Disguise the good old hearty female stench.

The episode of the typist was originally much longer and more laborious:

A bright kimono wraps her as she sprawls
In nerveless torpor on the window seat;
A touch of art is given by the false
Japanese print, purchased in Oxford Street.

Pound found the décor difficult to believe: "Not in that

lodging house?" The stanza was removed. When he read the later stanza,

—Bestows one final patronising kiss,
And gropes his way, finding the stairs unlit;
And at the corner where the stable is,
Delays only to urinate, and spit,

he warned that the last two lines were "probably over the mark," and Eliot acquiesced by cancelling them.

Pound persuaded Eliot also to omit a number of poems that were for a time intended to be placed between the poem's sections, then at the end of it. One was a renewed thrust at poor Bleistein, drowned now but still haplessly Jewish and luxurious under water:

Full fathom five your Bleistein lies
Under the flatfish and the squids.
Graves' Disease in a dead jew's/man's eyes!
Where the crabs have eat the lids...
That is lace that was his nose
Roll him gently side to side,
See the lips unfold unfold
From the teeth, gold in gold....

Pound urged that this, and several other mortuary poems, did not add anything, either to *The Waste Land* or to Eliot's previous work. He had already written "the longest poem in the English langwidge. Don't try to bust all records by prolonging it three pages further." As a result of this resmithying by *il miglior fabbro,* the poem gained immensely in concentration. Yet Eliot, feeling too solemnized by it, thought of prefixing some humorous doggerel by Pound about its composition. Later, in a more resolute effort to escape the limits set by *The Waste Land,* he wrote *Fragment of an Agon,* and eventually, "somewhere the other side of despair," turned to drama.

So it would have been about mid-January 1922, in London, that *The Waste Land* received its final form, and likely its title too. The state of the manuscripts Eliot had unpacked after his return from the continent may be readily summarized.

"The Burial of the Dead" had lost its Cambridge opening

but was otherwise lightly annotated. "A Game of Chess" had had its opening heavily worked over by Pound, to tighten the meter, and Vivien Eliot had supplied a few suggestions for improving the pub dialogue. "The Fire Sermon" was a shambles; it needed much work. "Death by Water" had been cut back to ten lines. "What the Thunder Said" was "OK."

Pondering these materials, Eliot perceived where the poem's centre of gravity now lay. Its centre was no longer the urban panorama refracted through Augustan styles. That had gone with the dismemberment of Part III.

Its centre had become the urban apocalypse, the great City dissolved into a desert where voices sang from exhausted wells, and the Journey that had been implicit from the moment he opened the poem in Cambridge and made its course swing via Munich to London had become journev through the Waste Land. Reworking Part III, and retyping the other parts with revisions of detail, he achieved the visionary unity that has fascinated two generations of readers. He then went to bed with the flu, "excessively depressed."

He was anxious. He thought of deleting Phlebas, and was told that the poem needed Phlebas "ABsolootly." "The card pack introduces him, the drowned phoen. sailor." He thought of using "Gerontion" as a prelude, and was told not to. "One don't miss it *at* all as the thing now stands." (Pound *Letters*, No. 182.) What seems to have bothered him was the loss of a schema.

"Gerontion" would have made up for that lack by turning the whole thing into "thoughts of a dry brain in a dry season." Later the long note about Tiresias attempted the same strategy: "What Tiresias *sees*, in fact, is the substance of the poem." The lost schema, if we have guessed about it correctly, had originated in a preoccupation with Dryden as the poem grew outward from "The Fire Sermon."

If Vergil had once sponsored the protagonist's journey as Homer sponsors the wanderings of Leopold Bloom, Vergil was pertinent to a poem prompted by Vergil's major English translator, John Dryden. Ovid, who supplied Tiresias and Philomel, and told the story of the Sibyl's terribly longevity which may underlie the line about fear in a handful of dust, was a favourite of Dryden's, and (on Mark Van Doren's showing) pertinent to Dryden's London and Eliot's.

Wren's churches, notably Magnus martyr, were built after the fire *Annus Mirabilis* celebrates, which is one reason Eliot works Magnus Martyr into his Fire Sermon. And in disposing ornate diction across the grid of a very tame pentameter, Eliot's original draft of the opening of Part II had rewritten in the manner of French decadence a Shakespearean passage ("... like a burnished throne") that Dryden had rewritten before him in a diction schooled by his own time's French decorum. No classroom exercise is more ritualized than the comparison of *Antony and Cleopatra* and *All for Love.*

But the centre from which such details radiate had been removed from the poem. What survived was a form with no form, and a genre with no name. Years later, on the principle that a form is anything done twice, Eliot reproduced the structural contours of *The Waste Land* exactly, though more briefly, in *Burnt Norton,* and later still three more times, to make the *Quartets,* the title of which points to a decision that such a form might have analogies with music.

That was *post facto.* In 1922, deciding somewhat reluctantly that the poem called *The Waste Land* was finished, he was assenting to a critical judgment, Pound's and his own, concerning which parts were alive in a sheaf of pages he had written.

Two years afterward, in "The Function of Criticism," he averted to "the capital importance of criticism in the work of creation itself," and suggested that "the larger part of the labour of an author in composing his work is critical labour; the labour of sifting, combining, constructing, expunging, correcting, testing." He called it "this frightful toil," and distinguished it from obedience to the Inner Voice. "The critical activity finds its highest, its true fulfilment in a kind of union with creation in the labour of the artist."

Chapter 7

On "The Hollow Men"

Although "The Hollow Men" is not a mere appendage to *The Waste Land,* it may most profitably be read as an extension of the same design of quest and failure. The quest has already failed once when the poem opens. The history of Kurtz in "Heart of Darkness" conforms to the general pattern. Conrad may often be understood best through the study of primitive rituals of succession, initiation, and fertility.

That Kurtz has been initiated into the tribe, becoming its shaman, its "rain and fine weather" maker, and that he has been ceremonially worshiped and appeased, seems an express symbol of his disastrous descent into the dark places. The gracious figure of his "Intended," from whom he has turned to immerse himself in the shadows, represents the light which Marlow, shaken by his own knowledge of the horror, is scarcely able to credit, except as either an illusion of the innocent or an ideal of the courageous.

What happens actually to Kurtz happens figuratively to Marlow, who voyages into a hell so dreadful that he comes back unconvinced of any other reality. The sheer Manichaeism of the revelation only narrowly fails to overwhelm with darkness Marlow as well as Kurtz.

Kurtz, after undertaking to combat darkness and devils, yields to them and is installed in the midst of them and, despite his final relative victory of self-knowledge, cannot avert his damnation. The whole design approximates that of hero myths, but it combines with curious subtlety the quest to subdue evil with a quest to restore the god overtaken by death in the guise of life. In a sense Kurtz is like the Fisher King and

Marlow is like the quester, but Kurtz has been a quester too.

The main parallel between "Heart of Darkness" and "The Hollow Men" consists in the theme, implicit throughout the latter, of debasement through the rejection of good, of despair through consequent guilt.

In Part II of the poem the speaker confesses the impossibility of facing "the eyes," even in dreams, in the dream kingdom of his world; and in his imagination he encounters only their symbolic counterparts—sunlight, a tree, voices in the wind.

The sunlight, however, shines only on "a broken column" among the broken desert images. His inability to return and brave the eyes resembles Tiresias' state after the scene in the Hyacinth garden. In *The Waste Land* the lost eyes are those of the protagonist himself; here they are the upbraiding eyes of one incarnating his lost redemption: the speaker takes refuge in apathy; he desires to think of himself only as a scarecrow. He shrinks from everything but concealment among the other hollow men and wears, with them,

Such deliberate disguises
Rat's coat, crowskin, crossed staves
In a field.
What he cannot contemplate is the reproach of
... that final meeting
In the twilight kingdom,
when at length he may meet the eyes in the real world of the dead.

The scarecrow symbol (like Hawthorne's "Feathertop") is appropriate to designate not only the ineptness and spiritual flaccidity of the speaker but, like the "tattered coat upon a stick" in Yeats's "Sailing to Byzantium", his inability to attain love. If one turns back to *The Golden Bough* and to some of the most ancient as well as most persistent rituals of pagan Europe, it is the straw man who seems to have functioned in certain of the fire festivals as a sacrificial representative of the vegetation spirit or as a scapegoat ridding his folk of accumulated ill-chance.

The commemoration of the fifth of November itself reflects

the custom of burning in effigy the bearer of local guilt; the accident of the season—for Guy Fawkes Day shortly follows All Souls'—may have suggested kindling traditional autumn fires for the modern culprit. A connection between the straw man and the Fisher King will be easily apparent, for Eliot's hollow men re-enact the distress of the mutilated Tiresias.

The figurative straw dummies of the poem suffer both physically and spiritually. How they themselves have erred, the poem does not demonstrate. It is plain enough, however, that they are all but damned; and not for nothing is there an allusion here, as in "The Burial of the Dead," to the third canto of the Inferno, where those, who "lived without blame, and without praise," are doomed to abide at Acheron without crossing into hell.

But it is meaningful that the hollow men are not bound to such a torment as theirs: to follow the whirling ensign, goaded by hornets and wasps. Instead they are like the throng awaiting (with "pennies for the Old 'Guy'") the barge of Charon to ferry them across to their everlasting sorrow in the depths.

The eyes, terrible and unrelenting, even resemble the glowing coals of Charon's eyes, as described in both the *Aeneid* and the *Commedia,* or the streaming eyes of the demon in Kipling's "At the End of the Passage." But the very possibility of descending, of not being forced to remain on the hither shore, paradoxically signifies hope.

Miraculously, the eyes that may reappear beyond the river portend salvation. As commentators have recognized, they are comparable to the eyes of Beatrice in the *Purgatorio.*

For the pattern of descent and ascent implies that having plunged into hell, the hollow men may find paradise. Part IV of the poem establishes a geography: the scarecrows, loitering beside "the tumid river" (a fixture also of "Heart of Darkness"), are trapped in Ezekiel's valley of bones, where, as in the "circular desert" of *The Family Reunion,* their suffering seems futile.

Theirs is the "dream kingdom" where the eyes are but a memory. They must invade the "other kingdom," the "twilight kingdom" of actual death, which, after further purgatorial trial, may vouchsafe to them, through the eyes of pain and joy, a way upward, even to the "multifoliate rose" of the final cantos of the *Paradiso,* to "the perpetual star," a symbol of the Holy Virgin. The way up and the way down are the same; the landscape is not Dantean except in so far as its moral and emotional processes match the allegory of the *Commedia.* And here, apparent hell is potential, though unrealized, purgatory.

In "Heart of Darkness" as in the *Commedia,* the feminine symbol, a prototype of the eyes in "The Hollow Men," charts the quester's pilgrimage into the region of pain; Kurtz's descent is irretraceable. But Dante's leads finally upward to his vision, beyond the eyes, beyond even the celestial spheres.

And "The Hollow Men" has a similar pattern; moreover, as Genevieve W. Foster has shown in her Jungian analysis, the eyes, the rose, and the star are equivalent to the "Grail" of *The Waste Land.*

So, too, is the tree, recurring in *Coriolan* and "New Hampshire," and, through the children in the leaves, in "Burnt Norton" also. (Here it ironically reminds one of Kurtz, "a tree swayed by the wind.")

"The Hollow Men" would re-express the affirmative way by abjuring lust, the false centre, the "prickly pear" of Part V, circled in a whirling or whirlpool motion, and by declaring the speaker's hope for the eyes. (In the negative way, the abandonment of lust would have to be ratified by renunciation of the affirmative symbol and by evacuation of desire.)

But attainment of the vision, according to "The Hollow Men," is remote indeed. The agony of "Lips that would kiss," the unalleviated "anguish of the marrow / The ague of the skeleton," lacerates the heart with proximate desire.

The first four lines of Part V parody "The Mulberry Bush," substituting for the fertility symbol connoting love (as in the legend of Pyramus and Thisbe) an image purely phallic. And echoing the chant of the May games, "Here we go gathering nuts in May... At five o'clock in the morning," with its reminiscence of the Maypole dance and the "country copulatives," they underscore the sexual nature of the plight with which the poem deals. In this terminal section, one is back, so to speak, in the marriage chamber of Eliot's "Ode," where sex has gone wrong. And in spite of the plain statement that the hollow men must remain "sightless" unless the rose reappears, love, along with powers of creation and repentance, is still sought in the world of nightmare.

With every effort to make the potential become actual a "Shadow" interferes. This, whatever its private value, has in the poem no clear conceptual reference. It implies Prufrockian inertia incapable of connecting imagination and reality, a defect of *kinesis,* in part a volitional weakness and in part an external constraint.

Deathlike, it hinders even the attempt at prayer through which the speaker might come into the "Kingdom" of pure actuality beyond. Eliot's threefold grouping of contrasts between prospect and fulfilment comprehends three failures.

The oppositions of potentiality and actuality are not the Aristotelian or Thomistic ones; they blur as the enumeration passes from "potency" and "existence" to "essence" and "descent," but each constitutes an antithesis compatible with Aristotelian dialectic.

Even "motion," normally actual, can fit into the potential category through its special meaning of "initial impulse," by which it contrasts with "act:" Each of the three groups (by ambiguities) recapitulates the preceding, until by accumulation all three groups combine in the third, just as, according to Aristotle, the soul includes in its highest powers those of the inferior species. Perhaps the first group chiefly connotes sex; the second, sex and creation; the last, sex, creation, and salvation.

Chapter 8

A Study in Sources and Meaning

In "The Hollow Men" all the richness and complexity of culture which gives "The Waste Land" such thickness of texture disappears. The poem takes place in a twilight realm of disembodied men and forces. The complexity of relations making up the subjective realm in Eliot's ideal descriptions of it is replaced by the vagueness and impalpability of "Shape without form, shade without colour, / Paralysed force, gesture without motion". The hollow men are walking corpses ("Mistah Kurtz - he dead"), and their emptiness is the vacuity of pure mind detached from any reality. They are cut off from one another. Their voices are whispers, "quiet and meaningless". Groping together, they "avoid speech". They are detached from nature, and live in a place which is devoid of any spiritual presence, a "dead land," a "cactus land," a "valley of dying stars," hollow like the men themselves.

The eyes of the hollow men are not only averted from one another, but from those other eyes, the returning look from the divine place which those who cross "with direct eyes" to "death's other Kingdom" will encounter. There are no eyes in the hollow valley, and the empty men are bereft of God. Even within their own hollowness detachment is the law.

The "Shadow" which falls between idea and reality, conception and creation, emotion and response, desire and spasm, potency and existence, is the paralysis which seizes men who live in a completely subjective world. Mind had seemed the medium which binds all things together in the unity of an organic culture. Now it is revealed to be the Shadow which isolates things from one another, reduces them to abstraction, and makes movement, feeling, and creativity impossible. "The Hollow Men" is an eloquent analysis of the vacuity of subjective idealism, and the state of the hollow men appears in Eliot's later work as the "distraction, delusion, escape into dream, pretence" of the unenlightened people in his plays, each one of whom is a "fugitive from reality", or as that horrid form of hell described in *Murder in the Cathedral,* the hell of "the Void," of "emptiness, absence, separation from God" in "the empty land/Which is no land," where "there are no objects, no tones,/No colours, no forms to distract, to divert the soul/From seeing itself, foully united forever, nothing with nothing".

If "The Hollow Men" shows where idealism leads, it offers a fleeting glimpse of a way out of emptiness. Though nature, other people, and God have an almost entirely negative existence in the poem, they do exist as something outside the hollow men. The poem places the "stuffed men" in the context of an external world, God's world.

Their state is defined as that of the trimmers in the third canto of the *Inferno,* those wretched souls, "gathered on this beach of the tumid river," who lived without blame or praise, and, like the neutral angels, were neither rebellious nor faithful to God, but lived for themselves. Far better to be one of the "lost/Violent souls", for they were at least capable of damnation, as Baudelaire, in Eliot's essay, "walked secure in this high vocation, that he was capable of a damnation denied to the politicians and newspaper editors of Paris". To recognize the possibility of damnation is in a way to become capable of it, and therefore capable of the salvation which is denied to the trimmers.

The trimmers in Dante have no hope of another death, but Eliot's hollow men understand dimly that if they endure the death which is prelude to rebirth they have some hope of salvation. Though Eliot's language is deliberately ambiguous, it implies that the sightless eyes of the hollow men may see again, and confront the divine eyes which are "The hope only/

Of empty men" and will reappear as "the perpetual star/ Multifoliate rose" of heaven itself. The idealists of "The Hollow Men" have stepped out of themselves into the barrenness of an external world, and the fragments of the Lord's prayer which they mutter at the end of the poem are moving appeals to a God who may be infinitely distant, but who is independent of their minds and therefore may have power to save them.

The Hollow Men (published 1925) portrays a poetic consciousness in which intense nostalgia for a state of Edenic purity conflicts with the paradoxical search for a more enduring form of order through acts of denial and alienation. To the common observation that *The Hollow Men* expresses the depths of Eliot's despair, one must add that the poet in a sense *chooses* despair as the only acceptable alternative to the inauthentic existence of the unthinking inhabitants of the waste land. Eliot himself saw this kind of metaphysical despair as more intellectual than emotional. He says of Pascal, a "Christian thinker" with whom be clearly identifies:

His despair, his disillusion, are... no illustration of personal weakness; they are perfectly objective, because they are essential moments in the progress of the intellectual soul; and for the type of Pascal they are the analogue of the drought, the dark night, which is an essential stage in the progress of the Christian mystic.

Principles of intellectual order control the despair of *The Hollow Men* as well, in the way the poem consciously evaluates experience in abstract terms, distinguishes between antithetical states of being, and establishes, both in form and subject matter, the archetype of the Negative Way as an alternative to disorder as well as to the illusory order of visionary experience. The following pages examine formal and thematic elements of the poem as representing the progress of Eliot's own "intellectual soul," and then show this progress as frustrated by the poet's attraction to a visionary imagery.

The Hollow Men replaces the richly chaotic style of *The Waste Land* with an austerity of expression that prepares for the contemplative mode of Ash-Wednesday. In what Bergonzi has called "a virtual surrender to the silence," the formal strategy of *The Hollow Men,* like its thematic content, seems designed to demonstrate how effectively the shadow of the inarticulate falls between the conception and the creation of an artistic work. Formal aspects of the poem imitate the characteristics of the hollow men it portrays. For example, their desire to "avoid speech" finds a counterpart in the poem's general paucity of utterance: the technique of constant repetition and negation—"The eyes are not here / There are no eyes here"—manages to employ only about 180 *different* words in a work 420 words long.

The "Paralysed force, gesture without motion" applies not only to the men themselves but also to the poem as a whole, which exhibits little narrative progression in the conventional sense and eschews verbs of direct action. As the hollow men grope together, form prayers to broken stone, and whisper meaninglessly, so the poem itself gropes toward a conclusion only to end in hollow abstraction, broken prayer, and the meaningless circularity of a child's rhyme. The conscious reduction of poetic expression to a bare minimum does away with metaphor and simile and produces a final section of the poem almost completely devoid of modifiers.

The poem avoids capitulation to the silence of the inarticulate by relying on a highly structured syntax that tends to order experience in terms of binary opposition: "Shape without form, shade without colour," or "Between the idea / And the reality / Between the motion / And the act."

The quality of a poetic style marked by verbal austerity and relentless negation forms a structural counterpart to a thematic strategy that repudiates the validity of human experience at every level. In this respect the poem expands upon the theme of denial explored as part of the individual's search for meaning in *The Waste Land*. In modern existential terms as well as those of traditional Christianity, the Negative Way leads ultimately to an encounter with nothingness which, paradoxically, can inspire the individual with faith in God.

Kierkegaard seeks to explain this paradox by showing that dread [*aengste*], the simultaneous fear and intense awareness of nothingness, opens up the possibility of faith in an infinite beyond human life by "laying bare all finite aims and discovering their deceptions," by revealing the "dead-endedness" of life itself: "When the discoveries of possibility are honestly administered, possibility will then disclose all finitudes and idealize them in the form of infinity in the individual who is overwhelmed by dread, until in turn be is victorious by the anticipation of faith." The *via negativa* brings the individual to a terminal point marking the boundary between the finite and the infinite. *The Hollow Men* explores this boundary situation in its images of finality or extremity and in a thematic structure comprising two different states of being. The poem's speaker anticipates with dread "that final meeting"; the men grope together "In this last of meeting places"; the final section, in its generalized abstraction of all that has gone before, tells us that "This is the way the world ends."

The Dantescan image of the lost souls "Gathered on this beach of the tumid river" belongs to a boundary motif that recurs throughout Eliot's poetry: Prufrock escapes from the world of skirts and teacups to the world of visionary imagination via a "walk upon the beach." The protagonist of *The Waste Land* sits down and weeps "By the waters of Leman," then upon the shore "with the arid plain behind me." The sea of *The Dry Salvages* "is the land's edge also." The persona of *The Hollow Men* has arrived, intellectually and imagistically, at the outer limit of one world only to find that its "deliberate disguises" conceal a finite lack of possibility: between the potency and existence "Falls the Shadow." The epigraph, "*A penny for the Old Guy,*" stresses that Eliot's poem relates to ceremonial effigies.

Here, as in *The Waste Land, Heart of Darkness* is important. "*Mistah Kurtz—he dead*" emphasizes a connection between savage ritual and Eliot's crossed staves. To obtain power by embracing darkness, Kurtz deified himself in line with primitive belief; ironically, Eliot's speaker dresses in relics of forgotten ritual out of a sense of total impotence, wishing to avoid a horrid dusk: "Not that final meeting / In the twilight kingdom." It is landscape like Dowson's, "Hollow Lands" where, in "the twilight of the year", "dead people with pale hands / Beckon" by a "weary river", "where pale stars shine" where, at passion's enactment, "There fell thy shadow."

But the poem's world, lit by the half-light of inaction, was a transmutation of Eliot's own suffering. Vivienne, who had felt *The Waste Land* to be a part of herself, saw 'The Hollow Men' as a fitting follow-on, and related it to her own nightmares. But, as before, the personal world and that of late nineteenth-century poetry are sieved through anthropological ideas, emotion distributed among unsettled voices, narrative, optative, and choral. The poem is typographically complex. The first section's 'Kingdom' may not be section three's 'kingdom'. Certainly 'death's *other* kingdom' (my italics) suggests that the speakers' inane life is only another form of death.

So, for Sweeney Agonistes 'Death or life or life or death / Death is life and life is death.' Cornford had quoted the Euripidean question, *'who knows if to be living be not death?* Through anthropology Eliot resuscitates the idea of the living dead, so common in late romantic poetry, where Death-in-Life is the eternal king. Eliot's Hollow Men share their hopelessness with the inhabitants of the City of Dreadful Night. The poem concerns degradation of language and ritual, failings of word and Word. Eliot's witty 1918 truncation of an Arnoldian phrase prefigures the Hollow Men's predicament; Clive Bell, 'lingering between two worlds, one dead', has the vice of inane mediocrity, incapable of 'icy inviolability, or violent fury'. His being 'the Matthew Arnold of his time' again connects, through the scarecrow image, with the Hollow Men who, like so many of Eliot's literary adversaries, are afflicted with a stuffed language, emptily 'poetic', the degradation of great poetry—

Leaning together
Headpiece filled with straw. Alas!

After the starkly factual 'Headpiece filled with straw' comes that most absurdly poetic word of all, indicating the speaker's weakness. Such childish poeticizing is reinforced, in directing us to the level of the infant, by the *'penny for the Old Guy'* epigraph, by the dressing up as a scarecrow, and by the nursery rhyme, 'Twinkle twinkle little star', which inescapably underlies the line 'Under the twinkle of a fading star'.

This use of nursery rhyme looks back to *The Waste Land* with its 'London Bridge is falling down falling down falling down' and anticipates another explicit nursery rhyme which, in slightly distorted form, opens section V of 'The Hollow Men'. Other forms of words instilled into the young are also present. The Lord's Prayer is quoted in the repeated fragment '*For Thine is the Kingdom*' but the earlier uses of the word kingdom, particularly when it has a capital 'K', must already have prompted questions about allusion to this fundamental Christian rite, and about how it relates to those `prayers to broken stone'. It is hard to avoid thinking that the hope of 'Thy Kingdom come' finds its opposite in

Let me be no nearer
In death's dream kingdom

which becomes an anti-Lord's Prayer, addressed to an unnamed hearer who may be the god of a universe of barrenness and death. 'The Hollow Men', not 'The Hippopotamus', is Eliot's most blasphemous poem. Ideas of childishness, linguistic degeneration, and confusion support the central theme of the degradation of essential ritual. The barely glimpsed possibility of Christian hope plunges to crazy childishness.

Here we go round the prickly pear
Prickly pear prickly pear
Here we go round the prickly pear
At five o'clock in the morning.

'Ritual,' Eliot wrote in 1923, 'consisting of a set of repeated movements, is essentially a dance.' He called *The Sacred Dance* '*an* excellent study of primitive religious dances', and read how these were performed round sacred trees, but also 'how often with the decay of old faiths the serious rites and pageants... have degenerated into the sports of children'. It was ten years since Eliot had been interested in *Ecstasy and Dance Hypnosis among the American Indians,* and had read in King about the lively 'moonlight dances' of Bushmen. These would resurface, bereft of fun, in the childish dance of 'The Hollow Men', as later, much more lightly in the Jellicle Cats' `Reserving their terpsichorean powers / To dance by the light of the jellicle Moon.'

Though anthropological theories of religious degeneration were becoming outdated, Eliot was familiar with the version propounded by, for instance, Andrew Lang in his *Making of Religion.* Tylor, about whose theories Eliot had been sceptical, was particularly strong on connecting the mental processes of savages with those of children, connections emphasized by Cornford, Frazer, Oesterley, Webb, Wundt, and others.

Cornford's book on some of the greatest Greek drama had as its frontispiece a Punch and Judy show. Eliot was fascinated by the idea which Cornford had put forward 'in "The Origin of Attic Comedy", [that] this [medicine-man] Doctor may be identical with the Doctor who is called in to assist Punch after he has been thrown by his horse'. Though primitive man may be something of a mystic, the distant voices and fading star in Eliot's poem show no 'prelogical mentality' from a golden age of childlike innocence. The distant fading signals a run-down age of degenerate belief. That it had paradisal origins is a simplistic assumption. His criticism of Oesterley's work makes it clear that for Eliot a ritual's origins may be as meaningless as is its present form. He attacks Oesterley for falling into 'the common trap of interpretation' by formulating intelligible reasons for the dancing of a primitive. Eliot asserts that it is perfectly possible to claim 'that primitive man acted in a certain way and then found a reason for it'.

The last section of 'The Hollow Men' in particular places its rituals in a crazy emptiness. The verve of the nursery rhyme spins us round in a sinister way, since it is disturbing to see the familiar 'mulberry bush' of the children's rhyme replaced with the arid 'prickly pear', making the rhyme like some distorted survival of a primitive chant. Eliot's substitution makes this seem an infertility dance. As an American plant, 'prickly pear' also connects with his own childhood in a society whose religious values seemed atrophied. Section V's voices are the most complex. First comes the choral nursery rhyme, linked typographically with the italicized passages placed against the right-hand margin to differentiate them from the rest of the text. These appear to be parts of the Lord's Prayer, but are confused by the addition of the complaint in the same typographical form, *'Life is very long,'* appropriately enough from the more primitive world of *An Outcast of the Islands.*

A third voice, represented by normal type and placed in the conventional part of the page, is itself like another ritual, a fact emphasized by the incantatory effect of semantic and lexical patterning in the repeated, only slightly varied form,

Between the a
And the b
Between the c
And the d
Falls the Shadow

This tripartite distinction, easy to uphold on the grounds of typography, is complicated, however, by the fact that fragments of the italicized Lord's Prayer passage find themselves brought in from the right-hand margin to form part of the body of the text when, further truncated, they make up the liturgical stutter of

For Thine is
Life is
For Thine is the

before a final all-embracing italicized section, looking back in its typography, placing, and, most importantly, its rhythm, recalls the opening nursery rhyme chorus, but gives it a universal voice which seems to include all that we have heard before in what is now a ritual chant ending with an appropriately childlike sound,

This is the way the world ends
This is the way the world ends
This is the way the world ends
Not with a bang but a whimper.

This combination of various voices, including the choric, makes the fifth section distinctly dramatic in its fragmentation, and, clearly deriving from the techniques employed in *The Waste Land,* also paves the way for the fragmentary drama of *Sweeney Agonistes.*

Chapter 9

On "The Journey of the Magi"

"Journey of the Magi" is the monologue of a man who has made his own choice, who has achieved belief in the Incarnation, but who is still part of that life which the Redeemer came to sweep away. Like Gerontion, he cannot break loose from the past.

Oppressed by a sense of death-in-life (Tiresias' anguish "between two lives"), he is content to submit to "another death" for his final deliverance from the world of old desires and gods, the world of "the silken girls." It is not that the Birth that is also Death has brought him hope of a new life, but that it has revealed to him the hopelessness of the previous life.

He is resigned rather than joyous, absorbed in the negation of his former existence but not yet physically liberated from it. Whereas Gerontion is "waiting for rain" in this life, and the hollow men desire the "eyes" in the next life, the speaker here has put behind him both the life of the senses and the affirmative symbol of the Child; he has reached the state of desiring nothing.

His negation is partly ignorant, for he does not understand in what way the Birth is a Death; he is not aware of the sacrifice. Instead, he himself has become the sacrifice; he has reached essentially, on a symbolic level true to his emotional, if not to his intellectual, life, the humble, negative stage that in a mystical progress would be prerequisite to union.

Although in the literal circumstances his will cannot be fixed upon mystical experience, because of the time and condition of his existence, he corresponds symbolically to the seeker as described by St. John of the Cross in *The Ascent of*

Mount Carmel. Having first approached the affirmative symbol, or rather, for him, the affirmative reality, he has experienced failure; negation is his secondary option.

The quest of the Magi for the Christ child, a long arduous journey against the discouragements of nature and the hostility of man, to find at last, a mystery impenetrable to human wisdom, was described by Eliot in strongly colloquial phrases adapted from one of Lancelot Andrewes' sermons of the Nativity:

A cold coming they had of it at this time of the year, just the worst time of the year to take a journey, and specially a long journey in. The ways deep, the weather sharp, the days short, the sun farthest off, *in solstitio brumali,* "the very dead of winter."

Also in Eliot's thoughts were the vast oriental deserts and the camel caravans and marches described in *Anabase,* by St.-J. Perse. He himself had begun work in 1926 on an English translation of that poem, publishing it in 1930. Other elements of his tone and imagery may have come from Kipling's "The Explorer" and from Pound's "Exile's Letter." The water mill was recollected from his own past; for in *The Use of Poetry,* speaking of the way in which "certain images recur, charged with emotion," he was to mention "six ruffians seen through an open window playing cards at night at a small French railway junction where there was a water-mill."

In vivifying the same incident, the fine proleptic symbolism of "three trees on the low sky," a portent of Calvary, with the evocative image of "an old white horse" introduces one of the simplest and most pregnant passages in all of his work:

Then we came to a tavern with vine-leaves over the lintel,
Six hands at an open door dicing for pieces of silver,
And feet kicking the empty wine-skins.

Here are allusions to the Communion (through the tavern "bush"), to the paschal lamb whose blood was smeared on the lintels of Israel, to the blood money of Judas, to the contumely suffered by Christ before the Crucifixion, to the soldiers casting lots at the foot of the Cross, and, perhaps, to the pilgrims at the open tomb in the garden. The arrival of the Magi at the place of Nativity, whose symbolism has been anticipated by the fresh vegetation and the mill "beating the darkness," is only a "satisfactory" experience. The narrator has seen and yet he does not fully understand; he accepts the fact of Birth but is perplexed by its similarity to a Death, and to death which he has seen before:

> *All this was a long time ago, I remember,*
> *And I would do it again, but set down*
> *This set down*
> *This: were we led all that way for*
> *Birth or Death?*

Were they led there for Birth or for Death? or, perhaps, for neither? or to make a choice between Birth and Death? And whose Birth or Death was it? their own, or Another's? Uncertainty leaves him mystified and unaroused to the full splendor of the strange epiphany. So he and his fellows have come back to their own Kingdoms, where,

> *... no longer at ease here, in the old dispensation,*
> *With an alien people clutching their gods*

(which are now alien gods), they linger not yet free to receive "the dispensation of the grace of God." The speaker has reached the end of one world, but despite his acceptance of the revelation as valid, he cannot gaze into a world beyond his own.

'Journey of the Magi', written in 1927, contains not only material quoted in Eliot's 1926 survey, 'Lancelot Andrewes', and recollections from Eliot's own life (some of which he catalogued when reminiscing in *The Use of Poetry and the Use of Criticism).* It also looks back towards his engagement with the primitive.

Like 'The Hollow Men' and parts of *The Waste Land,* this poem's setting is a desert one. The traditional landscape, however, is never mentioned, being involved indirectly through the details of 'the camels galled, sorefooted, refractory'. The poem is deliberately unconventional: no mention of gold, frankincense, and myrrh. But it is conventional in terms of Eliot's earlier poetry; though less dramatic, its conclusion is as apolcalyptic as before. The reader becomes aware that, Nemi-like, the birth of the new priest-king means the end of 'the old dispensation'— an entire world order — as 'this Birth was / Hard and bitter agony for us, like Death, our death'.

The 'Kingdoms' mentioned are perfectly sensible in the poem's context, but remind readers of Eliot's work of 'death's other Kingdom' and 'death's dream kingdom'. Though explicitly Christian, 'Journey of the Magi' forms between the earlier and later work a bridge over which the reader (with access to the gospel word) may cross into the release of Christianity, the new birth; but, denied that access, the speaker of the poem can only seek relief in death to escape from having to return to the old way in which he is 'no longer at ease'.

This old way, 'With an alien people clutching their gods', looks back to the savage world which Eliot had been exploring, the world trapped in the ritual of 'birth, and copulation, and death'. The word 'clutch' has particularly strong sexual connotations in Eliot's work, as when Saint Narcissus writhes 'in his own clutch'. Eliot had criticized Wundt for ignoring sexuality's part in religion. By 'Journey of the Magi', however, we have birth and death but not copulation.

The reader is faced with a renunciation both of the sexuality bound up with primitive rites and, for the moment at least, of modern sexuality. Vickery overemphasizes vegetation references by relating the 'temperate valley... smelling of vegetation' with its 'running stream' to a particular scene in *The Golden Bough,* and by insisting that the 'water-mill' is that 'in which Tammuz was ground' and thus functions as 'a reminder that death is the price of rebirth'.

General hints at fertility ceremonies may be present, demonstrating another continuity in theme between this and earlier poetry; but it is important to see that, though its death and rebirth are also related, Christianity is presented by Eliot as an escape from Frazerian cycles of fertility (in the way that the Buddhist 'Shantih shantih shantih' hinted at such an escape), not as its mere continuation.

The first paragraph presents the detail of the journey in a

manner which arrives at no vision of experience. The present participles and the paratactic syntax, presenting one thing after another in a simple narrative, hold us to the banalities of romantic travellers.

The voice recounting them is tired as if repeating the too well known. Only at the beginning and the end of the paragraph is there something to catch the attention of the modern reader, so far as he knows what the Magi did not know. Their 'cold coming' might suggest the cold coming Christ himself had, as the carols now tell it. Again, 'That this was all folly' becomes a commonplace Christian paradox when we know that they were seeking Christ. We are under some pressure to supply the meaning they missed.

In the rest of the poem that pressure increases. Are the images of the middle paragraph really charged with mysterious significance, some 'Symbolic value, but of what we cannot tell, for they come to represent the depths of feeling into which we cannot peer'?

They do have a dream-like clarity. At the same time they seem to offer themselves rather readily for allegorical exegesis; the valley of life; the three crosses of Calvary; the White Horse of the Second Coming; the Judas-like world. The immediate mystery of the images evaporates under such interpretation, to be replaced by 'the Christian mystery'. The primary sensory associations give way to an idea, and we find we are involved in a meaning beyond the Magi's actual experience.

It is the same in the final paragraph, except that here we are confronted directly with the abstract idea. The Magus is baffled by the apparent contradictions of Birth and Death, and is left simple wanting to die.

Chapter 10

On "Burnt Norton"

The more familiar we become with *Four Quartets,* however, the more we realise that the analogy with music goes much deeper than a comparison of the sections with the movements of a quartet, or than an identification of the four elements as 'thematic material'. One is constantly reminded of music by the treatment of images, which recur with constant modifications, from their context, or from their combination with other recurring images, as a phrase recurs with modifications in music. These recurring images, like the basic symbols, are common, obvious and familiar, when we first meet them. As they recur they alter, as a phrase does when we hear it on a different instrument, or in another key, or when it is blended and combined with another phrase, or in some way turned round, or inverted. A simple example is the phrase 'a shaft of sunlight' at the close of 'Burnt Norton'.

This image occurs in a rudimentary form in 'The Hollow Men', along with a moving tree and voices heard in the wind:

There, the eyes are
Sunlight on a broken column
There, is a tree swinging
And voices are
In the wind's singing
More distant and more solemn
Than a fading star.

At the close of 'Burnt Norton' a 'moment of happiness', defined in 'The Dry Salvages' as a 'sudden illumination' is made concrete by the image of a shaft of sunlight which transfigures the world:

Sudden in a shaft of sunlight
Even while the dust moves
There rises the hidden laughter
Of children in the foliage
Quick now, here, now, always —
Ridiculous the waste sad time
Stretching before and after.

This is the final concrete statement of what 'Burnt Norton' is about; but it recalls the experience we have been given in a different rhythm and with different descriptive accompaniments in the second half of the first movement, as the sun for a moment shines from the cloud, and the whole deserted garden seems to become alive:

Dry the pool, dry concrete, brown edged,
And the pool was filled with water out of sunlight,
And the lotos rose, quietly, quietly,
The surface glittered out of heart of light,
And they were behind us, reflected in the pool.
Then a cloud passed, and the pool was empty.

The image repeated, but with such a difference, at the close establishes the validity of the first experience. Brief and illusory as it appears in the first movement, it has not been dismissed. It has remained in thought and it returns. Though

Time and the bell have buried the day,
The black cloud carries the sun away
when the 'sudden shaft' falls, it is time that seems the illusion.

The subject of *Burnt Norton* can be defined in various ways. If we adopt the method of commentators on *The Divine Comedy,* we may distinguish a literal, a moral and a mystical meaning.

The literal meaning is simply that the poet has felt a moment of inexplicable joy, a moment of release, like the moment Agatha speaks of when she looked 'through the little door, when the sun was shining on the rose-garden'. It is a moment of escape from the endless walking 'down a concrete corridor'; or 'through the stone passages of an immense and empty hospital'.

This moment of release from the deadening feeling of

meaningless sequence, 'in and out, in an endless drift', 'to and fro, dragging my feet', into the present, the moment when, in Agatha's phrase, 'the chain breaks', is connected here with the memory of 'what might have been'.

The poem springs from this experience, and it sets by it another experience, which is sought deliberately, but which is the same, for 'the way up is the way down'. If we pass from the literal to the moral meaning we may say that the virtue to which *Burnt Norton* points us is the virtue of humility: a submission to the truth of experience, an acceptance of what is, that involves the acceptance of ignorance:

Internal darkness, deprivation
And destitution of all property,
Desiccation of the world of sense,
Evacuation of the world of fancy,
Inoperancy of the world of spirit.

If we pass then to the use of theological terms we may say that mystically the subject of *Burnt Norton* is grace: the gift by which we seek to discover what we have already been shown.

However, it is in the *Four Quartets* that the immanence theory of time is worked out fully in poetic terms. The first lines open on what seems to be the classical Augustinian conception of time, with its placing of the sense of the past and the future in the present; but the poem soon shifts to an orthodox neo-Platonic theory:

[Quotes first 10 lines of "Burnt Norton"]

The present and the past are perhaps already part of the future but the future is determined by the past. In this sense, all temporal experiences are in the present, at every moment, and we cannot redeem the temporal because it is never away from us to be redeemed.

Also, and this becomes clear in the total context, 'All time is unredeemable' has another meaning: There is no redemption if we recognize only the flux. Further, even the realm of pure possibilities, of things that might have happened, is no different from the temporal: Past, present, future and possibility point to one end which is always with us; that is, which end, as the Eternal or Timeless, immanent in the flux, is the ultimate source of explanation of it.

This notion of the Eternal or ultimate reality being immanent in the flux as the Logos which anyone can discern, but which only a few do discern, clarifies most of 'Burnt Norton'. Consider the following lines;

Footfalls echo in the memory
Down the passage which we did not take
Towards the door we never opened
Into the rose-garden. My words echo
Thus, in your mind.

The rose-garden is the key idea in this passage. Eliot has used this image in much of his poetry and there is cogent conflicting opinion about its meaning. Whatever the general meaning may be, if there is one, at least here it seems to function in a double sense, as an actual place — a rose-garden; and as a symbol of those temporal experiences which reveal most poignantly the immanent character of the ultimately real. Like the Christian 'Kairos', the rose-garden symbolizes those moments that show, more than any others, the meeting of the Eternal and the temporal.

Besides the echo of the Logos, which is the meaning of the temporal, there are other echoes in the garden. There is, first, the deception of the thrush, calling us to a world of mere temporality. But such a world is one of indolence and desiccation, a reiteration of the waste land and the land of the hollow men:

There they were, dignified, invisible,
Moving without pressure, over the dead leaves,
In the autumn heat, through the vibrant air....
There they were as our guests, accepted and accepting,
So we moved, and they, in a formal pattern,
Along the empty alley, into the box circle,
To look down into the drained pool.

There is also the echo of the undeceiving bird, who leads us to other, more alive voices, to those who are less dignified and patterned: to those who can *see* the reality of the roses, for the roses do have 'the look of flowers that are looked at'. These are the voices of the children, hidden excitedly in the apple tree, who are laughing and singing; but who are, as we realise in 'Little Gidding', 'Not known, because not looked for / But heard, half-heard, in the stillness / Between two waves of the sea.'

The bird is the messenger of Truth, telling us that the rose-garden echoes with life: and that this life itself is a manifestation of something which is more than the mere flux. But the bird also knows that man will not acquiesce to that which is true:

Go, go, go, said the bird: human kind
Cannot bear very much reality.

The second movement of 'Burnt Norton' sharpens the immanence conception of time: that the Eternal or Timeless is the ultimate dimension of the flux and gives it whatever reality and meaning it has. After an introductory passage, in which physical movement, 'The trilling wire in the blood', epitomized in the struggle between the boarhound and the boar that ends in death, is falsified as the only movement there is, we come to true, nonphysical movement:

At the still point of the turning world. Neither flesh nor fleshless;
Neither from nor towards; at the still point, there the dance is,
But neither arrest nor movement. And do not call it fixity,
Where past and future are gathered. Neither movement from nor towards,
Neither ascent nor decline. Except for the point, the still point,
There would be no dance, and there is only the dance.

The still point, of course, is the symbol of the Logos, but it is also the symbol of the Christian God. In God is the source of movement and the temporal. Not that God is movement; rather from Him emanates movement, to utilize a neo-Platonic idea. There is the temporal, the flux; but without God, the Timeless, there would be no temporal.

To experience the Eternal, the 'still point', is to transcend the temporal; it is to give up desire, action and suffering; to rise upto God, but with no physical action; and to understand both theTimeless and the temporal for the first time:

[Quotes from "I can only say, *there* we have been; but I

cannot say where" to "The resolution of its partial horror."] We must start with the temporal, the ever-changing experience; and come to see its dependence upon the Timeless:

Time past and time future
Allow but a little consciousness.
To be conscious is not to be in time
But only in time can the moment in the rose-garden,
The moment in the arbour where the rain beat,
The moment in the draughty church at smokefall
Be remembered; involved with past and future.
Only through time time is conquered.

In the final movement of 'Burnt Norton', the distinction between the Timeless and the temporal becomes the distinction between The Word and words. Words lie, but it is only through words that we can conquer them, to express the truth which is The Word. And what we want to say we cannot say because words are always changing, being in the flux; but even with words we can suggest The Word: That God, Who is the Final Cause, did initiate the first event and does determine the last event:

Desire itself is movement
Not in itself desirable;
Love is itself unmoving,
Only the cause and end of movement,
Timeless, and undesiring
Except in the aspect of time
Caught in the form of limitation
Between un-being and being.

The movement and the poem end with a concrete and visual return to the rose-garden with their contrast between the inadequate affirmation of the sole reality of the flux and the true recognition that there is something more, the Eternal, echoing in the laughter of the children. How ridiculous, then, the sole acceptance of 'the waste sad time Stretching before and after'.

It seems doubtful whether at the time of writing 'Burnt Norton', just after *Murder in the Cathedral,* Eliot had already projected the series. His creative energies for the next three years were to be largely taken up with *The Family Reunion,* which, to judge from the endless revisions in the manuscript, caused him about as much trouble as anything he has done. With 'East Coker' in the spring of 1940 he made his first experiment in a part for part parallel with an earlier work of his own.

Again Donne's practice is suggestive: when he had evolved a particularly intricate and irregular stanza, he invariably set himself the challenge of following it unchanged to the end of his poem. But in assigning himself a similar problem for a poem two hundred lines long, Eliot has tried something far more exacting, where failure could be caused by the parallels becoming merely mechanical, and by the themes and rhythms becoming not subtle variations but flat repetitions.

'East Coker' does indeed have something of the effect of a set piece. Just as its high proportion of prosaic lines seems to spring from partial exhaustion, so its resumption of themes from 'Burnt Norton' can occasionally sound as though the poet was merely imitating himself. But on the whole he had solved his problem. He had made a renewal of form that was to carry him successively in the next two years through 'The Dry Salvages' and 'Little Gidding'. The discrimination between repetition and variation ties primarily in the rhythm; and these last two poems reverberate with an increasing musical richness.

A double question that keeps insisting itself through any discussion of these structures is the poet's consciousness of analogies with music, and whether such analogies are a confusion of arts. One remembers that Eliot, in accepting Lawrence's definition of 'the essence of poetry' as a 'stark, bare, rocky directness of statement', drew an analogy with the later quartets of Beethoven.

This does not mean that he has ever tried to copy literally the effects of a different medium. But he knows that poetry is like music in being a temporal rather than a spatial art; and he has by now thought much about the subject, as the concluding paragraph of 'The Music of Poetry' shows:

I think that a poet may gain much from the study of music: how much technical knowledge of musical form is desirable I do not know, for I have not that technical knowledge myself. But I believe that the properties in which music concerns the poet most nearly, are the sense of rhythm and the sense of structure. I think that it might be possible for a poet to work too closely to musical analogies: the result might be an effect of artificiality.

But he insists — and this has immediate bearing on his own intentions — that 'the use of recurrent themes is as natural to poetry as to music'. He has worked on that assumption throughout his quartets, and whether he has proved that 'there are possibilities of transitions in a poem comparable to the different movements of a symphony or a quartet', or that 'there are possibilities of contrapuntal arrangement of subject-matter', can be known only through repeated experience of the whole series. All I wish to suggest here is the pattern made by some of the dominant themes in their interrelation and progression.

'Burnt Norton' opens as a meditation on time. Many comparable and contrasting views are introduced. The lines are drenched with reminiscences of Heraclitus' fragments on flux and movement. Some of the passages on duration remind us that Eliot listened to Bergson's lectures at the Sorbonne in the winter of 1911 and wrote an essay then criticizing his *durée réelle* as 'simply not final'.

Other lines on the recapture of time through consciousness suggest the aspect of Bergson that most stimulated Proust. But the chief contrast around which Eliot constructs this poem is that between the view of time as a mere continuum, and the difficult paradoxical Christian view of how man lives both 'in and out of time', how he is immersed in the flux and yet can penetrate to the eternal by apprehending timeless existence within time and above it.

But even for the Christian the moments of release from the pressures of the flux are rare, though they alone redeem the sad wastage of otherwise unillumined existence.

Eliot recalls one such moment of peculiar poignance, a

childhood moment in the rose-garden — a symbol he has previously used, in many variants, for the birth of desire. Its implications are intricate and even ambiguous, since they raise the whole problem of how to discriminate between supernatural vision and mere illusion.

Other variations here on the theme of how time is conquered are more directly apprehensible. In dwelling on the extension of time into movement, Eliot takes up an image he had used in 'Triumphal March': 'at the still point of the turning world'.

This notion of 'a mathematically pure point' (as Philip Wheelwright has called it) seems to be Eliot's poetic equivalent in our cosmology for Dante's 'unmoved Mover', another way of symbolising a timeless release from the 'outer compulsions' of the world. Still another variation is the passage an the Chinese jar in the final section. Here Eliot, in a conception comparable to Wallace Stevens' 'Anecdote of the Jar', has suggested how art conquers time:

Only by the form, the pattern,
Can words or music reach
The stillness, as a Chinese jar still
Moves perpetually in its stillness.

The third section of 'Burnt Norton' provides a second experience, located not in the Garden but in the City, or rather beneath the City, on an underground platform, no doubt of the Circle Line. The Underground's 'flicker' is a mechanical reconciliation of light and darkness, the two alternately exhibited very rapidly. The traveller's emptiness is 'neither plenitude nor vacancy'. In this 'dim light' we have

neither daylight
Investing form with lucid stillness
Turning shadow into transient beauty
With slow rotation suggesting permanence
Nor darkness to purify the soul
Emptying the sensual with deprivation
Cleansing affection from the temporal.

There is rotation, but it does not suggest permanence; there is darkness, purifying nothing; there is light, but it invests nothing with lucid stillness; there is a systematic parody of the wheel's movement and the point's fixity —

Men and bits of paper, whirled by the cold wind
That blows before and after time,

not like the souls of Paolo and Francesca, who were somewhere in particular throughout eternity for a particular reason known to them, nor even like de Bailhache, Fresca, and Mrs Cammel, who were disintegrated; but simply

The strained time-ridden faces
Distracted from distraction by distraction
Filled with fancies and empty of meaning
Tumid apathy with no concentration.

Light and darkness are opposites, apparently united by this flicker. Their actual reconciliation is to be achieved by 'descending lower', into an emptier darkness:

Descend lower, descend only,
Into the world of perpetual solitude,
World not world, but that which is not world,
Internal darkness, deprivation
And destitution of all property,
Desiccation of the world of sense,
Evacuation of the world of fancy,
Inoperancy of the world of spirit;
This is the one way...

Opposites falsely reconciled, then truly reconciled: in the central section of the poem its central structural principle is displayed. The false reconciliation parodies the true one, as the Hollow Men parody the saints, as Gerontion parodies Simeon, as Becket suicide would have parodied Becket martyr, as the leader's eyes in which there is no interrogation parody that certainty which inheres 'at the still point of the turning world'.

In this Underground scene curiously enough, the instructed reader may catch a glimpse of the author, sauntering through the crowd as Alfred Hitchcock does in each of his films. For its locale, Eliot noted, sharing a private joke with his brother in Massachusetts, is specifically the Gloucester Road Station, near the poet's South Kensington headquarters, the point of intersection of the Circle Line with the Piccadilly tube to Russell Square. Whoever would leave the endless circle and entrain for the offices of Faber & Faber must 'descend lower', and by spiral stairs if he chooses to walk. 'This is the one way, and the other is the same'; the other, adjacent to the stairs, is a lift, which he negotiates 'not in movement, but abstention from movement'. As Julia Shuttlethwaite observes in *The Cocktail Party*, 'In a lift I can meditate'.

After this whiff of the Possum's whimsy, section IV displays the flash of the kingfisher's wing, to offset an instance of the Light which rests. The sun is the still point around which the earth turns, and light is concentrated there; it subtly becomes (for Eliot does not name it) a type of the still point where every variety of light inheres, which transient phenomena reflect. And section V presents language itself as a transience on which sufficient form may confer endurance. The poem ends with a reassertion of the possibility, and the significance, of timeless moments:

Sudden in a shaft of sunlight
Even while the dust moves
There rises the hidden laughter
Of children in the foliage
Quick now, here, now, always —
Ridiculous the waste sad time
Stretching before and after.

In this elusive vision the moving dust in sunlight suggests the conditions of human existence, dust sustained and made visible by whatever power emanates from the still point; 'quick' means both instantaneous and alive; here and now acquire momentarily the significance of 'always'; and the 'before and after' which for Shelley contained those distracting glimpses of 'what might have been', cease to tantalize: they are merely aspects of 'the waste sad time' which the timeless moment has power to render irrelevant.

This remarkable poem, which no one, however well acquainted with Eliot's earlier work, could have foreseen, brings the generalizing style of the author of 'Prufrock' and the austere intuitions of the disciple of Bradley for the first time into intimate harmony. Suggestion does not outrun thought, nor design impose itself on what word and cadence are capable of suggesting. It was a precarious unobtrusive masterpiece, which had for some years no successor....

The five-parted dialectic of 'Burnt Norton' is exactly paralleled three times over, and so raised by iteration to the dignity of a form. Or so one would say, were not 'Burnt Norton', surprisingly enough, the exact structural counterpart of *The Waste Land.* That form, originally an accident produced by Pound's cutting,

Eliot would seem by tenacious determination to have analyzed, mastered, and made into an organic thing. 'Burnt Norton', terminating the 1935 *Collected Poems,* appears meant to bear the same relation to *The Waste Land* as Simeon to Gerontion.

Its rose-garden, for instance, with the passing cloud and the empty pool, corresponds to the Hyacinth garden and the despondent *'Oed' und leer das Meer',* while 'the heart of light, the silence' that was glimpsed in the presence of the hyacinth girl is the tainted simulacrum of that light which 'is still at the still point of the turning world'.

Each *Quartet* carries on this structural parallel. The first movement, like 'The Burial of the Dead', introduces a diversity of themes; the second, like 'A Game of Chess', presents first 'poetically' and then with less traditional circumscription the same area of experience; the third, like 'The Fire Sermon', gathers up the central vision of the poem while meditating dispersedly on themes of death: the fourth is a brief lyric; the fifth, a didactic and lyric culmination, concerning itself partly with language, in emulation of the Indo-European roots exploited in 'What the Thunder said'.

The fifth and last movement of the poem is its most contentious part, for reasons I'll try to explain. Much depends on the value we give to the first three lines: 'Words move, music moves / Only in time; but that which is only living / Can only die.' It recapitulates the statement about being conscious and remembering; as if to say that while of course we have to live in time, we are not obliged to live according to its chronometer or in deference to its 'metalled ways'. The distinction between Chronos (Yeats: 'the cracked tune that Chronos sings') and Kairos, the time of meaning and value, is much to the point here. The silence into which words reach is, so far as it is attended to, their meaning, not their defeat:

Only by the form, the pattern,
Can words or music reach
The stillness, as a Chinese jar still
Moves perpetually in its stillness.
Not the stillness of the violin, while the note lasts,
Not that only, but the co-existence,
Or say that the end precedes the beginning,
And the end and the beginning were always there
Before the beginning and after the end.
And all is always now.

In *The Living Principle* Leavis gives an account of this passage so invidious that it impels him beyond the necessity of his argument into a commentary, finally negative, on Eliot's entire later poetry. It is clear that he reached this position for many complicated reasons; including a radical shift in his scale of values, such that Eliot must be diminished by a revised comparison with Lawrence, a fate that Lawrence, too, suffered by still later comparison with the Tolstoy of *Anna Karenina.*

Leavis allowed himself to be scandalized, in his commentary on 'Burnt Norton', by Eliot's insistence — at least it appeared to Leavis to amount to insistence — that 'the really real... is the eternal'. Except by relation to the ultimately real, which is eternal, human life has no significance: this is what Leavis accused Eliot of believing, on the evidence of 'Burnt Norton'. Eliot, that is, 'insists on the unreality, the unlivingness, of life in time'.

I don't find Eliot believing anything of the kind: he couldn't have believed it and still be a communicant of a Church which is founded upon the redemption of time by the Annunciation. How Eliot judged those forms of temporal life which, were content to be, in every limiting sense, merely temporal, and to obey the call of punctuality and immediacy, is of course a different matter: on that, the evidence he has left is clear. In 'Burnt Norton', the words which induced Leavis to protest are those which seem to entail a claim, on Eliot's part, to know what 'the meaning' is; such words as 'form' and 'pattern', and, from an earlier movement, 'the dance'. 'The ultimate really real that Eliot seeks in *Four Quartets*', according to Leavis, 'is eternal reality, and *that* he can do little, directly, to characterize'.

Directly, of course not. Nor is there any pretence of 'characterizing'. Form, pattern and dance are merely analogies, ways of putting not 'eternal reality' but the poet's striving to apprehend it. Form, pattern and dance denote the point at which an otherwise mere event may be brought to disclose its meaning; brought, by exerting upon it the pressure of a more demanding moral and spiritual perspective than any judgement entailed in the immediacy of the event itself.

That the meaning is dynamic is clarified by the 'Chinese jar' which 'still / Moves perpetually in its stillness'. Where Eliot comes a cropper is in his attempt to be more specific than that, distinguishing between a visible and an audible stillness, and trying to go beyond the distinction. 'Not that only, but the co-existence': the co-existence of what? He finds it impossible to say just what he means; as the passage about the incapacity of words goes on to confess almost at once.

In the interval between *Murder in the Cathedral* and *The Family Reunion,* Eliot had temptation much on his mind; the temptation of Thomas á Becket, of Harry's father, of Christ in the desert and more generally the temptation of silence to dissolve in chatter. The last lines of this movement are perhaps melodramatic:

The Word in the desert
Is most attacked by voices of temptation,
The crying shadow in the funeral dance,
The loud lament of the disconsolate chimera.

I can't find any particular — or particularly cogent — meaning in the last two lines: what the shadow is, or who or what the disconsolate chimera is. Eliot is rattling old bones.

The poem ends more quietly in another attempt to represent the pattern as dynamic:

[Donoghue quotes from "The detail of the pattern is movement," to "Stretching before and after."]

Structurally, it is a return to the beginning, a discursive passage about time, love and desire; a passage in which the English language, in this respect like Mallarmé's French, seems to be intoning itself without requiring either a speaker or a listener to be in attendance.

As in the first movement, we are released from its monitions to the imagery of gardens, children and laughter. The figure of the ten stairs comes from St John of the Cross and may be left unglossed; it sustains the Heraclitean motif of the way up and the way down. It would be more useful to quote, from the third movement of 'Little Gidding', the passage about the use of memory:

This is the use of memory:
For liberation — not less of love but expanding
Of love beyond desire, and so liberation
From the future as well as the past.

This is what 'Burnt Norton', and indeed the other Quartets, are about: starting from the unquestionably rich ground of laughing children in the foliage, how to avoid losing or, worse still, humiliating the promise implicit in the sunshine and the laughter. How to convert the low dream of desire into the high dream of love.

In the chapter on *Alice in Wonderland* in *Some Versions of Pastoral* William Empson remarks how a certain feeling about children developed in England after the eighteenth-century settlement had come to seem narrow and inescapable; a feeling 'that no way of building up character, no intellectual system, can bring out all that is inherent in the human spirit, and therefore that there is more in the child than any man has been able to keep'.

This idea of the child, 'that it is in the night relation to Nature, not dividing what should be unified, that its intuitive judgment contains what poetry and philosophy must spend their time labouring to recover, was accepted by Dodgson and a main part of his feeling'.'Burnt Norton' is full of this feeling, along with a doomed conviction that it can't be recovered, and that the only thing possible is to invoke the plenitude of one's memory of such unity, and start again from there under better, because more exacting, auspices.

The success of 'Burnt Norton' is still in dispute. The reason is, I think, that none of the critical procedures developed and employed in the fifty years since the publication of the poem has been responsive to the kind of poetry we find in 'Burnt Norton'.

I can put this briefly by saying: nobody, not even Leavis, took up where D.W. Harding's account of the poem left off. Most of the critical procedures which have been used with success in the analysis of poems have concentrated upon one or another of a limited set of terms: image, symbol and structure.

No critical method has arisen which proposes to show the poetic character and potentiality of discourse? It is still an effort to take the harm out of the word 'discursive'; as reviews of John Ashbery's poems sufficiently indicate.

Here is part of the argument and imagery of *Four Quartets*. First there is the argument by Bergsonian, Christian and Indian mystics alike that the moment of illumination reveals (as in Plato's metaphor of the cave) the distinction between reality and its mere shadow. The sunlight fills the empty pool; presence is overcome by absence; meaning seems to be revealed.

Then there is Eliot's reservation about the Platonic language of light and shadow, for, given the values of light and shadow defined in the early essay, one finds a significant ambiguity in this mystical moment of illumination in 'Burnt Norton'. It is not clear what has been revealed, what truth it is that humankind cannot bear.

Is the light (presumably the light of the Gospel of John that becomes the Word by the end of this poem) real, marking all else as merely shadow? Or is shadow real (the darkness that comes with the cloud), marking the momentary light as merely an illusion? It is not clear which of these phenomena the bird is calling 'reality'. The ambiguity is no accident; it comes from Eliot's disenchantment with the 'meretricious captivation' of this sort of 'promise of immortality' that he had encountered in Bergsonism. His fear was that the inner light was no more trustworthy than the inner voice, I which breathes the eternal message of vanity, fear, and lust.' As always, the test is pragmatic; these moments 'can be judged only by their fruits.'

And yet pragmatism is no simple alternative to this mystical moment, Bergsonian or otherwise. One therefore also finds in 'Burnt Norton' the twenty-year fear of pragmatism's replacement of the spiritual part of our diet by fiction. The mysterious, lyrical fourth section of the poem focuses upon this fruitless option.

The puzzling rhetorical questions serve to mock the pragmatic proposition that reality is a function of human need. The passing away of the sun (as in the first section of the poem, symbolically the reality outside the human being) exposes the ludicrousness of the suggestion that we could replace the sun: 'Will the sunflower turn to us, will the clematis / Stray down, bend to us: tendril and spray / Clutch and cling?'

How can the world's being depend on human being? This section of the poem ironically reverses the bird's claim that humankind cannot bear very much reality: it is no longer to bear reality in the sense of 'to endure' reality; it is to bear reality in the sense of 'to sustain, support, create' reality.

Thus, in the first movement of *Burnt Norton,* the theme of Time and its end is introduced in the voice of impersonal thought, seeking a universal truth through abstraction, logical argument, and the resolution of paradox.

This modulates in the course of lines 11-19 into a personal voice with a contrasting sense of "What might have been and what has been," a sense arising from experience rather than from abstract argument. Memory and imagination combine in a sustained development of this second theme as a paradoxical experience of the world of light. At its close, ("a cloud passed and the pool was empty"), this voice rises in intensity - and then abruptly gives way to the detached voice of the opening lines. The arrangement of the voices in the second movement is the reverse of the first. It opens with a passage of taut lyrical writing in a symbolist manner, as if memory and imagination were essaying their own statement of the universal truth of sensual experience.

Then thought takes over and continues to the end in a sustained exploration of how time and the sensual body might be transcended. "At the still point of the turning world" appears at first to take up the conclusion of the lyric; but the series of paradoxes would have us conceive a realm beyond sense and contrary to sense.

In fact the meditation begun in the opening lines of the poem is being resumed. If there is a pattern in earthly experience it is because "the one end, which is always present" may be found "At the still point of the turning world." The meditation unfolds through three distinct sections: eight lines of paradoxes determined by negatives and exclusions are followed by nine lines positively affirming what is to be aspired to; then there is a return to the inescapable complications of a consciousness that is in time and in the sensual body.

Here memory and imagination re-enter, but now we find that they have been incorporated into the process of thought and subjected to its perspective and its ends: "only in time can the moment in the rose-garden... Be remembered; involved with past and future."

In the third movement the thought does what it will with the world of experience, determining its nature, and then dismissing it with outright satire. With "Descend lower, descend only" the meditation modulates rather suddenly into a third voice, that of prayer or exhortation.

The desire and direction of the will which have been present but in suspense from the beginning here reveal themselves as the motive-force behind the thought, from which they effectively take over now that it has done its work and prepared their way.

The fourth movement, like the lyric at the start of the second movement, is an account of the world of experience. But it differs from it in being informed by the thoughtful critique of experience, and it affirms the light that is beyond sense. Moreover, it does this with an air of desiring to be with that light, and thus to transcend time.

It would seem then that the three voices previously made out, and which have followed one upon another, are here heard in unison, thus producing the fourth voice which completes the quartet.

It is wholly characteristic of Eliot that there should be a hierarchy of instruments, that the lower should give rise to the higher, and then be caught up into the ultimate voice and vision. (In the fifth movement of *Burnt Norton* the three individual voices are heard both separately and together.)

Chapter 11

Tradition and the Individual Talent

In English writing we seldom speak of tradition, though we occasionally apply its name in deploring its absence. We cannot refer to "the tradition" or to "a tradition"; at most, we employ the adjective in saying that the poetry of So-and-so is "traditional" or even "too traditional." Seldom, perhaps, does the word appear except in a phrase of censure. If otherwise, it is vaguely approbative, with the implication, as to the work approved, of some pleasing archæological reconstruction. You can hardly make the word agreeable to English ears without this comfortable reference to the reassuring science of archæology.

Certainly the word is not likely to appear in our appreciations of living or dead writers. Every nation, every race, has not only its own creative, but its own critical turn of mind; and is even more oblivious of the shortcomings and limitations of its critical habits than of those of its creative genius.

We know, or think we know, from the enormous mass of critical writing that has appeared in the French language the critical method or habit of the French; we only conclude (we are such unconscious people) that the French are "more critical" than we, and sometimes even plume ourselves a little with the fact, as if the French were the less spontaneous.

Perhaps they are; but we might remind ourselves that criticism is as inevitable as breathing, and that we should be none the worse for articulating what passes in our minds when we read a book and feel an emotion about it, for criticizing our own minds in their work of criticism.

One of the facts that might come to light in this process is our tendency to insist, when we praise a poet, upon those aspects of his work in which he least resembles anyone else. In these aspects or parts of his work we pretend to find what is individual, what is the peculiar essence of the man.

We dwell with satisfaction upon the poet's difference from his predecessors, especially his immediate predecessors; we endeavour to find something that can be isolated in order to be enjoyed.

Whereas if we approach a poet without this prejudice we shall often find that not only the best, but the most individual parts of his work may be those in which the dead poets, his ancestors, assert their immortality most vigorously. And I do not mean the impressionable period of adolescence, but the period of full maturity.

Yet if the only form of tradition, of handing down, consisted in following the ways of the immediate generation before us in a blind or timid adherence to its successes, "tradition" should positively be discouraged. We have seen many such simple currents soon lost in the sand; and novelty is better than repetition.

Tradition is a matter of much wider significance. It cannot be inherited, and if you want it you must obtain it by great labour. It involves, in the first place, the historical sense, which we may call nearly indispensable to anyone who would continue to be a poet beyond his twenty-fifth year; and the historical sense involves a perception, not only of the pastness of the past, but of its presence; the historical sense compels a man to write not merely with his own generation in his bones, but with a feeling that the whole of the literature of Europe from Homer and within it the whole of the literature of his own country has a simultaneous existence and composes a simultaneous order.

This historica sense, which is a sense of the timeless as well as of the temporal and of the timeless and of the temporal together, is what makes a writer traditional. And it is at the same time what makes a writer most acutely conscious of his place in time, of his contemporaneity.

No poet, no artist of any art, has his complete meaning alone. His significance, his appreciation is the appreciation of his relation to the dead poets and artists. You cannot value him alone; you must set him, for contrast and comparison, among the dead. I mean this as a principle of æsthetic, not merely historical, criticism.

The necessity that he shall conform, that he shall cohere, is not one-sided; what happens when a new work of art is created is something that happens simultaneously to all the works of art which preceded it. The existing monuments form an ideal order among themselves, which is modified by the introduction of the new (the really new) work of art among them.

The existing order is complete before the new work arrives; for order to persist after the supervention of novelty, the *whole* existing order must be, if ever so slightly, altered; and so the relations, proportions, values of each work of art toward the whole are readjusted; and this is conformity between the old and the new.

Whoever has approved this idea of order, of the form of European, of English literature, will not find it preposterous that the past should be altered by the present as much as the present is directed by the past. And the poet who is aware of this will be aware of great difficulties and responsibilities.

In a peculiar sense he will be aware also that he must inevitably be judged by the standards of the past. I say judged, not amputated, by them; not judged to be as good as, or worse or better than, the dead; and certainly not judged by the canons of dead critics. It is a judgment, a comparison, in which two things are measured by each other.

To conform merely would be for the new work not really to conform at all; it would not be new, and would therefore not be a work of art. And we do not quite say that the new is more valuable because it fits in; but its fitting in is a test of its value—a test, it is true, which can only be slowly and cautiously applied, for we are none of us infallible judges of conformity. We say: it appears to conform, and is perhaps individual, or it appears individual, and may conform; but we are hardly likely to find that it is one and not the other.

To proceed to a more intelligible exposition of the relation of the poet to the past: he can neither take the past as a lump, an indiscriminate bolus, nor can he form himself wholly on one or two private admirations, nor can he form himself wholly upon one preferred period.

The first course is inadmissible, the second is an important experience of youth, and the third is a pleasant and highly desirable supplement.

The poet must be very conscious of the main current, which does not at all flow invariably through the most distinguished reputations. He must be quite aware of the obvious fact that art never improves, but that the material of art is never quite the same.

He must be aware that the mind of Europe—the mind of his own country—a mind which he learns in time to be much more important than his own private mind—is a mind which changes, and that this change is a development which abandons nothing *en route*, which does not superannuate either Shakespeare, or Homer, or the rock drawing of the Magdalenian draughtsmen.

That this development, refinement perhaps, complication certainly, is not, from the point of view of the artist, any improvement. Perhaps not even an improvement from the point of view of the psychologist or not to the extent which we imagine; perhaps only in the end based upon a complication in economics and machinery. But the difference between the present and the past is that the conscious present is an awareness of the past in a way and to an extent which the past's awareness of itself cannot show.

Some one said: "The dead writers are remote from us because we *know* so much more than they did." Precisely, and they are that which we know. I am alive to a usual objection to what is clearly part of my programme for the *métier* of poetry. The objection is that the doctrine requires a ridiculous amount of erudition (pedantry), a claim which can be rejected by appeal to the lives of poets in any pantheon. It will even be affirmed that much learning deadens or perverts poetic sensibility. While, however, we persist in believing that a poet ought to know as much as will not encroach upon his necessary receptivity and necessary laziness, it is not desirable to confine knowledge to whatever can be put into a useful shape for examinations, drawing-rooms, or the still more pretentious modes of publicity.

Some can absorb knowledge, the more tardy must sweat for it. Shakespeare acquired more essential history from Plutarch than most men could from the whole British Museum. What is to be insisted upon is that the poet must develop or procure the consciousness of the past and that he should continue to develop this consciousness throughout his career.

What happens is a continual surrender of himself as he is at the moment to something which is more valuable. The progress of an artist is a continual self-sacrifice, a continual extinction of personality. There remains to define this process of depersonalization and its relation to the sense of tradition. It is in this depersonalization that art may be said to approach the condition of science. I shall, therefore, invite you to consider, as a suggestive analogy, the action which takes place when a bit of finely filiated platinum is introduced into a chamber containing oxygen and sulphur dioxide.

Honest criticism and sensitive appreciation is directed not upon the poet but upon the poetry. If we attend to the confused cries of the newspaper critics and the susurrus of popular repetition that follows, we shall hear the names of poets in great numbers; if we seek not Blue-book knowledge but the enjoyment of poetry, and ask for a poem, we shall seldom find it. In the last article I tried to point out the importance of the relation of the poem to other poems by other authors, and suggested the conception of poetry as a living whole of all the poetry that has ever been written.

The other aspect of this Impersonal theory of poetry is the relation of the poem to its author. And I hinted, by an analogy, that the mind of the mature poet differs from that of the immature one not precisely in any valuation of "personality," not being necessarily more interesting, or having "more to say," but rather by being a more finely perfected medium in which special, or very varied, feelings are at liberty to enter into new combinations.

The analogy was that of the catalyst. When the two gases previously mentioned are mixed in the presence of a filament of platinum, they form sulphurous acid. This combination takes place only if the platinum is present; nevertheless the newly formed acid contains no trace of platinum, and the platinum itself is apparently unaffected; has remained inert, neutral, and unchanged.

The mind of the poet is the shred of platinum. It may partly or exclusively operate upon the experience of the man himself; but, the more perfect the artist, the more completely separate in him will be the man who suffers and the mind which creates; the more perfectly will the mind digest and transmute the passions which are its material.

The experience, you will notice, the elements which enter the presence of the transforming catalyst, are of two kinds: emotions and feelings. The effect of a work of art upon the person who enjoys it is an experience different in kind from any experience not of art. It may be formed out of one emotion, or may be a combination of several; and various feelings, inhering for the writer in particular words or phrases or images, may be added to compose the final result. Or great poetry may be made without the direct use of any emotion whatever: composed out of feelings solely. Canto XV of the *Inferno* (Brunetto Latini) is a working up of the emotion evident in the situation; but the effect, though single as that of any work of art, is obtained by considerable complexity of detail.

The last quatrain gives an image, a feeling attaching to an image, which "came," which did not develop simply out of what precedes, but which was probably in suspension in the poet's mind until the proper combination arrived for it to add itself to. The poet's mind is in fact a receptacle for seizing and storing up numberless feelings, phrases, images, which remain there until all the particles which can unite to form a new compound are present together.

If you compare several representative passages of the greatest poetry you see how great is the variety of types of combination, and also how completely any semi-ethical criterion of "sublimity" misses the mark. For it is not the "greatness," the intensity, of the emotions, the components, but the intensity of the artistic process, the pressure, so to speak, under which the fusion takes place, that counts.

The episode of Paolo and Francesca employs a definite emotion, but the intensity of the poetry is something quite different from whatever intensity in the supposed experience it may give the impression of.

It is no more intense, furthermore, than Canto XXVI, the voyage of Ulysses, which has not the direct dependence upon an emotion. Great variety is possible in the process of transmution of emotion: the murder of Agamemnon, or the agony of Othello, gives an artistic effect apparently closer to a possible original than the scenes from Dante.

In the *Agamemnon,* the artistic emotion approximates to the emotion of an actual spectator; in *Othello* to the emotion of the protagonist himself. But the difference between art and the event is always absolute; the combination which is the murder of Agamemnon is probably as complex as that which is the voyage of Ulysses.

In either case there has been a fusion of elements. The ode of Keats contains a number of feelings which have nothing particular to do with the nightingale, but which the nightingale, partly, perhaps, because of its attractive name, and partly because of its reputation, served to bring together.

The point of view which I am struggling to attack is perhaps related to the metaphysical theory of the substantial unity of the soul: for my meaning is, that the poet has, not a "personality" to express, but a particular medium, which is only a medium and not a personality, in which impressions and experiences combine in peculiar and unexpected ways. Impressions and experiences which are important for the man may take no place in the poetry, and those which become important in the poetry may play quite a negligible part in the man, the personality.

I will quote a passage which is unfamiliar enough to be regarded with fresh attention in the light—or darkness—of these observations:

And now methinks I could e'en chide myself
For doating on her beauty, though her death
Shall be revenged after no common action.
Does the silkworm expend her yellow labours
For thee? For thee does she undo herself?
Are lordships sold to maintain ladyships
For the poor benefit of a bewildering minute?
Why does yon fellow falsify highways,
And put his life between the judge's lips,
To refine such a thing—keeps horse and men
To beat their valours for her?...

In this passage (as is evident if it is taken in its context) there is a combination of positive and negative emotions: an intensely strong attraction toward beauty and an equally intense fascination by the ugliness which is contrasted with it and which destroys it. This balance of contrasted emotion is in the dramatic situation to which the speech is pertinent, but that situation alone is inadequate to it. This is, so to speak, the structural emotion, provided by the drama. But the whole effect, the dominant tone, is due to the fact that a number of floating feelings, having an affinity to this emotion by no means superficially evident, have combined with it to give us a new art emotion. It is not in his personal emotions, the emotions provoked by particular events in his life, that the poet is in any way remarkable or interesting. His particular emotions may be simple, or crude, or flat. The emotion in his poetry will be a very complex thing, but not with the complexity of the emotions of people who have very complex or unusual emotions in life.

One error, in fact, of eccentricity in poetry is to seek for new human emotions to express; and in this search for novelty in the wrong place it discovers the perverse. The business of the poet is not to find new emotions, but to use the ordinary ones and, in working them up into poetry, to express feelings which are not in actual emotions at all. And emotions which he has never experienced will serve his turn as well as those familiar to him. Consequently, we must believe that "emotion recollected in tranquillity" is an inexact formula.

For it is neither emotion, nor recollection, nor, without distortion of meaning, tranquillity. It is a concentration, and a new thing resulting from the concentration, of a very great number of experiences which to the practical and active person would not seem to be experiences at all; it is a concentration which does not happen consciously or of deliberation. These experiences are not "recollected," and they finally unite in an atmosphere which is "tranquil" only in that it is a passive attending upon the event. Of course this is not quite the whole story. There is a great deal, in the writing of poetry, which must be conscious and deliberate. In fact, the bad poet is usually unconscious where he ought to be conscious, and conscious where he ought to be unconscious. Both errors tend to make him "personal." Poetry is not a turning loose of emotion, but an escape from emotion; it is not the expression of personality, but an escape from personality. But, of course, only those who have personality and emotions know what it means to want to escape from these things.

This proposes to halt at the frontier of metaphysics or mysticism, and confine itself to such practical conclusions as can be applied by the responsible person interested in poetry. To divert interest from the poet to the poetry is a laudable aim: for it would conduce to a juster estimation of actual poetry, good and bad.

There are many people who appreciate the expression of sincere emotion in verse, and there is a smaller number of people who can appreciate technical excellence. But very few know when there is expression of *significant* emotion, emotion which has its life in the poem and not in the history of the poet. The emotion of art is impersonal. And the poet cannot reach this impersonality without surrendering himself wholly to the work to be done. And he is not likely to know what is to be done unless he lives in what is not merely the present, but the present moment of the past, unless he is conscious, not of what is dead, but of what is already living.

Chapter 12

T.S. Eliot and Anti-Semitism

Some years ago I attempted to repudiate the critical charge that first America's and then England's leading poet of the twentieth century – see the dictum in Time magazine, for example, in a 'best-of-the-century' compilation – was a blatant anti-Semite. My main essay appeared in the Yeats Eliot Review (1990) and then led to a chapter in my second Eliot book (T. S. Eliot and the Heritage of Africa, 1992). Recently a lengthy study by Ranen Omer, "'It is I who have been defending a Religion called Judaism":

The T. S. Eliot and Horace M. Kallen Correspondence,' in Texas Studies in Literature and Language (1997). helped to respond to this dastardly contention. Still, references in many journals have taken the adverse criticism as a matter of course now, referring to the 'anti-Semitic T. S. Eliot' as if that was universally accepted. Probably the main stimulant has been Anthony Julius' T. S. Eliot, Anti-Semitism, and Literary Form (Cambridge Univ. Press, 1995). Yet he had previously admitted, even in The Times (9 Aug. 1988), how the poet 'wrote publicly, and in stirring terms, condemning anti-Semitism.'

In the recent biography of A. L. Rowse by Richard Ollard, mention is made of a letter from Eliot to Rowse in January 1934 trying to organise help for German Jewish refugees. Eliot had been asked to do this by a Jewish friend in New York. So is the fact that a few Jews are cited in Eliot's poetry, and not admittedly in complimentary ways, sufficient evidence that he was of two minds? If so, on the same grounds we would have to condemn great writers like Chaucer, Shakespeare, and

Dickens. No doubt the close association with Ezra Pound constitutes a major factor (Pound having eventually confessed to having been anti-Semitic, as is well known), but it is also widely recognized that Eliot wrote Pound a strong letter deploring the latter's anti-Semitism. Positive proof for this I happen to have seen in the material assembled from Pound's stay at St. Elizabeth's mental hospital in Washington, D.C., now available in the Rare Books and Manuscripts Division of the Hamilton College Library, Pound having been a student there once. He referred, for example, to his Jewish psychiatrist as a 'kike.'

To cover in detail all the many things Eliot had said which would dispute the charge would mean reiterating material very well known, so at this stage it might be just as well to stick to some basic concepts, as well as a few personal items.

With regard to the latter, it might be mentioned that Mrs. Valerie Eliot happened to remark to me, at the International T. S. Eliot Symposium at the University of London (July 1996), that in all the years she had known Tom she never had found him guilty of making any anti-Semitic remark. Such evidence could be taken as a form of special pleading perhaps, and so would hold little scholarly weight, but to me at least it was a memorable reminiscence.

One other personal note is that I happened once to hear him speak at the Poetry Centre, Young Men's Hebrew Association, in New York after the war (the second time he had been there for that purpose). The subject of race or ethnicity did not arise then, though admittedly some Jewish members boycotted the event and picketed it.

Now because the charge of racism has been applied to his purported anti-Semitic portrayals (admittedly this term being a bit controversial with regard to Jewish people, though some Jews have defended it in particular contexts), we surely should not deny some connections with his attitude toward African people in general, the partial subject of my second Eliot book (incidentally acclaimed, as the official announcement for it demonstrates, by Henry Louis Gates, Jr., Director of the Harvard DuBois Centre for African Studies). The point here is that he was on record for asserting that poetry originally derives from the African beating his drum in a jungle.

That, in itself, may seem to be a statement which could be taken in different ways, but at any rate it need not be considered in any literal, palaeontological sense. For it points really to the inherent talent of the black race, and it is surely common knowledge by now that Eliot was inspired, especially in his early work, by African anthropology (which he the n had studied at Harvard).

All this is germane enough to my present thesis particularly because some Africans traditionally have been considered Semitic as well (for example, Ethiopians and certain North African Tribes).

When personally accosted of being anti-Semitic in some of his poetry, he is known for having claimed that his writings occasionally involving Jewish people had been, as he put it, 'misrepresented.'

A neighbouring colleague of mine at another institution has tried to defend this for me on the grounds that if Eliot deplored some common associations of Jewish people with being good in moneymaking, he had nothing against them religiously, ethnically, or in any other cultural context. Whether such a distinction is always socially acceptable is another matter, one a bit subtle to consider here at any length.

In any event, it must be admitted that he felt that the speaker in a poem (the persona, not merely the 'person') does not represent the poet himself or his own possible prejudices. This viewpoint is clearly seen in his well-known essay 'The Three Voices of Poetry.' True, he later conceded that this principle sometimes worked better in theory than in practice.

At this point it might be helpful to resort to some particular instances in his writings which have been a cause for alarm and see just what we can make of them objectively. The most notorious is probably his use of the phrase 'freethinking Jews' in a talk at the University of Virginia, which was printed then in his collection After Strange Gods (but then never reprinted because he admitted that he had composed some things that were not well enough written). One of

America's leading Eliot scholars, whose name I hereby reserve the right to withhold in print, has instructed me at a T. S. Eliot Society annual meeting in St.

Louis a few years ago that the very title of Eliot's book represents in fact a give-away. In other words, what Eliot meant to suggest was that Jews who were 'free-thinking' represented followers of such liberal prototypes as Freud and Marx (not Abraham).

Later he was known for admitting that, in such a respect, it would seem he did not mean to single out merely Jews as being such 'free-think ers.' It is arguable, by some, whether Marx himself was much of a Jew, his heritage notwithstanding. In any case, it might be contended that such an expression as 'free-thinking Jews' when taken by itself does sound bigoted. The immediate context qualifies this appreciably, though the term itself might better now be dropped.

Another example worth some scrutiny is his reference to a 'jew merchant' in a familiar letter to Pound. Again the expression when taken by itself is defamatory. But again context has to be seen for what it is as well.

The main point here is that evidently he was playing up to Pound's own proclivities with his phrase, trying to placate him in other words. Such an 'occasion' would not totally excuse the term in question, but at least it gives it an understandably more human touch.

Along with this is the fact that such an expression was more or less endemic among his fellow Americans. If that was so, he was probably trying to conform to a colloquialism, one which in one form or another was used and quoted even in poetry.

This is notably true, I have found, with the anthologizer Louis Untermeyer, himself Jewish, insofar as he included Southern poetry with the expression jewboy, for one, in his collection Modern American Poetry. Because of my having had some of my graduate school training in the South, I witnesse d the use of the term cited by Untermeyer even in a private conference by one of the most distinguished professors of English at the University of North Carolina in Chapel Hill (a personal friend of Frost's, it so happened, not Eliot's). So the key point again is that if terms like 'jewboy' and 'jew merchant' (even in the uncapitalized form, used by Eliot in his earlier poetic references but later revised) derived from a certain cultural heritage, the heritage itself was basically to blame, not Eliot himself necessarily.

Another example worth momentary treatment at least is the fact that one original section of The Waste Land, which he then later discarded, was entitled 'Dirge' and contained a passing, plausibly offensive reference to the money-making Bleistein. Having examined the original manuscript in the Berg Collection at the New York Public Library, I can verify that even Pound himself had qualms about this short verse, assigning there the label of 'doubtful' to it.

Fortunately Eliot did not have the lyric printed because of possible overtones it had. In a word, he himself recognized the dangers inherent in such a stereotyped association of a Jew (with a German name) and money-making. The basic issue, however, is whether in fact proper conservation of money is not a fundamental human prerogative, hardly one limited to any one ethnic group, though (granted) one may be more talented at it than another.

Aware of sinister implications of the name of Bleistein, Eliot widely discarded this jeu d' esprit of his from his most impressive overall assemblage which warranted the modernist label of The Waste Land. Besides, 'Dirge' was simply not well enough written.

How finally can this attempt to rehabilitate Eliot from charges of antiSemitism be profitably concluded? The recent attempt to revive interest in his output through publication of Inventions of the March Hare, edited by Christopher Ricks, now has to be mentioned, at least in passing, if only because reviewers have pointed out how some of these hitherto unpublished poems contained possibly racist overtones, for instance notably the 'King Bob' collection.

(That, of course, would have amounted to a good reason for his original decision to desist from further publication.) A final verdict on this gathering has yet to be made. So let us conclude rather on a more positive note by ascribing value to the poet's well-received statements that his fundamental purpose, at least after his conversion from Unitarianism, was said to be a true Christian poet.

The particular relevance of this admission here is that he emphasized, as is well known, how his therefore being 'Christian' (that is, not just 'a Christian') meant tha t he could not thereby be anti-Semitic (or racist at all for that matter).

This point is subtler than it might at first seem. It does not refer merely to a particular religious belief in itself: numerous critics would have to counter that many self-professed Christians have in fact acted in an un-Christ-like manner regardless.

Yet his use of the adjective Christian implies that not merely his formal affiliation but his heart is what is at stake. In other words, if one is truly Christian, not merely a baptized one, then by definition he cannot be biased toward other ethnic or racial groups owing to his faith in God as Love.

Maybe this all sounds rather idealistic at times, but at least it has that needed sincere ring to it. And that is what can revamp Eliot's status as a true believer and not a bigot.

Chapter 13

The Sacred Wood

Three conclusions at least issue from the perusal of Swinburne's critical essays: Swinburne had mastered his material, was more inward with the Tudor-Stuart dramatists than any man of pure letters before or since; he is a more reliable guide to them than Hazlitt, Coleridge, or Lamb; and his perception of relative values is almost always correct. Against these merits we may oppose two objections: the style is the prose style of Swinburne, and the content is not, in an exact sense, criticism.

The faults of style are, of course, personal; the tumultuous outcry of adjectives, the headstrong rush of undisciplined sentences, is the index to the impatience and perhaps laziness of a disorderly mind.

But the style has one positive merit: it allows us to know that Swinburne was writing not to establish a critical reputation, not to instruct a docile public, but as a poet his notes upon poets whom he admired. And whatever our opinion of Swinburne's verse, the notes upon poets by a poet of Swinburne's dimensions must be read with attention and respect.

In saying that Swinburne's essays have the value of notes of an important poet upon important poets, we must place a check upon our expectancy. He read everything, and he read with the single interest in finding literature. The critics of the romantic period were pioneers, and exhibit the fallibility of discoverers.

The selections of Lamb are a successful effort of good taste, but anyone who has referred to them after a thorough reading of any of the poets included must have found that some of the best passages—which must literally have stared Lamb in the face—are omitted, while sometimes others of less value are included.

Hazlitt, who committed himself to the judgment that the *Maid's Tragedy* is one of the poorest of Beaumont and Fletcher's plays, has no connected message to deliver. Coleridge's remarks—too few and scattered—have permanent truth; but on some of the greatest names he passes no remark, and of some of the best plays was perhaps ignorant or ill-informed. But compared with Swinburne, Coleridge writes much more as a poet might be expected to write about poets. Of Massinger's verse Swinburne says:

It is more serviceable, more businesslike, more eloquently practical, and more rhetorically effusive—but never effusive beyond the bounds of effective rhetoric—than the style of any Shakespearean or of any Jonsonian dramatist.

It is impossible to tell whether Webster would have found the style of Massinger more "serviceable" than his own for the last act of the *White Devil,* and indeed difficult to decide what "serviceable" here means; but it is quite clear what Coleridge means when he says that Massinger's style is much more easily constructed [than Shakespeare's], and may be more successfully adopted by writers in the present day.

Coleridge is writing as a professional with his eye on the technique. I do not know from what writing of Coleridge Swinburne draws the assertion that "Massinger often deals in exaggerated passion," but in the essay from which Swinburne quotes elsewhere Coleridge merely speaks of the "unnaturally irrational passions," a phrase much more defensible.

Upon the whole, the two poets are in harmony upon the subject of Massinger; and although Coleridge has said more in five pages, and said it more clearly, than Swinburne in thirty-nine, the essay of Swinburne is by no means otiose: it is more stimulating than Coleridge's, and the stimulation is never misleading. With all his superlatives, his judgment, if carefully scrutinized, appears temperate and just.

With all his justness of judgment, however, Swinburne is

an appreciator and not a critic. In the whole range of literature covered, Swinburne makes hardly more than two judgments which can be reversed or even questioned: one, that Lyly is insignificant as a dramatist, and the other, that Shirley was probably unaffected by Webster. The *Cardinal* is not a cast of the *Duchess of Malfi,* certainly; but when Shirley wrote

the mist is risen, and there's none
To steer my wandering bark. (Dies.)
he was probably affected by
My soul, like to a ship in a black storm,
Is driven, I know not whither.

Swinburne's judgment is generally sound, his taste sensitive and discriminating. And we cannot say that his thinking is faulty or perverse—up to the point at which it is thinking. But Swinburne stops thinking just at the moment when we are most zealous to go on. And this arrest, while it does not vitiate his work, makes it an introduction rather than a statement.

We are aware, after the *Contemporaries of Shakespeare* and the *Age of Shakespeare* and the books on Shakespeare and Jonson, that there is something unsatisfactory in the way in which Swinburne was interested in these people; we suspect that his interest was never articulately formulated in his mind or consciously directed to any purpose.

He makes his way, or loses it, between two paths of definite direction. He might as a poet have concentrated his attention upon the technical problems solved or tackled by these men; he might have traced for us the development of blank verse from Sackville to the mature Shakespeare, and its degeneration from Shakespeare to Milton.

Or he might have studied through the literature to the mind of that century; he might, by dissection and analysis, have helped us to some insight into the feeling and thought which we seem to have left so far away. In either case, you would have had at least the excitement of following the movements of an important mind groping towards important conclusions. As it is, there are to be no conclusions, except that Elizabethan literature is very great, and that you can have pleasure and even ecstasy from it, because a sensitive poetic talent has had the experience.

One is in risk of becoming fatigued by a hubbub that does not march; the drum is beaten, but the procession does not advance.

If, for example, Swinburne's interest was in poetry, why devote an essay to Brome? "The opening scene of the *Sparagus Garden,*" says Swinburne, "is as happily humorous and as vividly natural as that of any more famous comedy." The scene is both humorous and natural.

Brome deserves to be more read than he is, and first of all to be more accessible than he is. But Swinburne ought to suggest or imply (I do not say impose) a reason for reading the *Sparagus Garden* or the *Antipodes,* more sufficient than any he has provided. No doubt such reason could be found.

When it is a matter of pronouncing judgment between two poets, Swinburne is almost unerring. He is certainly right in putting Webster above Tourneur, Tourneur above Ford, and Ford above Shirley.

He weighs accurately the good and evil in Fletcher: he perceives the essential theatricality, but his comparison of the *Faithful Shepherdess* with *Comus* is a judgment no word of which can be improved upon:

The difference between this poem [*i.e.* the *Faithful Shepherdess*] and Milton's exquisitely imitative *Comus* is the difference between a rose with a leaf or two faded or falling, but still fragrant and radiant, and the faultless but scentless reproduction of a rose in academic wax for the admiration and imitation of such craftsmen as must confine their ambition to the laurels of a college or the plaudits of a school.

In the longest and most important essay in the *Contemporaries of Shakespeare,* the essay on Chapman, there are many such sentences of sound judgment forcibly expressed. The essay is the best we have on that great poet. It communicates the sense of dignity and mass which we receive from Chapman. But it also illustrates Swinburne's infirmities. Swinburne was not tormented by the restless desire to penetrate to the heart and marrow of a poet, any more than he was tormented by the desire to render the finest shades of difference and resemblance between several poets. Chapman is a difficult author, as Swinburne says; he is far more difficult than Jonson, to whom he bears only a superficial likeness. He is difficult beyond his obscurity.

He is difficult partly through his possession of a quality comparatively deficient in Jonson, but which was nevertheless a quality of the age. It is strange that Swinburne should have hinted at a similarity to Jonson and not mentioned a far more striking affinity of Chapman's—that is, Donne. The man who wrote

Guise, O my lord, how shall I cast from me
The bands and coverts hindering me from thee?
The garment or the cover of the mind
The humane soul is; of the soul, the spirit
The proper robe is; of the spirit, the blood;
And of the blood, the body is the shroud:

and

Nothing is made of nought, of all things made,
Their abstract being a dream but of a shade,

is unquestionably kin to Donne. The quality in question is not peculiar to Donne and Chapman. In common with the greatest—Marlowe, Webster, Tourneur, and Shakespeare—they had a quality of sensuous thought, or of thinking through the senses, or of the senses thinking, of which the exact formula remains to be defined.

If you look for it in Shelley or Beddoes, both of whom in very different ways recaptured something of the Elizabethan inspiration, you will not find it, though you may find other qualities instead. There is a trace of it only in Keats, and, derived from a different source, in Rossetti. You will not find it in the *Duke of Gandia*. Swinburne's essay would have been all the better if he had applied himself to the solution of problems like this.

He did not apply himself to this sort of problem because this was not the sort of problem that interested him. The author of Swinburne's critical essays is also the author of Swinburne's verse: if you hold the opinion that Swinburne was a very great poet, you can hardly deny him the title of a great critic. There is the same curious mixture of qualities to produce Swinburne's own effect, resulting in the same blur, which only the vigour of the colours fixes.

His great merit as a critic is really one which, like many signal virtues, can be stated so simply as to appear flat. It is that he was sufficiently interested in his subject-matter and knew quite enough about it; and this is a rare combination in English criticism.

Our critics are often interested in extracting something from their subject which is not fairly in it. And it is because this elementary virtue is so rare that Swinburne must take a very respectable place as a critic.

Critics are often interested—but not quite in the nominal subject, often in something a little beside the point; they are often learned—but not quite to the point either. (Swinburne knew some of the plays almost by heart.) Can this particular virtue at which we have glanced be attributed to Walter Pater? or to Professor Bradley? or to Swinburne's editor?

A ROMANTIC ARISTOCRAT

It is impossible to overlook the merits of scholarship and criticism exhibited by George Wyndham's posthumous book, and it is impossible to deal with the book purely on its merits of scholarship and criticism. To attempt to do so would in the first place be unfair, as the book is a posthumous work, and posthumous books demand some personal attention to their writers.

This book is a collection of essays and addresses, arranged in their present order by Mr. Whibley; they were intended by their author to be remodelled into a volume on "romantic literature"; they move from an ingenious search for the date of the beginning of Romanticism, through the French and English Renaissance, to Sir Walter Scott. In the second place, these essays represent the literary work of a man who gained his chief distinction in political life. In the third place, this man stands for a type, an English type. The type is interesting and will probably become extinct. It is natural, therefore, that our primary interest in the essays should be an interest in George Wyndham.

Mr. Charles Whibley, in an introduction the tone of which is well suited to the matter, has several sentences which throw light on Wyndham's personality. What issues with surprising clearness from Mr. Whibley's sketch is the unity of Wyndham's mind, the identity of his mind as it engaged in apparently unrelated occupations. Wyndham left Eton for the army; in barracks he "taught himself Italian, and filled his leisure with the reading of history and poetry." After this Coldstream culture there was a campaign in Egypt; later, service in South Africa accompanied by a copy of Virgil.

There was a career in the Commons, a conspicuous career as Irish Secretary. Finally, there was a career as a landowner—2400 acres. And throughout these careers George Wyndham went on not only accumulating books but reading them, and occasionally writing about them. He was a man of character, a man of energy. Mr. Whibley is quite credible when he says:

Literature was for him no parergon, no mere way of escape from politics. If he was an amateur in feeling, he was a craftsman in execution; and, more significantly,

With the same zest that he read and discoursed upon *A Winter's Tale* or *Troilus and Cressida,* he rode to hounds, or threw himself with a kind of fury into a "point to point," or made a speech at the hustings, or sat late in the night talking with a friend.

From these and other sentences we chart the mind of George Wyndham, and the key to its topography is the fact that his literature and his politics and his country life are one and the same thing. They are not in separate compartments, they are one career. Together they made up his world: literature, politics, riding to hounds. In the real world these things have nothing to do with each other. But we cannot believe that George Wyndham lived in the real world. And this is implied in Mr. Whibley's remark that:

George Wyndham was by character and training a romantic. He looked with wonder upon the world as upon a fairyland.

Here is the manifestation of type.

There must probably be conceded to history a few "many-sided" men. Perhaps Leonardo da Vinci was such. George Wyndham was not a man on the scale of Leonardo, and his writings give a very different effect from Leonardo's notebooks. Leonardo turned to art or science, and each was what it was and not another thing.

But Leonardo was Leonardo: he had no father to speak of, he was hardly a citizen, and he had no stake in the community. He lived in no fairyland, but his mind went out and became a part of things. George Wyndham was Gentry. He was chivalrous, the world was an adventure of himself. It is characteristic that on embarking as a subaltern for Egypt he wrote enthusiastically:

I do not suppose that any expedition since the days of Roman governors of provinces has started with such magnificence; we might have been Antony going to Egypt in a purple-sailed galley.

This is precisely the spirit which animates his appreciation of the Elizabethans and of Walter Scott; which guides him toward Hakluyt and North. Wyndham was enthusiastic, he was a Romantic, he was an Imperialist, and he was quite naturally a literary pupil of W. E. Henley.

Wyndham was a scholar, but his scholarship is incidental; he was a good critic, within the range allowed him by his enthusiasms; but it is neither as Scholar nor as Critic that we can criticize him. We can criticize his writings only as the expression of this peculiar English type, the aristocrat, the Imperialist, the Romantic, riding to hounds across his prose, looking with wonder upon the world as upon a fairyland.

Because he belongs to this type, Wyndham wrote enthusiastically and well about North's Plutarch. The romance of the ancient world becomes more romantic in the idiomatic prose of North; the heroes are not merely Greek and Roman heroes, but Elizabethan heroes as well; the romantic fusion allured Wyndham. The charms of North could not be expounded more delightfully, more seductively, with more gusto, than they are in Wyndham's essay.

He appreciates the battles, the torchlight, the "dead sound" of drums, the white, worn face of Cicero in his flight peering from his litter; he appreciates the sharp brusque phrase of North: "he roundly trussed them up and hung them by their necks." And Wyndham is learned.

Here, as in his essays on the Pléiade and Shakespeare, the man has read everything, with a labour that only whets his enjoyment of the best. There are two defects: a lack of balance and a lack of critical profundity.

The lack of balance peeps through Wyndham's condemnation of an obviously inferior translation of Plutarch: "He dedicated the superfluity of his leisure to enjoyment, and used his Lamia," says the bad translator. North: "he took pleasure of Lamia."

Wyndham makes a set upon the bad translator. But he forgets that "dedicated the superfluity of his leisure" is such a phrase as Gibbon would have warmed to life and wit, and that a history, in the modern sense, could not be written in the style of North. Wyndham forgets, in short, that it is not, in the end, periods and traditions but individual men who write great prose. For Wyndham is himself a period and a tradition.

The lack of balance is to be suspected elsewhere. Wyndham *likes* the best, but he likes a good deal. There is no conclusive evidence that he realized all the difference, the gulf of difference between lines like:

En l'an trentiesme de mon aage
Que toutes mes hontes j'ay beues;

and even the very best of Ronsard or Bellay, such as:

Le temps s'en va, le temps s'en va, madame;
Las! le temps, non, mais nous nous en allons
Et tost serons estendus sous la lame.

We should not gather from Wyndham's essay that the *Phoenix and Turtle* is a great poem, far finer than *Venus and Adonis;* but what he says about *Venus and Adonis* is worth reading, for Wyndham is very sharp in perceiving the neglected beauties of the second-rate.

There is nothing to show the gulf of difference between Shakespeare's sonnets and those of any other Elizabethan.

Wyndham overrates Sidney, and in his references to Elizabethan writings on the theory of poetry omits mention of the essay by Campion, an abler and more daring though less common-sense study than Daniel's.

He speaks a few words for Drayton, but has not noticed that the only good lines (with the exception of one sonnet which may be an accident) in Drayton's dreary sequence of "Ideas" occur when Drayton drops his costume for a moment and talks in terms of actuality:

Lastly, mine eyes amazedly have seen
Essex' great fall; Tyrone his peace to gain;
The quiet end of that long-living queen;
The king's fair entry, and our peace with Spain.

More important than the lack of balance is the lack of critical analysis. Wyndham had, as was indicated, a gusto for the Elizabethans. His essay on the Poems of Shakespeare contains an extraordinary amount of information. There is some interesting gossip about Mary Fitton and a good anecdote of Sir William Knollys.

But Wyndham misses what is the cardinal point in criticizing the Elizabethans: we cannot grasp them, understand them, without some understanding of the pathology of rhetoric.

Rhetoric, a particular form of rhetoric, was endemic, it pervaded the whole organism; the healthy as well as the morbid tissues were built up on it. We cannot grapple with even the simplest and most conversational lines in Tudor and early Stuart drama without having diagnosed the rhetoric in the sixteenth- and seventeenth-century mind. Even when we come across lines like:

There's a plumber laying pipes in my guts, it scalds,we must not allow ourselves to forget the rhetorical basis any more than when we read:

Come, let us march against the powers of heaven
And set black streamers in the firmament
To signify the slaughter of the gods.

An understanding of Elizabethan rhetoric is as essential to the appreciation of Elizabethan literature as an understanding of Victorian sentiment is essential to the appreciation of Victorian literature and of George Wyndham.

Wyndham was a Romantic; the only cure for Romanticism is to analyse it. What is permanent and good in Romanticism is curiosity—

...l' ardore
Ch' i' ebbe a divenir del mondo esperto
E degli vizii umani e del valore—a curiosity which recognizes that any life, if accurately and profoundly penetrated, is interesting and always strange. Romanticism is a short cut to the strangeness without the reality, and it leads its disciples only back upon themselves.

George Wyndham had curiosity, but he employed it romantically, not to penetrate the real world, but to complete the varied features of the world he made for himself. It would be of interest to divagate from literature to politics and inquire to what extent Romanticism is incorporate in Imperialism; to inquire to what extent Romanticism has possessed the imagination of Imperialists, and to what extent it was made use of by Disraeli.

But this is quite another matter: there may be a good deal to be said for Romanticism in life, there is no place for it in letters. Not that we need conclude that a man of George Wyndham's antecedents and traditions must inevitably be a Romanticist writer.

But this is the case when such a man plants himself firmly in his awareness of caste, when he says "The gentry must not abdicate." In politics this may be an admirable formula. It will not do in literature. The Arts insist that a man shall dispose of all that he has, even of his family tree, and follow art alone.

For they require that a man be not a member of a family or of a caste or of a party or of a coterie, but simply and solely himself. A man like Wyndham brings several virtues into literature. But there is only one man better and more uncommon than the patrician, and that is the Individual.

THE LOCAL FLAVOUR

In a world which is chiefly occupied with the task of

keeping up to date with itself, it is a satisfaction to know that there is at least one man who has not only read but enjoyed, and not only enjoyed but read, such authors as Petronius and Herondas. That is Mr.

Charles Whibley, and there are two statements to make about him: that he is not a critic, and that he is something which is almost as rare, if not quite as precious. He has apparently read and enjoyed a great deal of English literature, and the part of it that he has most enjoyed is the literature of the great ages, the sixteenth and seventeenth centuries. We may opine that Mr.

Whibley has not uttered a single important original judgment upon any of this literature. On the other hand, how many have done so? Mr. Whibley is not a critic of men or of books; but he convinces us that if we read the books that he has read we should find them as delightful as he has found them; and if we read them we can form our own opinions.

And if he has not the balance of the critic, he has some other equipoise of his own. It is partly that his tastes are not puritanical, that he can talk about Restoration dramatists and others without apologizing for their "indecency"; it is partly his sense for the best local and temporal flavours; it is partly his healthy appetite.

A combination of non-critical, rather than uncritical, qualities made Mr. Whibley the most appropriate person in the world for the work by which he is best known. We should be more grateful for the "Tudor Translations Series" if we could find copies to be bought, and if we could afford to buy them when we found them.

But that is not Mr. Whibley's fault. The introductions which he wrote for some of the translators are all that such introductions should be. His Urquhart's *Rabelais* contains all the irrelevant information about that writer which is what is wanted to stimulate a taste for him. After reading the introduction, to read Urquhart was the only pleasure in life. And therefore, in a country destitute of living criticism, Mr. Whibley is a useful person: for the first thing is that English literature should be read at all.

The few people who talk intelligently about Stendhal and Flaubert and James know this; but the large number of people who skim the conversation of the former do not know enough of English literature to be even insular. There are two ways in which a writer may lead us to profit by the work of dead writers. One is by isolating the essential, by pointing out the most intense in various kinds and separating it from the accidents of environment.

This method is helpful only to the more intelligent people, who are capable of a unique enjoyment of perfect expression, and it concentrates on the very best in any art. The other method that of Mr. Whibley, is to communicate a taste for the period— and for the best of the period so far as it is of that period.

That is not very easy either. For a pure journalist will not know any period well enough; a pure dilettante will know it too egotistically, as a fashion of his own. Mr. Whibley is really interested; and he has escaped, without any programme of revolt, from the present century into those of Tudor and Stuart. He escapes, and perhaps leads others, by virtue of a taste which is not exactly a literary taste.

The "Tudor Translations" form part of a pronounced taste. Some are better written than others. There is, of course, a world of difference—of which Mr. Whibley is perhaps unaware—between even Florio and his original. The French of Montaigne is a mature language, and the English of Florio's living translation is not. Montaigne could be translated into the English of his time, but a similar work could not have been written in it.

But as the English language matured it lost something that Florio and all his inferior colleagues had, and that they had in common with the language of Montaigne. It was not only the language, but the time. The prose of that age had life, a life to which later ages could not add, from which they could only take away.

You find the same life, the same abundance, in Montaigne and Brantôme, the alteration in Rochefoucauld as in Hobbes, the desiccation in the classic prose of both languages, in

Voltaire and in Gibbon. Only, the French was originally richer and more mature—already in Joinville and Commines—and we have no prose to compare with Montaigne and Rabelais. If Mr.

Whibley had analysed this vitality, and told us why Holland and Underdowne, Nashe and Martin Marprelate are still worth reading, then he could have shown us how to recognize this quality when it, or something like it, appears in our own lifetime. But Mr. Whibley is not an analyst. His taste, even, becomes less certain as he fixes it on individuals within his period.

On Surrey's blank verse he is feeble; he does not even give Surrey the credit of having anticipated some of Tennyson's best effects. He has no praise for Golding, quite one of the best of the verse translators; he apologizes for him by saving that Ovid demands no strength or energy! There is strength and energy, at least, in Marlowe's *Amores.* And he omits mention of Gawain Douglas, who, though he wrote in Scots, was surely a "Tudor" translator.

Characteristically, Mr. Whibley praises Chapman because it gives proof of an abounding life, a quenchless energy. There is a grandeur and spirit in Chapman's rendering, not unworthy the original...

This is commonplace, and it is uncritical. And a critic would not use so careless a phrase as "Tasso's masterpiece." The essay on Congreve does not add much to our understanding:

And so he set upon the boards a set of men and women of quick brains and cynical humours, who talked with the brilliance and rapidity wherewith the finished swordsman fences. We have heard of this conversation like fencing before. And the suspicion is in our breast that Mr. Whibley might admire George Meredith. The essay on Ralegh gives still less. The reality of that pleasing pirate and monopolist has escaped, and only the national hero is left. And yet Ralegh, and Swift, and Congreve, and the underworld of sixteenth and seventeenth-century letters, are somehow kept alive by what Mr. Whibley says of them.

Accordingly, Mr. Whibley does not disappear in the jungle of journalism and false criticism; he deserves a "place upon the shelves" of those who care for English literature. He has the first requisite of a critic: interest in his subject, and ability to communicate an interest in it. His defects are both of intellect and feeling.

He has no dissociative faculty. There were very definite vices and definite shortcomings and immaturities in the literature he admires; and as he is not the person to tell us of the vices and shortcomings, he is not the person to lay before us the work of absolutely the finest quality. He exercises neither of the tools of the critic: comparison and analysis.

He has not the austerity of passion which can detect unerringly the transition from work of eternal intensity to work that is merely beautiful, and from work that is beautiful to work that is merely charming. For the critic needs to be able not only to saturate himself in the spirit and the fashion of a time—the local flavour—but also to separate himself suddenly from it in appreciation of the highest creative work.

And he needs something else that Mr. Whibley lacks: a creative interest, a focus upon the immediate future. The important critic is the person who is absorbed in the present problems of art, and who wishes to bring the forces of the past to bear upon the solution of these problems. If the critic consider Congreve, for instance, he will have always at the back of his mind the question: What has Congreve got that is pertinent to our dramatic art?

Even if he is solely engaged in trying to understand Congreve, this will make all the difference; inasmuch as to understand anything is to understand from a point of view. Most critics have some creative interest—it may be, instead of an interest in any art, an interest (like Mr. Paul More's) in morals. These remarks were introduced only to assist in giving the books of Mr. Whibley a place, a particular but unticketed place, neither with criticism, nor with history, nor with plain journalism; and the trouble would not have been taken if the books were not thought to be worth placing.

Mr. Paul More is the author of a number of volumes which

he perhaps hopes will break the record of mass established by the complete works of Sainte-Beuve. The comparison with Sainte-Beuve is by no means trivial, for Mr. More, and Professor Irving Babbitt also, are admirers of the voluminous Frenchman.

Not only are they admirers, but their admiration is perhaps a clue both to much of their merit and to some of their defects. In the first place, both of these writers have given much more attention to French criticism, to the study of French standards of writing and of thought, than any of the notable English critics since Arnold; they are therefore much nearer to the European current, although they exhibit faults which are definitely transatlantic and which definitely keep them out of it.

The French influence is traceable in their devotion to ideas and their interest in problems of art and life as problems which exist and can be handled apart from their relations to the critic's private temperament. With Swinburne, the criticism of Elizabethan literature has the interest of a passion, it has the interest for us of any writing by an intellectual man who is genuinely moved by certain poetry. Swinburne's intelligence is not defective, it is impure.

There are few ideas in Swinburne's critical writings which stand forth luminous with an independent life of their own, so true that one forgets the author in the statement. Swinburne's words must always be referred back to Swinburne himself.

And if literature is to Swinburne merely a passion, we are tempted to say that to George Wyndham it was a hobby, and to Mr. Whibley almost a charming showman's show (we are charmed by the urbanity of the showman). The two latter have gusto, but gusto is no equivalent for taste; it depends too much upon the appetite and the digestion of the feeder.

And with one or two other writers, whom I have not had occasion to discuss, literature is not so much a collection of valuable porcelain as an institution—accepted, that is to say, with the same gravity as the establishments of Church and State.

That is, in other words, the essentially uncritical attitude. In all of these attitudes the English critic is the victim of his temperament. He may acquire great erudition, but erudition easily becomes a hobby; it is useless unless it enables us to see literature all round, to detach it from ourselves, to reach a state of pure contemplation.

Now Mr. More and Mr. Babbitt have endeavoured to establish a criticism which should be independent of temperament.

This is in itself a considerable merit. But at this point Mr. More particularly has been led astray, oddly enough, by his guide Sainte-Beuve. Neither Mr. More nor Sainte-Beuve is primarily interested in art.

Of the latter M. Benda has well observed that on sait—et c'est certainement un des grands éléments de son succès—combien d'études l'illustre critique consacre à des-auteurs dont l'importance littéraire est quasi nulle (femmes, magistrats, courtisans, militaires), mais dont les écrits lui sont une occasion de pourtraiturer une âme; combien volontiers, pour les maîtres, il s'attache à leurs productions secondaires, notes, brouillons, lettres intimes, plutôt qu'à leurs grandes oeuvres, souvent beaucoup moins expressives, en effet, de leur psychologie.

Mr. More is not, like Sainte-Beuve, primarily interested in psychology or in human beings; Mr. More is primarily a moralist, which is a worthy and serious thing to be. The trouble with Mr. More is that you cannot disperse a theory or point of view of morals over a vast number of essays on a great variety of important figures in literature, unless you can give some more particular interest as well. Sainte-Beuve has his particularized interest in human beings; another critic—say Remy de Gourmont—may have something to say always about the art of a writer which will make our enjoyment of that writer more conscious and more intelligent.

But the pure moralist in letters—the moralist is useful to the creator as well as the reader of poetry—must be more concise, for we must have the pleasure of inspecting the beauty of his structure. And here M. Julien Benda has a great advantage over Mr. More; his thought may be less profound, but it has more formal beauty.

Mr. Irving Babbitt, who shares so many of the ideals and opinions of Mr. More that their names must be coupled, has expressed his thought more abstractly and with more form, and is free from a mystical impulse which occasionally gets out of Mr. More's hand.

He appears, more clearly than Mr. More, and certainly more clearly than any critic of equal authority in America or England, to perceive Europe as a whole; he has the cosmopolitan mind and a tendency to seek the centre. His few books are important, and would be more important if he preached of discipline in a more disciplined style. Although he also is an admirer of Sainte-Beuve, he would probably subscribe to this admirable paragraph of Othenin d'Haussonville:

Il y a une beauté littéraire, impersonnelle en quelque sorte, parfaitement distincte de l'auteur lui-même et de son organisation, beauté qui a sa raison d'être et ses lois, dont la critique est tenue de rendre compte. Et si la critique considère cette tâche comme au-dessous d'elle, si c'est affaire à la rhétorique et à ce que Sainte-Beuve appelle dédaigneusement les Quintilien, alors la rhétorique a du bon et les Quintilien ne sont pas à dédaigner.

There may be several critics in England who would applaud this notion; there are very few who show any evidence of its apprehension in their writings. But Mr. More and Mr. Babbitt, whatever their actual tastes, and although they are not primarily occupied with art, are on the side of the artist. And the side of the artist is not the side which in England is often associated with critical writing. As Mr. More has pointed out in an interesting essay, there is a vital weakness in Arnold's definition of criticism as "the disinterested endeavour to know the best that is known and thought in the world, irrespectively of practice, politics, and everything of the kind."

The "disinterested endeavour to know" is only a prerequisite of the *critic,* and is not *criticism,* which may be the result of such an endeavour. Arnold states the work of the critic merely in terms of the personal ideal, an ideal for oneself—and an ideal for oneself is not disinterested. Here Arnold is the Briton rather than the European.

Mr. More indicates his own attitude in praising those whom he elevates to the position of masters of criticism:

If they deal much with the criticism of literature, this is because in literature more manifestly than anywhere else life displays its infinitely varied motives and results; and their practice is always to render literature itself more consciously a criticism of life.

"Criticism of life" is a facile phrase, and at most only represents one aspect of great literature, if it does not assign to the term "criticism" itself a generality which robs it of precision. Mr. More has, it seems to me, in this sentence just failed to put his finger on the right seriousness of great literary art; the seriousness which we find in Villon's *Testament* and which is conspicuously absent from *In Memoriam;* or the seriousness which controls *Amos Barton* and not *The Mill on the Floss.*

It is a pity that Mr. More does not write a little oftener about the great literary artists, it is a pity that he takes the reputations of the world too solemnly. This is probably due in part to remoteness in space from the European centre. But it must be observed that English solemnity and American solemnity are very different.

I do not propose to analyse the difference (it would be a valuable chapter in social history); the American solemnity, it is enough to say, is more primitive, more academic, more like that of the German professor. But it is not the fault of Mr. More or Mr. Babbitt that the culture of ideas has only been able to survive in America in the unfavourable atmosphere of the university.

THE FRENCH INTELLIGENCE

As the inspection of types of English irresistibly provoked a glance at two American critics, so the inspection of the latter leads our attention to the French. M. Julien Benda has the formal beauty which the American critics lack, and a close affinity to them in point of view. He restricts himself, perhaps, to a narrower field of ideas, but within that field he manipulates the ideas with a very exceptional cogency and clarity. To notice his last book (*Belphégor: essai sur l'esthétique de la présente société française*) would be to quote from it.

M. Benda is not like Remy de Gourmont, the critical consciousness of a generation, he could not supply the conscious formulas of a sensibility in process of formation; he is rather the ideal scavenger of the rubbish of our time. Much of his analysis of the decadence of contemporary French society could be applied to London, although differences are observable from his diagnosis.

Quant à la société en elle-même, on peut prévoir que ce soin qu'elle met à éprouver de l'émoi par l'art, devenant cause à son tour, y rendra la soif de ce plaisir de plus en plus intense, l'application à la satisfaire de plus en plus jalouse et plus perfectionnée.

On entrevoit le jour où la bonne société française repudiera encore le peu qu'elle supporte aujourd'hui d'idées et d'organisation dans l'art, et ne se passionera plus que pour des gestes de comédiens, pour des impressions de femmes ou d'enfants, pour des rugissements de lyriques, pour des extases de fanatiques....

Almost the only person who has ever figured in England and attempted a task at all similar to that of M. Benda is Matthew Arnold. Matthew Arnold was intelligent, and by so much difference as the presence of one intelligent man makes, our age is inferior to that of Arnold.

But what an advantage a man like M. Benda has over Arnold. It is not simply that he has a critical tradition behind him, and that Arnold is using a language which constantly tempts the user away from dispassionate exposition into sarcasm and diatribe, a language less fitted for criticism than the English of the eighteenth century.

It is that the follies and stupidities of the French, no matter how base, express themselves in the form of ideas—Bergsonism itself is an intellectual construction, and the mondaines who attended lectures at the College de France were in a sense using their minds. A man of ideas needs ideas, or pseudo-ideas, to fight against. And Arnold lacked the active resistance which is necessary to keep a mind at its sharpest.

A society in which a mind like M. Benda's can exercise itself, and in which there are persons like M. Benda, is one which facilitates the task of the creative artist. M. Benda cannot be attached, like Gourmont, to any creative group. He does not wholly partake in that "conscious creation of the field of the present out of the past" which Mr. More considers to be part of the work of the critic.

But in analysing the maladies of the second-rate or corrupt literature of the time he makes the labour of the creative artist lighter. The Charles Louis Philippes of English literature are never done with, because there is no one to kill their reputations; we still hear that George Meredith is a master of prose, or even a profound philosopher. The creative artist in England finds himself compelled, or at least tempted, to spend much of his time and energy in criticism that he might reserve for the perfecting of his proper work: simply because there is no one else to do it.

Chapter 14

Painting and Idealization of Character

Both in theory and in practice George Eliot's realism welcomed the idealization of character. "Paint us an angel, if you can," urges the narrator of Adam Bede, "paint us yet oftener a Madonna..." (17: 270). And as if to heed his own advice, he thrice associates Dinah Morris with the angel at Christ's sepulchre in Adam's new illustrated Bible ((10:162, 14:208, 51:319). By the same token, Milly Barton is "a large, fair, gentle Madonna" (2:24), and Lucy Deane in The Mill on the Floss has "a face breathing playful joy, like one of Correggio's cherubs" (VI, 9:267).

As these examples suggest, George Eliot habitually idealized her characters by associating them with sacred and heroic history painting and classical sculpture. Her work well exemplifies what Jean Hagstrum calls "the unshakeable association that has existed between literary idealization and ideal form in the graphic arts" (Sister Arts, p. 8). This chapter will discuss the rationale for George Eliot's pictorial idealization of character, and relate her techniques to the revival of typological iconography in the nineteenth-century visual arts.

Particular attention will be paid to Eliot's characteristic ambivalence toward such idealization as it is expressed in Middlemarch, and to her complex resolution of that ambivalence in the double plot of Daniel Deronda.

Not all Victorian novelists believed in the compatibility of the ideal and the real. Trollope, for example, assumed that the terms are antithetical. Transvaluing Reynolds's famous contrast between Italian and Dutch painting, Trollope contended in The Last Chronicle of Barset that the High Renaissance art of Italy depicts what is unreal:

We are, most of us, apt to love Raphael's madonnas better than Rembrandt's matrons. But though we do so, we know that Rembrandt's matrons existed; but we have a strong belief that no such woman as Raphael painted ever did exist. In that he painted... for Church purposes, Raphael was justified; but had he painted so for family portraiture he would have been false." [London: Smith, Elder, (1867), II, 84:383]

This conception of realism was very different from George Eliot's. She believed that Raphael's madonnas sometimes belong in family portraiture, and she pointedly denied that the ideal is antithetical to the real. "Any real observation of life and character must be limited, and the imagination must fill in and give life to the picture," she told John Blackwood in 1861 (Letters, III, 427).

Eliot agreed with G.H. Lewes's argument, in his important essay on "Realism in Art" (1858), that the opposite of realism is not idealism but falsism. Lewes illustrates the compatibility of idealism,with realism by citing Raphael's Sistine Madonna:

In the figures of the Pope and St. Barbara we have a real man and woman, one of them a portrait, and the other not elevated above sweet womanhood. Below, we have the two exquisite angel children, intensely childlike, yet something more, something which renders their wings congruous with our conception of them.

In the never-to-be-forgotten divine babe, we have at once the intensest realism of presentation, with the highest idealism of conception: the attitude is at once grand, easy, and natural; the face is that of a child, but the child is divine... we feel that humanity in its highest conceivable form is before us. Here is a picture which from the first has enchained the hearts of men, which is assuredly in the highest sense ideal, and which is so because it is also in the highest sense real — a real man, a real woman, real angel-children, and a real Divine Child; the last a striking contrast to the ineffectual attempts of other painters to spiritualize and idealize the babe — attempts which represent no babe at all.

The Leweses valued highly the ideal realism of High Renaissance painting, and George Eliot strove to create a similar effect in many parts of her own fiction.

Eliot was of course no Christian, but her idealization had a rationale in the secular religion of humanity which replaced her Evangelicalism. This humanism rejected Christian theology but sought to retain the ethics, emotional culture, and social bonding of the older religion. Feuerbach, whose Essence of Christianity strongly influenced Eliot on these points, argued that since the Christian god is a projection of mankind, mankind itself should be worshipped in a religious spirit. Christian devotion should be transferred to secular subjects, and human experience should be venerated and sanctified.[7] George Eliot favored this redirection of emotion, and promoted it in her fiction by associating her characters with sacred and heroic visual] art. Thus she attempted to hallow Romola's experience by visualizing her moral growth as a progression from "The Unseen Madonna" to "The Visible Madonna" to "the Holy Mother with the Babe, fetching water for the sick" in a plague-stricken village (43:131, 44:141, 68:406). Feuerbach himself suggested a didactic and affective rationale for literary pictorialism when he defined imagination as the "type-creating [bildliche], emotional, and sensuous" part of the human mind, and argued that "man, as an emotional and sensuous being, is governed and made happy only by images, by sensible representations."

George Eliot took something of a liberty when she rendered Feuerbach's term bildliche as "type-creating." But her translation points up one important element of traditional Christian thought which she sought to preserve and secularize in her religion of humanity: the concept of types. George Eliot's pictorial idealization may be viewed in the context of efforts by other nineteenth-century artists to redefine typological symbolism so that it might serve the religious and aesthetic needs of the age. Typological symbolism attracted many of the best minds of the period because it offered a way of conferring spiritual meaning upon the representation of phenomenal experience? of affirming the existence of design while yet respecting the integrity of history. Strictly speaking, a type is an Old Testament prefiguration of a New Testament truth. It is not a vehicle of allegory; a type retains its identity as a historical reality at the same time that it foreshadows the divinely ordained event which fulfills it.

The Victorians often used the term more loosely, however, to denote any exemplary moral or religious norm which finds successive incarnations in history. In the visual arts the revaluation of typological symbolism was a sign of dissatisfaction with established conceptions of sacred and heroic history painting.

This dissatisfaction had grown steadily since the middle of the eighteenth century. In the later eighteenth century, history painters began boldly to combine the inherited motifs of Christian art with scenes of contemporary heroism.[12] By the mid-nineteenth century, a creative and nontraditional typological symbolism was widely employed in English painting.

Obscure or invented incidents in the early life of Christ were made to foreshadow famous later events, and Christian types were often applied postfiguratively to secular and contemporary situations. Such symbolism is a prominent feature in Pre-Raphaelite painting, where it balances the tendency of empirical realism toward fragmentation and atomism. The iconography of the Deposition in Holman Hunt's A Converted British Family Sheltering a Christian Missionary from the Persecution of the Druids (1850), of the Pieta in Henry Wallis's The Death of Chatterton (1856), of the Madonna and Child in Ford Madox Brown's The Pretty Baa-Lambs (1852) or Take Your Son, Sir! (1857), of the emblematic pilgrimage in Millais's The Blind Girl (1856), suggests in each case a connection between a concrete historical moment and a recurrent type of spiritual activity.

George Eliot came to art, then, in an atmosphere congenial to "the notion that Types in their continuing cycles can be found in contemporary reality" (Fletcher, p. 680). Her education had introduced her to the traditional exegesis of biblical types, which was still widespread in nineteenth-century Evangelical circles. In Scenes of Clerical Life, Amos Barton finds it difficult to communicate "instruction through familiar types and symbols." Attempting to explain the Christian significance of unleavened bread, he carries the imagination of his audience "to the dough-tub, but unfortunately was not able to carry it upwards from that well-known object to the unknown truths which it was intended to shadow forth" (2:39). In "Janet's Repentance" the residents of Milby "had not yet heard that the schismatic ministers of Salem [the Dissenters' chapel] were obviously typified by Korah, Dathan, and Abiram" (2:60). George Eliot was obviously familiar enough with typological thinking to draw upon it for humorous effects.

The novelist often used the word type in connection with the representation of sublime and religious ideas in contemporary art. At Weimar she saw a portrait head of Goethe at seventy which she thought "might serve as a type of sublime old age". Also at Weimar she saw Liszt in concert, and thereafter understood why "the type of Liszt's face seems to haunt [Ary Scheffer] in so many of his compositions." She particularly recalled Scheffer's Die drei Weisen aus dem Morgenlande (1844), a picture "in which he expressly intended to introduce an idealization of Liszt" as one of the three Magi, "gazing in ecstasy at the guiding light above them." She herself thought Liszt looked like "a perfect model of a St. John" or "a prophet in the moment of inspiration" (Essays, p. 98).

This kind of idealization, which ennobles without falsifying its subject, and which associates admirable human faces with established Christian exemplars, violates neither George Eliot's atheism nor her conception of realism.

She used the word type even more revealingly when defending her presentation of Mordecai in Daniel Deronda: "The effect that one strives after is an outline as strong as that of Balfour of Burley [in Scott's Old Mortality] for a much more complex character and a higher strain of ideas. But such an effect is just the most difficult thing in art-to give new elements-i.e. elements not already used up — in forms as vivid as those of long familiar types" (Letters, VI, 223). Here is a clear statement of the rationale for the pictorial idealization of character in George Eliot's fiction: she seeks to give the new elements of her religion of humanity in forms as vivid as those of the long familiar types of traditional religious culture.

Eliot was well aware of the revaluation of typological symbolism in the nineteenth-century visual arts, especially within the German Nazarene and English Pre-Raphaelite movements.[20] She began to follow the work of the Pre-Raphaelites in 1852, when she commended Millais's A Huguenot on Saint Bartholomew's Day in May and read the famous essay on "Pre-Raphaelitism in Art and Literature" in the British Quarterly Review for November (Letters, II, 29-30, 48).

This essay helped to shape her most basic beliefs about [77/78] the movement: that it represented a salutary return to nature, truth, and realism in art, but that its strengths were sapped by its weakness for medieval ecclesiasticism and archaism.

Thus Eliot had mixed reactions to the work of her favourite Pre-Raphaelite painter, William Holman Hunt. In 1856 she described him as "one of the greatest painters of the pre-eminently realistic school" (Essays, p. 268), and she remained interested in his work at least until 1864, when she sent to Sara Hennell a sympathetic critique of his Afterglow in Egypt (Letters, IV, 159). But her lack of sympathy with the theistic religious aims of Hunt's painting sometimes made her indifferent or oblivious to the workings of its figural symbolism.[21] She had no use for The Light of the World (1853) because "it is too mediaeval and pietistic to be rejoiced in as a product of the present age" (Letters, II, 156).

She praised The Hireling Shepherd (1851) for the "marvellous truthfulness" of its landscape (Essays, p. 268), but quite misread the moral iconography of the shepherd and the wench, failing to see that, like Adam Bede, the painting is profoundly critical of false and idyllic notions of pastoral; see John Duncan Macmillan, "Holman Hunt's Hireling Shepherd:

Some Reflections on a Victorian Pastoral," The Art Bulletin, 54 (1972), 187-97, and chapter 8, n. 46, below. Her doctrinal antipathy probably accounts for her inability to perceive the similarity between her own mode of didactic symbolism and that of her more orthodox contemporaries.[23]

She was even less receptive to the typological history painting of the German Nazarenes, which she encountered on her trips to Berlin, Munich, and Rome in 1854-60. She was sympathetic with the early Nazarene revolt against the German neoclassical style, and once compared it (borrowing an argument from the author of "Pre-Raphaelitism in Art and Literature") with Wordsworth's rebellion against eighteenth-century poetic diction. Thus she defended "an early poem of Wordsworth's, or an early picture of Overbeck's" on the ground that "the attempt at an innovation reveals a want that has not hitherto been met" (Essays, pp. 99-100).

But Eliot strongly disliked the monumental style of history painting which Nazarene artists and their disciples began to practice in the 1820s and perfected in the 1840s; G.H. Lewes was referring to this style when he spoke of "celebrated paintings of the Modern German school... in which a great deal is meant and very little executed, full of symbol and historical meaning, which require a long commentary before they can be rendered intelligible, and which before and after the commentary leave the emotions untouched and the eye ungratified" ("Realism in Art," p. 497).

Because George Eliot's critique of Nazarene history painting is central both to the question of her pictorial idealization of character and to the meaning of Middlemarch, it is worth discussing in some detail.

It has long been recognized that Adolf Naumann, the German painter of the Rome chapters of Middlemarch, represents the Nazarene or revivalist tradition, which was the branch of German Romantic art best known in Victorian England; see William Vaughan, "The German Manner in English Art, 1815-1861," Diss. Courtauld Institute 1977, pp. 18, 25, 35.

Naumann is modeled upon two identifiable Nazarenes:

Johann Friedrich Overbeck (1789-1869) and Josef von Führich (1800-76). Naumann's link with Overbeck is twofold. First, Naumann portrays Mr. Casaubon in a "picture in which Saint Thomas Aquinas sat among the doctors of the Church in a disputation too abstract to be represented, but listened to with more or less attention by an audience above" (22:332).,/P.

Gordon S. Haight has noted the resemblance between this fictive painting and Overbeck's The Triumph of Christianity in the Arts (1840), a picture that George Eliot had hoped to see during her trip to Germany in 1854-55 (Haight, p. 151; fig. 7). Both of these idealized history paintings are patterned after Raphael's Disputa in the Vatican Stanze. The second link between Naumann and Overbeck is a detail of the costume worn by Overbeck on the day George Eliot visited his Roman studio in 1860 — a connection first noticed in a review of Cross's Life by Joseph Jacobs (George Eliot...: Essays and Reviews from the 'Athenaeum ' [London: D. Nutt, 1891], p. 72). The venerable painter had on "a maroon velvet cap, and a grey scarf over his shoulders."

On display in Overbeck's studio, the Leweses saw cartoons of The Savior Withdraws from His Followers on the Hill at Nazareth (1857) and Allegory of the Arts (1860). Duly recorded in the novelist's journal (Cross, II,158), these items reappeared eleven years later as "a dove-coloured blouse and a maroon velvet cap" worn by Naumann when the Casaubons visit his studio in Middlemarch (22:327). Having seen the greatest of the Nazarenes in his own milieu, George Eliot knew how to dress a character partly modeled upon him.

Although Overbeck lived to be visited by George Eliot, he was nevertheless too old to be Naumann's sole original. The distinguished Nazarene was already forty in 1829, the year of Dorothea's honeymoon (For 1829 as the year of Dorothea's honeymoon, see Jerome Beaty, "History by Indirection: The Era of Reform in Middlemarch," Victorian Studies, 1 (1957), 173-79). Chronologically, Naumann more closely resembles Josef von Fuhrich, who was born in Bohemia in 1800 and worked under Overbeck in Rome from 1827 to 1829, helping to finish the frescoes [79/80] in the Casino Massimo. One of the paintings attributed to Naumann in the novel is modeled upon a painting of Fuhrich's that George Eliot had seen during her own honeymoon trip to Berlin in 1854-55.

Ladislaw tells us that Naumann is painting "the Saints drawing the Car of the Church" (22:326). This processional allegory recalls Führich's The Triumph of Christ. George Eliot saw the painting in Graf Raczinsky's famous collection of modern art, and described it in her journal with a charmingly Dorothean incomprehension of the iconography, which derives from Titian's Triumph of Faith:

Under this picture was one by a Viennese artist [Führich had become Professor of History Painting at Vienna] also shewing a great amount of misapplied power. Jesus sits in a chariot, drawn by a bullock and a lion (I think), Popes in their robes pushing along the wheels, and a saintly female figure — the Virgin, I suppose, sitting opposite him" ["Recollections of Berlin," Beinecke Library; for the iconography.

The lion and "bullock" are, of course, two of the four evangelists drawing the chariot, and the "Popes" at the wheels are the four fathers of the church, of whom only Gregory wears the papal habit. Dorothea's ignorance of Christian iconography in Middlemarch clearly mirrors a stage in her creator's own education.

Nevertheless, George Eliot was almost certainly remembering Führich's Triumphzug when she attributed "the Saints drawing the Car of the Church" to Naumann. She may also have remembered Otto van Veen's Der Triumph der katholischen Kirche in sechs Bildern allegorisch dargestellt, which she might have seen at Munich in 1858; Verzeichnis der Gemalde in der koniglichen Pinakothek zu Munchen (Munich,1858), pp. 197-200. 36 Vaughan, "The German Manner in English Art," p. 46.

The year of Dorothea's wedding journey was a year of great change in the Nazarene movement. It marked the end of the Roman phase of the movement, which had begun in 1810, when Overbeck first moved to the Eternal City to live and paint in the spirit of late medieval Christianity with his fellows in the Brotherhood of Saint Luke. After the completion of the Casino Massimo frescoes in 1829, the remaining Nazarenes disbanded to various cities in Germany, leaving Overbeck to carry on alone in Rome. By then Nazarene artists were in great demand for the decoration of public buildings and monuments, and the staffing of various academies and art institutes.

Official recognition and patronage prompted a change toward a programmatic, didactic, monumental style of art [80/81] suitable to the decoration of cities that had grown culturally ambitious, intensely nationalistic, and historically self-conscious. This later phase of German art, known to George Eliot chiefly through Overbeck's Triumph of Christianity and the fresco cycles in Berlin and Munich of Peter Cornelius and his pupil Wilhelm von Kaulbach, is clearly anticipated by Naumann's theory and practice of history painting in Middlemarch.

George Eliot's critique of Naumann's art involves a sophisticated version of the standard Victorian charge that modern German art contains too much mind and not enough nature. The Leweses thought of the Nazarenes and their followers essentially as Pre-Raphaelites who lacked the saving grace of naturalism. Eliot's principal objection to German monumental art was that its symbolism is insufficiently grounded in an empirically observed and represented order of nature. This tendency to depict things "too abstract to be represented" is suggested by Ladislaw's introduction of Naumann as "one of the chief renovators of Christian Art, one of those who had not only revived but expanded that grand conception of supreme events as mysteries at which the successive ages were spectators, and in relation to which the great souls of all periods became as it were contemporaries" (22:332,326). We are meant to take this vague but grandiose neotypological theory of history painting with a large grain of salt. Idealization must not be confused with Teutonic mystification. (For a different view of Naumann's achievement, see Barbara Hardy, "Middlemarch: Public and Private Worlds," English, 25 (1976), 22.)

Naumann's pictures are open to the same objections that

George Eliot made to Wilhelm von Kaulbach's weltgeschichtliche Bilder when she saw them at Berlin and Munich. Kaulbach's "allegorical-historical compositions... intended to represent the historical development of culture," she declared, "leave one entirely cold as all elaborate allegorical compositions must do."[41] Kaulbach's frescoes employ "a regular child's puzzle of symbolism," she complained to Sara Hennell; "instead of taking a single moment of reality and trusting to the infinite symbolism that belongs to all nature, he attempts to give at one view a succession of events, each represented by some group which may mean 'whichever you please, my dear"' (Letters, II, 454-55).

In other words, Kaulbach's symbolism does not sufficiently incarnate the ideal in the real. It ignores what Ruskin termed the naturalist ideal, and it violates Lessing's prohibition against representing events separated by time in a single picture; see Laokoon, sec. xviii. The engravings of "mystic groups where far-off ages made one moment" in Mrs. Meyrick's front parlor in Daniel Deronda (20:313) are probably reproductions of modern German history paintings such as Kaulbach's.

First articulated in the 1850s, George Eliot's reaction to Nazarene art remained relatively unchanged. Reappearing in Middlemarch, her critique of the indeterminacy and arbitrariness of German typological symbolism amusingly unites Mr. Brooke's fuzzy response to the "Dispute" with Will Ladislaw's parody of the "Saints."

Brooke, echoing Browning's Duke of Ferrara, says to Casaubon: "And we'll go down and look at the picture. There you are to the life: a deep subtle sort of thinker with his forefinger on the page, while Saint Bonaventure or somebody else, rather fat and florid, is looking up at the Trinity. Everything is symbolical, you know — the higher style of art: I like that up to a certain point, but not too far — it's rather straining to keep up with, you know" (34:86). As interpreted by Mr. Brooke, the "symbolical" style of Naumann's "Dispute" affords more delight than instruction.

Ladislaw's parody of the "Saints" likewise stresses the

indeterminacy and arbitrariness of its symbolism, but does so more instructively:

"I have been making a sketch of Marlow's Tamburlaine Driving the Conquered Kings in his Chariot. I am not so ecclesiastical as Naumann, and I sometimes twit him with his excess of meaning. But this time I mean to outdo him in breadth of intention. I take Tamburlaine in his chariot for the tremendous course of the world's physical history lashing on the harnessed dynasties. In my opinion that is a good mythical interpretation." Will here looked at Mr. Casaubon, who received this offhand treatment of symbolism very uneasily, and bowed with a neutral air. [22:326-27]

Will's statement is not, as Richard Ellmann and others have assumed, a description of an actual project.[43] Rather, it describes a purely imaginary allegory of secular history concocted by Will to parody the symbolic pretensions of Nazarene allegories of church history. Will's fantastic "Tamburlaine" belongs to the same genre as Kaulbach's "allegorical-historical compositions... intended to represent the historical development of culture." The point of the parody is essentially the same point that Will makes when he accuses Naumann of thinking "that all the universe is straining towards the obscure significance of your pictures" (19:290).

What weakens Naumann's history painting is precisely what vitiates Mr. Casaubon's key to all mythologies. Proceeding from dogmatic Christian preconceptions, both men approach history deductively and categorically rather than inductively and empirically. As a follower of Jacob Bryant's A New System, or an Analysis of Ancient Mythology (1774-76), Casaubon finds his key to all mythologies in the revealed truth of Holy Scripture, and seeks to interpret the pagan mythologies as corruptions of the one true myth.

Both he and Naumann read the past as a symbolic record of Christian certitudes. Their agreement on the Christian interpretation of myth and history is signified by Casaubon's decision to appear in the "Dispute" and to buy the finished painting. In Scenes of Clerical Life, George Eliot noted the bond between Nazarene art and Anglican sensibilities when she described a clergyman's study in which "a refined Anglican taste is indicated by a German print from Overbeck" (I 1: 170). One wonders whether she knew that Charles Pusey visited Overbeck in Rome in 1829 (Vaughan, "German Manner in English Art," p. 48).

To associate Naumann with Casaubon in this context is to see how Naumann's career fits the historical pattem of aspiration and failure established by the careers of the major characters in Middlemarch. Naumann's ambition to renovate Christian art is comparable to Casaubon's ambition to find the key to all mythologies. But like the mythographer, the painter is working along lines that future generations will judge to have been misguided and retrogressive.

In George Eliot's view, Naumann's achievement belongs to a reactionary eddy in the mainstream progression of nineteenth-century painting toward a Ruskinian naturalism. She had little sympathy with the deliberate imitation of archaic pictorial styles, and less with the attempt to revive medieval Catholicism; thus she once criticized Overbeck for evoking "all the barbarisms of the Pre-Raphaelite period." The Nazarene programme ran dead against George Eliot's belief in humanistic empiricism and evolutionary development.

Tempering this judgment with a characteristic admixture of sympathy, however, Eliot perceived many virtues in the Nazarene movement. She certainly admired the learning, energy, and commitment of its adherents. What she said of Overbeck in 1860 might well be applied to Naumann: "The man himself is more interesting than his pictures" (Cross, II, 158). Eliot agreed with Lewes's observation in Life and Works of Goethethat German revivalist art had not only "a retrograde purpose which was bad" but also a "critical purpose which was good (II, 216).

The critical purpose to which Lewes referred was the recovery of last traditions of Christian art, an educational endeavor which helped to overcome precisely the kind of ignorance displayed by George Eliot's description of Führich's Triumphzug According to Lewes, Overbeck and Cornelius '1ent real genius to the attempt to revive the dead forms of early Christian art" (II, 219). They did so not only in their own works but also by inspiring an important body of research into the history and iconography of European Pre-Raphaelite painting.

Such studies were no doubt in Lewes's mind when he spoke in 1855 of "the services rendered by Romanticism in making the Middle Ages more thoroughly understood" (Life and Works of Goethe, II, 220). By Romanticism in this context, he and George Eliot meant a German, Catholic, neomedieval movement whose "main feature... was the exaltation of the Medieval above the Classic, of art animated by Christian spiritualism above the art animated by Greek humanism."

Largely published between 1835 and 1855, the scholarship inspired by Romanticism divided Dorothea's England of the first Reform Bill from George Eliot's of the second. Readers of Middlemarch are reminded that in Dorothea's day travelers to Rome did not often carry full information on Christian art either in their heads or their pockets; and even the most brilliant English critic of the day mistook the flower-flushed tomb of the ascended Virgin for an ornamental vase due to the painter's fancy. Romanticism, which has helped to fill some dull blanks with love and knowledge, had not yet penetrated the times with its leaven and entered into everybody's food; it was fermenting still as a distinguishable vigorous enthusiasm in certain long-haired German artists at Rome.... [19:287]

George Eliot's example of English ignorance is accurate and well-chosen. In Notes of a Journey through France and Italy (1826), a book Dorothea might well have carried to Rome, William Hazlitt grossly misreads the iconography of Raphael's The Coronation of the Virgin in the Vatican Museum. Referring indeed to a "vase of flowers," Hazlitt fails to recognize the Marian resurrection symbolism of the lilies and roses that spring from the Virgin's sarcophagus. And he describes the twelve apostles as a "crowd".

Readers of Middlemarch would almost certainly have possessed better "information on Christian art" than Hazlitt's. For example, Mrs. Jameson's popular Legends of the Madonna as Represented in the Fine Arts (1852) mentions five versions of the Coronation in which "the miraculous flowers" appear. Of Raphael's treatment Mrs. Jameson says: "Here we have the tomb below, filled with flowers; and around it the twelve apostles."[54] For such gains in precision George Eliot thanked the "long-haired German artists" of the early nineteenth century.

In Middlemarch Naumann dramatizes the educational function of Romanticism when he plays the kindly didact to Dorothea. Her pre-Romantic ignorance of the conventions of Christian art prevents her from appreciating the "walls... covered with frescoes, or with rare pictures" that she sees in Rome (21:315). Although Dorothea's conscience is troubled by aesthetic apprehension per se, part of her difficulty is that often she simply does not know what the pictures represent. By explicating the iconography of his own neomedieval works, Naumann comes nearer than anyone else in the novel to teaching Dorothea how to look at traditional paintings which are not simple portraits or landscapes:

The painter in his confident English gave little dissertations on his finished and unfinished subjects... and Dorothea felt that she was getting quite new notions as to the significance of madonnas seated under inexplicable canopied thrones with the simple country as a background, and of saints with architectural models in their hands, or knives accidentally wedged in their skulls. Some things which had seemed monstrous to her were gathering intelligibility and even a natural meaning.

Although the narrator's dry tone suggests considerable sympathy with Dorothea's distaste for such subjects, the last sentence affirms a positive and welcome enlightenment. Here Naumann does in small what Romanticism will soon do for Europe at large: he gives "intelligibility and even a natural meaning" to symbols of Christian art that had come to seem unintelligible and unnatural.

Whether the conventions of medieval Christian art should determine the direction of nineteenth-century painting was, however, a different question in George Eliot's mind. On balance she felt they should not, because they distort more than they clarify. To teach Dorothea how to look at Madonnas is one thing; to paint her as one is another. Both Naumann and the narrator of Middlemarch present idealizing portraits of Dorothea as a Christian heroine, but the novel calls all such portraiture into doubt. One side of George Eliot's mind remained skeptical toward the pictorial idealization of character even as she was practicing it.

When Naumann first encounters Dorothea in the Vatican Museum, her "Quakerish" costume and meditative expression inspire him to paint her as a personification of the Christian spirit, "dressed," since Naumann is Catholic, "as a nun" (19:289). Then he sees Dorothea as a "perfect young Madonna," and eventually he settles for painting her as Santa Clara (19:290, 22:331). But Dorothea's figure and attitude resemble those of the statue of Ariadne near which she stands, so there are pagan elements in the scene which prompt Naumann to a more comprehensive definition. He envisions Dorothea as "antique form animated by Christian sentiment — a sort of Christian Antigone — sensuous force controlled by spiritual passion" (19:290). This formulation unites the classical and the medieval, reconciling the great antitheses of German aesthetic debate in a higher synthesis.

Though suggestive, Naumann's exalted and schematic vision is only partly valid. Will Ladislaw immediately warns his friend not to confuse a symbolic conception of Dorothea with her human reality. Actually Naumann's allegorizing distorts his subjects, much as the fantasies of the male egoists in Adam Bede distort Hetty. Ladislaw alludes to Naumann's egoism when he accuses the painter of "looking at the world entirely from the studio point of view" (21:317), of thinking that art perfects life, and of believing that his picture of Dorothea would be "the chief outcome of her existence — the divinity passing into higher completeness and all but exhausted in the act of covering [a] bit of canvas" (19:290).

This is a critique of the solipsistic tendency inherent in Romantic aestheticism. It no doubt reflects the many charges of spiritual pride which Ruskin laid against the Nazarenes.

George Eliot quoted the third of these passages in her review of Ruskin, "Art and Belles Lettres," Westminster Review, 65 (1856), 628.

This critique may also entail a more contemporary reference to the Victorian philosophy of art-for-art's-sake that had begun to spin off from Pre-Raphaelitism by the later 1860s. The critique also aligns Naumann with one of the grand themes of the novel: the inescapable corruption of aspiration by egoism. Compare, for example, Naumann's description of Dorothea with Walter Pater's description of Leonardo's Mona Lisa; in both, the lady's beauty is a synthesis of the major phases of western civilization, an incarnation of the collective wisdom and experience of her kind. Pater's essay on Leonardo was first published in 1869; in 1870 George Eliot dined at Oxford with "Mr. Pater, writer of articles on Leonardo da Vinci, Morris, etc." (Letters, V, 100).

Naumann's Christianizing aestheticism, then, is one of the many modes of human intellection tested and found wanting in Middlemarch Idealizing portraiture provides no coherent vision in this novel of incomplete insights. Ultimately Dorothea eludes all of the analogies that attempt to characterize her as Santa Clara, Santa Teresa, Santa Barbara, the Madonna, and a Christian Antigone, just as Mr. Casaubon more obviously eludes Naumann's vision of him as Saint Thomas Aquinas or Dorothea's comparison of him with "the portrait of Locke" (2:21).

In The Art of George Eliot (1969), W. J. Harvey has argued that in Middlemarch such comparisons border upon the mock-heroic (pp. 193-95; for a different interpretation of the mythological allusions in chapter 19 of Middlemarch. George Eliot sometimes wished passionately to affirm the persistence of ideal types in everyday life (G.H. Lewes often called her "Madonna"), but at other times she was skeptical and satirical about just such affirmations; and her skepticism is by no means confined to Middlemarch. In Felix Holt, for example, she gently satirizes her own response to religious art in a scene between Felix and Esther Lyon: "He was looking up at her quite calmly, very much as a reverential Protestant might look at a picture of the Virgin, with a devoutness suggested by the type rather than by the image" (27:39).

Usually, of course, George Eliot tried to be as attentive to the image as to the type, and this attention often complicated her responses. She was, for instance, no indiscriminate admirer of Raphael's madonnas.

Although she worshipped the Sistine Madonna, she disliked some of its earlier "sisters" for "their sheep-like look" (Cross, II, 189). In The Mill on the Floss she draws an unflattering analogy between these images and Mrs. Tulliver: "I have often wondered whether those early Madonnas of Raphael, with the blond faces and somewhat stupid expression, kept their placidity undisturbed when their strong-limbed, strong-willed boys got a little too old to do without clothing" (I, 2:15).

Eliot's ambivalent vision sometimes issued in contradictory treatments of the same picture. Raphael's Saint Catherine, for example, was an early favourite of hers. At the age of twenty-five she told a friend that "you are a bright spot in my memory, like Raphael's Saint Catherine" (Letters, I, 188); and she may well have had the same painting in mind when Arthur Donnithorne refers to Dinah Morris as "St. Catherine in a Quaker dress" (5:91), and when one of the characters in Romola says that the heroine is "fit to be a model for a wise Saint Catherine of Egypt". But Raphael's famous picture is treated much less reverently in Middlemarch when Dorothea, recuperating from her bereavement, begins to grow restless: "After three months Freshitt had become rather oppressive: to sit like a model for Saint Catherine looking rapturously at Celia's baby would not do for many hours in the day: (54:3-4). Viewed from this perspective, Raphael's saint seems posed and a bit silly.

George Eliot's ambivalence toward idealization also complicates her attitude toward sculpture. Her visit to Weimar in 1854 convinced her that she did not care for "classical idealising in portrait sculpture." She saw there several distasteful examples of the technique, including a "colossal statue of Goethe, executed after Bettina's design," which represents him "as a naked Apollo with a Psyche at his knee!" Any work in which the "artist tells us that the ideal of a Greek god divides his attention with his immediate subject" must be taken, Eliot warned, with a grain of salt. She declared herself particularly "irritated with idealization in portrait when, as in Dannecker's bust of Schiller, one has been misled into supposing that Schiller's brow was square and massive, while, in fact, it was receding".

In other words, idealization must not exceed the bounds of phrenological realism. Yet in other moods Eliot was not at all averse to classical idealizing in portrait sculpture. She was particularly fond of heroic and monumental images of women, such as the cockle-woman she once saw at Swansea: "the grandest woman I ever saw — six feet high, carrying herself like a Greek Warrior, and treading the earth with unconscious majesty". This taste for massive, Amazonian figures also manifests itself in Eliot's admiration of several pieces of contemporary sculpture: August Kiss's Mounted Amazon Attacked by a Tiger and Ludwig Schwanthaler's Bavaria (Cross, II, 21-22). Given her predilection for grand, statuesque female forms, she naturally visualized her own heroines as imposing creatures.

Dorothea, for example, resembles the reclining Ariadne in the Vatican Museum, and the similarity is of amplitude as well as attitude. The full-grown Maggie Tulliver is a tall, queenly figure whose arm resembles either one of the Parthenon sculptures or a classical sculpture that George Eliot saw in Berlin. In "Janet's Repentance" we pause with the heroine's mother to admire Janet's "tall rich figure, looking all the grander for the plainness of the deep mourning dress, and the noble face with its massy folds of black hair, made matronly by a simple white cap. Janet had that enduring beauty which belongs to pure majestic outline and depth of tint".

In a word, Janet's beauty, like that of Isola Churchill, the heroine of G. H. Lewes's Ranthorpe, is "more sculpturesque than picturesque". In Daniel Deronda the heroine is visualized in terms of Roman colored sculpture: "Dressed in black, without a single ornament, and with the warm whiteness of her skin set off between her light-brown coronet of hair and her square-cut bodice, she might have tempted an artist to try again the Roman trick of a statue in black, white, and tawny marble. Seeing her image slowly advancing, she thought, 'I am beautiful'". As usual, Gwendolen is the first to admire her own aesthetic effects.

Herein she differs from Mirah Cohen, who is all unconsciously transformed from "immovable, statue-like des" to "a coloured statue of serenity" (17:280, 52:159). On a smaller scale, Mirah is visualized as "an onyx cameo" (17:281), "a perfect cameo" (32: 144). As in the case of Mirah's suicidal despair, George Eliot often represents states of extreme emotional stress through an imagery of sculpture. See, for example, Adam Bede (27:10, 27:19, 43:223). Roman sculpture figures, too, in the presentation of Felix Holt: "Felix might have come from the hands of a sculptor in the later Roman period, when the plastic impulse was stirred by the grandeur of barbaric forms" (46:309). Although pagan sculptural idealization obviously does not involve the renewal of biblical types, it nevertheless serves much the same function as George Eliot's Christian pictorialism. Both modes of literary portraiture hallow character by associating it with venerated traditional norms.

Eliot also elicited exemplary values from her literary portraits by grouping them in contrasting pairs. For example, the description just quoted of Felix Holt as a late-Roman statue occurs in combination with a description of Harold Transome as "a handsome portrait by Sir Thomas Lawrence." The two Radicals, we are told, "certainly made a striking contrast" (46:309).

A similar pairing takes place in Daniel Deronda: "Deronda, turning to look straight at Grandcourt who was on his left hand, might have made a subject for those old painters who liked contrasts of temperament" (15:240). Or again, in Adam Bede: "The family likeness between [Mrs. Poyser] and her niece Dinah Morris, with the contrast between her keenness and Dinah's seraphic gentleness of expression, might have served a painter as an excellent suggestion for a Martha and Mary" (6: 10',7).

In George Eliot's work such contrasts are usually moral as well as visual, and sometimes they border on the emblematic in their clear-cut, monitory juxtaposition of virtue and vice, altruism and egoism. In "Amos Barton," for example, Milly is compared in physiognomy and moral temperament with the Countess Czerlaski: "Look at the two women on the sofa together! The large, fair, mild-eyed Milly is timid even in friendship: it is not easy to her to speak of the affection of which her heart is full.

The lithe, dark, thin-lipped countess is racking her small brain for caressing words and charming exaggerations" (3:48). Exemplary pairings of women may be found among George Eliot's earliest published writings (Essays, pp. 21-22), and as Constance Marie Fulmer points out in "Contrasting Pairs of Heroines in George Eliot's Fiction," they are an important device for unifying parallel plots in her mature fiction (Studies in the Novel, 6 (1974), 288-94).

Perhaps the best-known of Eliot's double portraits is the "Two Bed-Chambers" scene in chapter 15 of Adam Bede. Here Hetty Sorrel and Dinah Morris are contrasted in great visual and moral detail. Their surroundings, their appearances, and their physical and mental activities are set forth with a painstaking realism that emulates the spirit of Dutch painting. Yet these concrete descriptive details compose themselves into coherent symbolic patterns as well, so that Hetty's portrait incorporates many traditional symbols of vanity, whereas Dinah's abounds with familiar signs of contemplation [90/91] and spiritual rebirth. After describing the two women separately, George Eliot brings them together, as if joining two wings of a diptych.

What a strange contrast the two figures made! Visible enough in that mingled twilight and moonlight. Hetty, her cheeks flushed and her eyes glistening from her imaginary drama, her beautiful neck and arms bare, her hair hanging in a curly tangle down her back, and the baubles in her ears. Dinah, covered with her long white dress, her pale face full of subdued emotion, almost like a lovely corpse into which the soul has returned charged with sublimer secrets and a sublimer love.

The uncharacteristic absence of predication in Eliot's syntax here reinforces the impression of static, juxtaposed icons. Although vanitas symbolism is common enough in seventeenth-century Dutch genre painting, this sort of stark moral contrast is not common. Eliot's description is so emblematic that one critic has actually proposed a direct iconographic parallel with Francis Quarles's emblem III, 14.

This is not a convincing analogy, however. R. T. Jones is closer to the mark when he compares the scene to a hypothetical nineteenth-century painting: "It might be called 'Sacred and Profane Love,' and it might have been painted by, say, Holman Hunt" (George Eliot, Cambridge: Cambridge University Press, 1970, p. 17). This is a perceptive suggestion, especially if Jones is thinking of Hunt's famous pair of moral pictures, The Light of the World and The Awakening Conscience.

Yet Hunt never depicted two women together in quite the way that Eliot does here. A better pictorial analogy for "The Two Bed-Chambers" scene, if one need be sought, is Wilhelm von Schadow's Pietas und Vanitas: Parabel der klugen und törichten Jungfrauen (1842), a painting displayed at the great Munich exhibition of 1858 within two months of George Eliot's visit to the Bavarian capital. Schadow's wise and foolish virgins are juxtaposed as if in a diptych, equipped with contrasting symbolic accoutrements and differentiated by the directions of their gazes.

Although the painting does not resemble George Eliot's text in every detail, the correspondences are nonetheless suggestive. A comparable Victorian painting, though done too late to have influenced Adam Bede, is Arthur D. Lemon's Pure Innocence and Pure in No Sense (ca. 1880); see Rodee, "Scenes of Rural and Urban Poverty," p. 141 and illus. 52.

This sort of contrast attains massive proportions in the structure of Daniel Deronda, where the English and Jewish parts of the novel incorporate two distinctive and antithetical modes of literary portraiture. Both modes involve the idealization of character and the reincarnation of sacred types, but the novel treats one mode as false and the other as true. Throughout Deronda, George Eliot regularly visualizes Gwendolen and the other English characters in terms of the English portrait tradition, and especially of the "fancy" portraits that were fashionable among the upper classes in the seventeenth and eighteenth centuries.

Conversely, Eliot visualizes Daniel and other Jewish characters in terms of Italian Renaissance painting, especially that of Titian and the Venetian school. The contrasts between these two schools of painting reflect moral contrasts between the two races and cultures represented.

George Eliot's characteristic ambivalence toward the pictorial idealization of character finds a complex resolution in the double plot of Daniel Deronda: her ironic portraiture has full play in the English half of the novel, while her ennobling portraiture finds a more ardent and affirmative expression in the Jewish part than anywhere else in her fiction.

Gwendolen, as we have seen, likes to imagine herself as the central subject of attractive pictures. Her favourite attitudes in these imaginary self-portraits are borrowed from the allegorical society portraiture of the Van Dyck tradition. In the seventeenth and eighteenth centuries it was fashionable to idealize sitters by depicting them in costumes, poses, and settings that recall heroic, mythical, or religious figures from earlier works of art.

Van Dyck popularized this technique of pictorial quotation in England when he transferred the baroque style of his Genoese religious work into his society portraiture. Thus he painted Lady Venetia Digby as Prudence, Rachel, Countess of Southampton, as Fortuna, and Mary, Duchess of Lenox, as Saint Agnes. Continuing the fashion,

Sir Peter Lely drew the Duchess of Cleveland as Juno, Mrs. Middleton as Pomona, Jane Kelleway as Diana, the Duchess of Rutland as Saint Agnes. Godfrey Kneller drew Anne, Lady Middleton, and Mrs. Voss and her daughter as Arcadian shepherdesses bearing staffs in their hands, and, on another occasion, the same Mrs. Voss as St. Agnes holding a prayer book in her hand and cuddling a lamb.

Reynolds, in his turn, portrayed Mrs. Quarrington as St. Agnes, Mrs. Crewe as St Genevieve, The Daughters of Sir William Montgomery as the Graces Adorning a Term of Hymen, The Duchess of Manchester as Diana, Mrs. Blake as Juno, and the famous courtesan Kitty Fisher as Cleopatra.[74] Because they allude to the subjects of historical or "fancy" painting, these pictures are often referred to as "fancy portraits" (Tinker, Painter and Poet, p. 14). That George Eliot was familiar with the term is shown by the fact that Latimer, the narrator of "The Lifted Veil," has been "the model of a dying minstrel in a fancy-picture" (1:295).

It is with fancy portraits that Gwendolen is most prominently associated in Daniel Deronda. At the Archery Meeting in Brackenshaw Park, for example, it was the fashion to dance in the archery dress, throwing off the jacket; and the simplicity of [Gwendolen's] white cashmere with its border of pale green set off her form to the utmost. A thin line of gold round her neck, and the gold star on her breast, were her only ornaments. Her smooth soft hair piled up into a grand crown made a clear line about her brow. Sir Joshua would have been glad to take her portrait.... [11:170]

Clearly Sir Joshua would have entitled the portrait Miss Harleth as Diana. Earlier in the same scene, a comparable portrait is evoked when we are told that "Gwendolen seemed a Calypso among her nymphs. It was in her attitudes and movements that every one was obliged to admit her surpassing charm" (10:147). We are dealing once more with Ovidian mythological fantasies of the sort that were treated so ironically in Adam Bede and Romola.

The self-indulgence of the fantasies is underlined by the fact that Gwendolen is critical of other women who might figure in the same sort of painting. After observing that Charlotte Arrowpoint "would make quite a fine picture in that gold-coloured dress," Gwendolen decides that the picture would be "perhaps a little too symbolical — too much like the figure of Wealth in an allegory" (10:151). Too many allegorical figures might crowd Gwendolen's canvas. Gwendolen's most memorable borrowed attitudes are Hermione and Saint Cecilia. The famous tableau of Hermione in Daniel Deronda is indebted to a similar scene in Goethe's Die Wahlverwandtschaften, which was in turn inspired by the drawing-room attitudes of Lady Emma Hamilton.

In her tableau Gwendolen chooses to imitate the attitude in which Mrs. Siddons and other eighteenth-century actresses regularly played the statue scene in The Winter's Tale: "Hermione, her arm resting on a pillar, was elevated by about six inches, which she counted on as a means of showing her pretty foot and instep, when at the given signal she should advance and descend" (6:85).

Edgar Wind, in his classic essay on English heroic portraiture in the eighteenth century, reproduces engravings of Mrs. Siddons and Miss Farren in the role of Hermione, holding precisely this pose. He shows that the attitude descends from classical representations of the Muses, and that it was "an established formula" for all actresses who played the statue scene in the eighteenth century. Gwendolen, then, is imitating pictures of Mrs. Siddons as Hermione. As Wind notes, in society masquerades the ladies "often learned the attitudes which they assumed from actresses on the stage" ("Humanitatsidee," pp. 222, 224). Wind reproduces a drawing of Mrs. Siddons as Hermione from the sketchbook of a young lady, Mary Hamilton, who depicted the attitudes and costumes of Mrs. Siddons in a variety of roles, with a view to recreating them in private entertainments.

Gwendolen's Hermione is designed primarily to allow her to display "a statuesque pose" in her Greek dress (6:82). The planned effect perfectly exemplifies Ruskin's assertion in Modern Painters, vol. III that "the modern 'ideal' of high art is a curious mingling of the gracefulness and reserve of the drawing-room with a certain measure of classical sensuality" (V, 96). But it is Gwendolen's expression, not her attitude, that is affected by the sudden apparition of the prophetic picture of the dead face and fleeing figure. Instead of assuming the radiant face of comedy appropriate to the end of The Winter's

Tale, Gwendolen unwittingly dons the mask of tragedy:

Gwendolen... stood without change of attitude, but with a change of expression that was terrifying in its terror. She looked like a statue into which a soul of Fear had entered: her pallid lips were parted; her eyes, usually narrowed under their long lashes, were dilated and fixed. [6:86]

The complacent beauty has now become a study in physiognomical expression, a sculpturesque representation of Terror, one of the two passions appropriate to Aristotelian tragedy. Instead of Miss Harleth as Hermione, we have, still in the Reynolds tradition, Miss Harleth as the Tragic Muse. The picture distinctly recalls Piero di Cosimo's picture of Tito as a terror-stricken reveller in Romola.

More to Gwendolen's taste is the attitude of Saint Cecilia:

"Here is an organ. I will be Saint Cecilia: some one shall paint me as Saint Cecilia. Jocosa (this was her name for Miss Merry), let down my hair. See, mamma!"

She had thrown off her hat and gloves, and seated herself before the organ in an admirable pose, looking upward; while the submissive and sad Jocosa took out the one comb which fastened the coil of hair, and then shook out the mass till it fell in a smooth light-brown stream far below its owner's slim waist. Mrs Davilow smiled and said, "A charming picture, my dear!" not indifferent to the display of her pet, even in the presence of a housekeeper. Gwendolen rose and laughed with delight. All this seemed quite to the purpose on entering a new house which was so excellent a background. [3:33-34]

Here the imaginary portrait is in the style of Kneller's Lady Elizabeth Cromwell as Saint Cecilia (1703), Reynolds's Mrs. Sheridan as Saint Cecilia (1775), or Reynolds's Mrs Billington as Saint Cecilia. The aristocratic life to which Gwendolen aspires is again presented as an eighteenth-century affair. The attitude of Saint Cecilia in society portraiture was familiar enough by 1735 to be an object of Pope's satire in Moral Essay II, "On the Characters of Women":

How many pictures of one Nymph we view,
All how unlike each other, all how true!

....

Let then the Fair one beautifully cry,
In Magdalen's loose hair and lifted eye,
Or drest in smiles of sweet Cecilia shine,
With simp'ring Angels, Palms, and Harps divine;
Whether the Charmer sinner it or saint it,
If folly grows romantic, I must paint it.81

Hagstrum's The Sister Arts cites this passage after listing the representations of Saint Cecilia best known in the seventeenth century. Fancy portraits were also satirized by Oliver Goldsmith in chapter 16 of The Vicar of Wakefield. Edgar Wind argues that English allegorical portraiture reflects a heroic conception of mankind, and other scholars have defended them. But Pope and George Eliot see in such portraiture mainly the affectation and folly of the social class depicted. Indeed, for the middle-class Victorian intellectual, fancy portraits must have epitomized all that was Dandy about the fashionable classes under George III and George IV.

Ruskin strikes the characteristic Victorian tone in the third volume of Modern Painters when he speaks of paintings which introduce pretty children as cherubs, and handsome women as Magdalens and Maries of Egypt, or portraits of patrons in the character of the more decorous saints; but more frequently, for direct flatteries of this kind, recurring to pagan mythology, and painting frail ladies as goddesses or graces, and foolish kings in radiant apotheosis. [V, 93-94]

The portraits in which Gwendolen loves to see herself do not in George Eliot's view truly idealize their subjects; they falsify in order to please the vanity of their subjects. Hans Meyrick temporarily resists Sir Hugo Mallinger's advice to take up portraiture because the sort of painter Sir Hugo has in mind "has a little truth, and a great facility in falsehood — [his] idealism will never do for gods and goddesses and heroic story, but it may fetch a high price as flattery" (52:152). That Hans has higher standards of truthfulness in portraiture is perhaps suggested by the fact that he is "christened after Holbein" and that "only to look at his pinched features and blond hair dangling over his collar reminded one of pale quaint heads by early German painters" (16:270).

Early German is not the only school to be contrasted with the English in Daniel Deronda Before discussing George Eliot's Italian sources, we should glance briefly at her use of the Dutch school in the presentation of Mordecai. Eliot's idealization of Mordecai is pictorial and overtly typological. Daniel's first impression of the consumptive scholar is that "such a physiognomy as that might possibly have been seen in a prophet of the Exile, or in some New Hebrew poet of the medieval time" (33:165). Later Daniel sees Mordecai as "an illuminated type of bodily emaciation and spiritual eagerness" (40:327).

For Hebrew portraiture Eliot turned naturally to Rembrandt's pictures of rabbis. G. H. Lewes spoke of "a Rembrandtish background to her dramatic presentation" of the Jews in Daniel Deronda (Letters, Vl, 196), and certainly a Rembrandtish chiaroscuro is suggested by the first glimpse of Mordecai's face, "with its dark, far-off gaze, and yellow pallor in relief on the gloom of the backward shop". Later Hans Meyrick, who is painting the picturesque figure, says: "Our prophet is an uncommonly interesting sitter — a better model than Rembrandt had for his Rabbi" (52:147).

It is difficult to know which of Rembrandt's so-called rabbis Hans has in mind, but perhaps he is referring to the only one in the collection of the National Gallery, purchased under the title A Jewish Rabbi in 1844. The picturesque caps of Rembrandt's sitters were probably in George Eliot's memory when she wrote of Mordecai: "he commonly wore a cloth cap with black fur round it, which no painter would have asked him to take off" (38: 298). Mordecai himself may be thinking of Rembrandt when he envisions his messiah "from his memory of faces seen among the Jews of Holland and Bohemia, and from the pictures which revived that memory" (38:300).

Nevertheless, Dutch art does not dominate the Jewish part of Daniel Deronda as completely as might be expected. It is an exaggeration to say, as Harold Fisch does in "Daniel Deronda, or Gwendolen Harleth?" that "the Jewish portraiture of Rembrandt" is "the true prototype" of George Eliot's treatment of the Jews (Nineteenth-Century Fiction, 19 (1965),

354-55). Except for Mordecai, no important character in the novel is associated with Rembrandt's portraiture. Eliot's use of Dutch painting is highly selective, no doubt because the idealization she wished to confer upon her Jewish characters was incompatible with her audience's preconceptions about the limitations of the Dutch school.

No one did more than Eliot herself had done in Adam Bede to foster the notion that the province of Dutch art is "the faithful rendering of commonplace things," and that it depicts "few prophets... few sublimely beautiful women; few heroes" (17:270). In Adam Bede Dutch models sufficed for the mundane range of experience she wised to present. But in Daniel Deronda she ventures into precisely those extraordinary reaches of experience which she chose to avoid in Adam Bede. She could not make an extensive use of Dutch models because she shared with a substantial part of her audience the venerable prejudice that Dutch painting rarely achieves the sublime.

Instead she relies heavily upon Italian, especially Venetian, models. So persistently does she associate Jews with Italians that the Anglo-Saxon reader of Daniel Deronda is induced almost subliminally to grant the Jews whatever tolerance and respect he is accustomed to grant the Italians. It is as though George Eliot were saying to her Protestant English audience: you have learned to appreciate the Italians despite their ethnic, religious, and cultural foreignness; you can learn to appreciate the Jews in the same way: both peoples are of Mediterranean origin, both have distinguished non-Protestant religious traditions, and the Italian Renaissance painting you admire realizes many motifs of the Hebrew scriptures. (Disraeli's hero in Lothair (1870) makes a similar point when discussing the influence of "Semitism" upon "Aryan art" [chap. 29].)

Eliot's pictorialism, in other words, here becomes a sophisticated rhetorical device employed in the service of a liberal social vision. The Italian connection affects major and minor characters alike. An elderly man at the synagogue in Frankfurt, for example, has an "ample white beard and felt hat framing a profile of that fine contour which may as easily be Italian as Hebrew" (32:136). Of Klesmer, the Jewish pianist, the narrator says: "draped in a loose garment with a Florentine berretta on his head, he would have been fit to stand by the side of Leonardo da Vinci" (10:149).

Even Mirah Cohen is associated with Italians in Hans Meyrick's Titus and Berenice series; she is to be the model for the Jewish mistress of the prospective emperor of Rome. The series was originally suggested, as Hans explains, by "a splendid woman in the Trastevere — the grandest women there are half Jewesses — and she set me hunting for a fine situation of a Jewess at Rome" (37:276). The fusion of Jewish and Roman identities here is threefold: in Berenice, in the Trasteverina, and by association in Mirah.

Finally, Daniel Deronda himself, who learns in Genoa that he is a Jew, has "a face not more distinctively oriental than many a type seen among what we call the Latin races" (40:332). Gwendolen's mother says the same thing more concisely: "he puts me in mind of Italian paintings" (29: 83). That Deronda does not belong pictorially to the English school is made clear when Gwendolen notices that "hardly any face could be less like Deronda's than that represented as Sir Hugo's in a crayon portrait at Diplow" (29:84).

Of the regional schools of Italian painting evoked in Daniel Deronda, the most prominent is the Venetian. Venetian painting regained its prestige in England in the 1860s and 1870s after the rage for Pre-Raphaelite styles had run its course. Ruskin's revaluation of the Venetian school in the last volume of Modern Painters (1860) concludes that "the Venetian mind... and Titian's especially, as the central type of it, was wholly realist, universal, and manly.... In all its roots of power, and modes of work... I find the Venetian mind perfect" (VII, 296-98.). Earlier in the same work Ruskin contrasted Venetian Renaissance portraiture to modern English portraiture in terms that parallel George Eliot's handling of the two schools in Daniel Deronda:

> the first step towards the ennobling of any face is the ridding it of its vanity; to which aim there cannot be anything more contrary than that principle of portraiture which prevails

with us in these days, whose end seems to be the expression of vanity throughout, in face and in all circumstances of accompaniment; tending constantly to insolence of attitude, and levity and haughtiness of expression, and worked out farther in mean accompaniments of worldly splendour and possession... whence has arisen such a school of portraiture as must make the people of the nineteenth century the shame of their descendants, and the butt of all time. To which practices are to be opposed both the glorious severity of Holbein, and the mighty and simple modesty of Raffaelle, Titian, Giorgione, and Tintoret, with whom armour does not constitute the warrior, neither silk the dame. And from what feeling the dignity of that portraiture arose is best traceable at Venice.

According to Ruskin, painting done before 1600 embodies a greater purity of religious spirit than painting done since, and the Venetians "were the last believing school of Italy" (VII, 286). Hence the Venetian school is appropriate to the Jewish characters in Daniel Deronda, who have preserved a vital contact with their ancient religion; whereas the modern school is appropriate to the English characters, who are vain and worldly. In characterizing modern portraiture as an art of vanity, Ruskin anticipates George Eliot's pictures of Gwendolen.

Among the Victorians the chief technical excellence of the Venetian painters was generally held to be their colour. In The Stones of Venice [100/101] Ruskin spoke of "that mighty spirit of Venetian colour, which was to be consummated in Titian," and argued that there is always a "connexion of pure colour with profound and noble thought" (X, 64, 174. In Deronda George Eliot draws upon the pure colour values of Venetian painting when she describes Daniel's visit to the family of Ezra Cohen:

When she showed him into the room behind the shop he was surprised at the prettiness of the scene.... The ceiling and walls were smoky, and all the surroundings were dark enough to throw into relief the human figures, which had a Venetian glow of colouring. The grandmother was arrayed in yellowish brown with a large gold chain in lieu of the necklace, and by this light her yellow face with its darkly-marked eyebrows and framing roll of grey hair looked as handsome as was necessary for picturesque effect. Young Mrs Cohen was clad in red and black, with a string of large artificial pearls wound round and round her neck: the baby lay asleep in the cradle under a scarlet counterpane; Adelaide Rebekah was in braided amber; and Jacob Alexander was in black velveteen with scarlet stockings. As the four pairs of black eyes all glistened a welcome at Deronda, he was almost ashamed of the supercilious dislike these happy-looking creatures had raised in him by daylight.

Here the Venetian aura of colour in the group portrait dignifies the London Jewish family in Deronda's eyes and is meant to have the same effect upon the reader. Structurally, the scene is a conversation piece. It may recall Simeon Solomon's "Illustrations of Jewish Customs," The Leisure Hour, vol 15 (1866). Once again we see "Hebrew dyed Italian" (55:213). No doubt the coloristic style of Venetian painting seemed to George Eliot more exotic, more "oriental," and therefore more appropriate to her Jewish characters than did the linear styles of other Italian schools.

If Reynolds dominates the English portraiture in Daniel Deronda, then Titian dominates the Jewish. "One can," says Jean Hagstrum, "almost always count on a literary Englishman's admiration of Titian" (SisterArts, p. 164). In a sense, the entire novel was inspired by a Titian painting — the Annunciation at the Scuola di San Rocco in Venice, which gave George Eliot the theme she developed first in The Spanish Gypsy and later in Deronda. In "this small picture of Titian's," she found "a great dramatic motive": a young person chosen to fulfil a great destiny... chosen, not by any momentary arbitrariness, but as a result of foregoing hereditary conditions... I came home with this in my mind, meaning to give the motive a clothing in some suitable set of historical and local conditions. [Cross, III, 34-35]

Here is an excellent example of the typological thinking that underlies so much of Eliot's art. Titian's handling of a traditional biblical type inspires Eliot to reincarnate the same type in a more contemporary setting.

Small wonder, then, that the literary portraiture of George Eliot's hero derives principally from two of Titian's paintings. In the early part of the novel, before he has accepted his Zionist mission, Daniel is associated with a secular portrait in the Louvre — The Young Man with a Glove. In the later part of the novel, after his destiny has been revealed, Daniel is associated with a religious painting at Dresden — The Tribute Money. The change of portraits symbolizes Daniel's progression from a life of aimless upper-class ease to a life of religious commitment. Deronda comes to exemplify G. H. Lewes's belief that "a well-painted face, with a noble expression, is the highest reach of art" ("Realism in Art," p. 499). Earlier in the novel the Meyrick girls create their own portrait of "Deronda as an ideal" when they set about "to paint him as Prince Camaralzaman," hero of one of the Arabian Nights (16:275).

The Young Man with a Glove is evoked in chapter 17 as Deronda rows on the Thames:

Look at his hands: they are not small and dimpled, with tapering fingers that seem to have only a deprecating touch: they are long, flexible, firmly-grasping hands, such as Titian has painted in a picture where he wished to show the combination of refinement with force. And there is something of a likeness, too, between the faces belonging to the hands — in both the uniform pale-brown skin, the perpendicular brow, the calmly-penetrating eyes. [17:277-78]

George Eliot might have seen this portrait during visits to the Louvre in 1859 and again in 1864 (Cross, II, 96 and "Italy 1864," Beinecke Library, entry 6 May). Here is Deronda as handsome young gentleman, idle perhaps but potentially energetic and less affected than he might be if he belonged to the English school. The young man's potential is fully realized in the painting that represents Deronda's later, more spiritual aspect. Titian's Tribute Money is evoked immediately after Deronda is recognized by Mordecai as the incarnation of his messianic vision:

In ten minutes the two men, with as intense a consciousness as if they had been two undeclared lovers, felt themselves alone in the small gas-lit book-shop and turned face to face, each baring his head from an instinctive feeling that they wished to see each other fully.... I wish I could perpetuate those two faces, as Titian's "Tribute Money" has perpetuated another type of contrast.

Imagine — we all of us can — the pathetic stamp of consumption with its brilliancy of glance to which the sharply-defined structure of features reminding one of a forsaken temple, give already a far-off look as of one getting unwillingly out of reach; and imagine it on a Jewish face naturally accentuated for the expression of an eager mind-the face of a man little above thirty, but with that age upon it which belongs to time lengthened by suffering, the hair and beard still black throwing out the yellow pallor of the skin, the difficult breathing giving more decided marking to the mobile nostril, the wasted yellow hands conspicuous on the folded arms.... Seeing such a portrait you would see Mordecai. And opposite to him was a face not more oriental than many a type seen among what we call the Latin races: rich in youthful health, and with a forcible masculine gravity in its repose, that gave the value of judgment to the reverence with which he met the gaze of this mysterious son of poverty who claimed him as a long-expected friend. [40: 33 1-32]

The scene in the bookshop is analogous, not identical, to the scene in The Tribute Money. In particular, Mordecai does not resemble·the tax-collecting Pharisee through whom Jesus renders unto Caesar what is Caesar's. Yet Titian's Christ looks enough like The Young Man with a Glove to resemble Deronda as well, and Deronda is bearded. Probably we are meant to visualize Deronda in terms of Titian's Christ. "In this way," to borrow a remark made by Albert R. Cirillo in another context, "Eliot fleshes out Daniel's portrait as a paragon, as a symbol, or personal savior." That Daniel's Portrait involves a form of typological incarnation is strongly suggested by the language of the novel. Deronda is "the antitype of [the] visionary image in Mordecai's mind" (41:352).

An antitype is not the opposite of a type but its fulfillment. As soon as he meets Daniel, Mordecai is struck by "a face and frame which seemed to him to realise the long-conceived type... Deronda had that sort of resemblance to the preconceived type which a finely individual bust or portrait has to the more generalised copy left in our minds after a long interval" (38:307-08). The type in question reveals its virtues through its expression; it has "a face at once young, grand, and beautiful, where, if there is any melancholy, it is no feeble passivity, but enters into the foreshadowed capability of heroism" (38:298).

This face, at once contemplative and active, belongs both to Mordecai's messiah and to Titian's Christ in The Tribute Money. In effect, Eliot seeks to make Deronda a convincing postfiguration of Christ in her secular religion of humanity by contrasting his unconscious pictorial fulfillment of the role with Gwendolen's self-conscious fulfillment of the pictorial roles of saints and goddesses in fashionable society portraiture.

Deronda's literary portrait associates him with one of George Eliot's favourite paintings in all the world. During her extended stay at Dresden in the summer of 1858, she and G. H. Lewes visited the Gemäldegalerie "three mornings in the week" and "looked at the Zinsgroschen (Titian's), too, every day" (Cross, II, 47). In an essay written that summer, Lewes explained their reasons for admiring the picture. He cites The Tribute Money to illustrate the compatibility of idealism with realism in art:

Titian's unsurpassable head of Christ, in the famous "Christo del Moneta," if compared with all other heads by other painters, will likewise be found to have its profound significance and idealism in the wonderful reality of the presentation: the head is more intensely human than that of any other representation of Christ, but the humanity is such as accords with our higher conceptions. ["Realism in Art," p. 494]

In other words, The Tribute Money is a supreme example of the ideal in the real. It successfully achieves the idealization which fancy portraits fail to achieve when they depict their sitters as saints or mythological divinities. And it realizes a higher conception of humanity than does The Young Man with a Glove, as Lewes made clear when he ranked the two paintings on a Ruskinian scale of "greatness" in "The Principles of Success in Literature":

Titian's portrait of "The Young Man with a Glove" is a great work of art, though not of great art. It is infinitely higher than a portrait of Cromwell, by a painter unable to see into the great soul of Cromwell, and to make us see it; but it is infinitely lower than Titian's "Tribute Money," "Peter the Martyr," or the "Assumption." During the story, Deronda traverses the spiritual distance that separates The Young Man with a Glove from The Tribute Money on Lewes's scale. Deronda moves from a secular to a religious life, from a poised sitter in a portrait to a dramatic actor in a sacred history painting. With this bold pictorial affirmation George Eliot's career as a novelist ends. The techniques we have observed call into doubt Henry James's influential description of George Eliot's idealization in his review of Cross's Life. We feel in her, always," wrote James, that she proceeds from the abstract to the concrete: that her figures and situations are evolved, as the phrase is, from her moral consciousness, and are only indirectly the products of observations. They are deeply studied and elaborately justified, but they are not seen in the irresponsible plastic way. [Atlantic Monthly, 55 (May 1885); rpt. Carroll, ed., George Eliot: The Critical Heritage, p. 498.]

James's metaphors do not provide an altogether accurate account of the process which produced such characters as Dinah Morris, Romola, Mordecai, and Daniel Deronda. To be sure, these figures were evolved from Eliot's moral consciousness; but they were also seen in a plastic way virtually from the moment of their conception. They are not abstract or indirectly observed in any visual sense of the terms; on the contrary, as Ian Milner has observed, they are highly particularized and often modeled upon specific, identifiable pictures (The Structure of Values in George Eliot (Prague: Universita Karlova, 1968), p. 121). If we judge the characters to be failures, our verdict may be based upon our distaste for exemplary typological characterization rather than upon George Eliot's failure to achieve presentational concreteness.

Chapter 15

Inheriting the Empire After Morant Bay

When we reflect on the nineteenth century, the mid-1860s does not immediately spring to mind as a moment of great crisis in British domestic and imperial affairs. The mobilization that led up to the Second Reform Bill in 1867 lacks the revolutionary drama of the first round of Reform agitation and the great Chartist movement in the 1830s and 40s; the Morant Bay uprising in Jamaica in late 1865 was hardly on the same scale as the Sepoy Rebellion in India in 1857 or the Anglo-Boer War that brought the Victorian age to an end.

Nevertheless, social commentators and cultural critics of the 1860s believed themselves to be living through a period of major upheaval. And although some anticipated a positive outcome from the winds of change they sensed blowing through musty old Britain, others saw only threats and possible catastrophe. Thomas Carlyle, for instance, blustery as ever in his old age, fired off a letter in August 1866 promising support for the Eyre Testimonial and Defence Fund, set up to defend the governor of Jamaica against criticism of his methods in suppressing the Morant Bay rebellion:

> The clamour raised against Governor Eyre appears to me to be disgraceful to the good sense of England; and if it rested on any depth of conviction... I should consider it of evil omen to the country, and to its highest interests, in these times.... The English nation never loved anarchy; nor was wont to spend its sympathy on miserable mad seditions, especially of this inhuman and half-brutish type; but always loved order

and prompt suppression of seditions. (Workman 91-2). The shift to the past tense in the second of Carlyle's sentences here nicely conveys the sense that anarchy may actually be the new order of the day, and the disturbing fact that the opposition to Eyre not only rested on strongly held convictions but also had mass appeal. This second sentence also recalls (anachronistically, as it turns out) that most famous statement of the troubles of the 1860s, Matthew Arnold's *Culture and Anarchy*, first published as a series of magazine essays in 1867-68 and printed in book form in 1869.

In the conclusion to that work, writing about the disorder in Hyde Park in 1866 during a massive rally for Reform, Arnold demonstrates his firm conviction that seditions of any kind must be put down forcefully:

> For us the framework of society, that theatre on which this august drama has to unroll, is sacred; and whoever administers it... we steadily and with undivided heart support them in repressing anarchy and disorder; because without order there can be no society, and without society there can be no human perfection. (180-1)

In the original magazine version of this essay, and in the first edition of *Culture and Anarchy*, this passage is immediately followed by these notorious lines:

> With me, indeed, this rule of conduct is hereditary. I remember my father, in one of his unpublished letters of more than forty years ago, when the political and social state of the country was gloomy and troubled and there were riots in many places, goes on, after strongly insisting on the badness and foolishness of the government, and on the harm and dangerousness of our feudal and aristocratical constitution of society, and ends thus: "As for rioting, the old Roman way of dealing with that is always the right one; flog the rank and file and fling the ringleaders from the Tarpeian Rock!" (qtd. in Super 526)

In later editions of the book, Arnold deleted this passage, for reasons that have never been entirely clear. Perhaps the country seemed less gloomy and troubled by the time of the second edition (1875), and thus less in need of Thomas

Arnold's lawgiving. Or perhaps Matthew revised his text in response to the answer, now lost, that his mother gave to this letter that he sent to her on July 25, 1868:

In the passage quoted from Papa, [Arthur Penrhyn] Stanley's impression is that Papa's words were "Crucify all the slaves" instead of "Flog the rank & file"—but as the latter expression is the milder, and I have certainly got it in my memory as what he said, I have retained it. Do you remember which the words were, and in what letter they occur? (qtd. in Super 455)

Buried deep within Arnold's text, we find a connection between the unrest in the Caribbean—"Crucify all the slaves"—and the sometimes unruly agitation for working-class enfranchisement and parliamentary reform—"Flog the rank and file." It is this conjuncture, this alchemy of race and rights, that forms the subject of this essay.

I argue that what has come to be known, rather misleadingly, as the Governor Eyre controversy enabled the articulation of the discourses of class, race, and empire in Britain, discourses that were all in a state of major transition. It was these connections, more or less explicitly made, that gave the Jamaica uprising such a disproportionate significance at the time, and produced the sense of crisis that Arnold and Carlyle felt compelled to respond to. And it is out of this sense of crisis, I argue, after the Morant Bay rebellion, that the modern notion of the British Empire as a single conceptual, territorial, and political unit emerges.

Jamaica in the 1860s had been in serious economic decline for half a century; the days when ownership of a Jamaican sugar plantation was virtually a licence to print money were a distant memory. The Afro-Jamaican labouring classes, however, were beginning to leave behind the legacies of chattel slavery, establishing an internal island economy based on foodstuffs grown on small plots of land (often the same fields cultivated during slavery days, known as provision grounds). A combination of drought and ruling-class attempts to push squatters and poor tenants from abandoned estate lands led, in the southeast of the island in the mid-1860s, to a volatile situation. In October 1865, a group of Afro-Jamaicans, led by Paul Bogle, rescued one of their friends from punishment before the hated magistrates in the nearby town of Morant Bay; then they overwhelmed the police sent to arrest them the following day; finally, several hundred of them marched on the town to demand justice.

The local worthies, expecting trouble, had called out the volunteer militia; shots were fired, and several rebels were killed; then the rebels laid siege to the courthouse and took over the town, killing eighteen and wounding dozens, predominately whites. The insurgents, however, were never well organized, and they were no match for the might of the colonial military machine once it rolled into action. The British governor of the island, Edward Eyre, declared martial law in the district, and in the month-long suppression of the abortive uprising that followed, upwards of 400 people were killed, most without trial, hundreds were flogged, and a thousand houses were burned. Bogle, along with the other leaders of the rebellion, was quickly captured and executed.

The response to the Jamaica events in England was initially predictable: the governor was generally praised for saving the island from destruction. It seemed unlikely that much controversy would ensue; this was just another in a long line of colonial rebellions put down with brutal force and then conveniently forgotten—except by its victims. But as more details began to emerge, opposition from liberals in England began to grow against Eyre's handling of the crisis, and by the end of 1865 the "Governor Eyre Case" had become the hottest topic of national debate.

A coalition of antislavery activists, radical politicians, and lawyers formed the Jamaica Committee, chaired by John Stuart Mill; public pressure led to the government sending a Royal Commission of inquiry to Jamaica to gather evidence on the uprising and its suppression. It delivered its report in April 1866, and while it broadly exonerated Eyre, it concluded that British and Jamaican troops had often used excessive force. The controversy raged throughout 1866, coinciding with the intense debates over parliamentary reform and the enfrancisement of the working classes in England—indeed, this was a connection that was frequently made at the time.

I argue in this essay that the relationship between national and imperial histories needs to be rethought. With "Britain"—or, still worse, "England"—no longer the unexamined organizing principle of cultural and historical studies, events in "the colonies" will have a relevance beyond their traditional marginal locations. Affairs in the colonies will no longer be relegated to the discrete field of "imperial history" and to those rare moments in British national history when they happen to illuminate English questions. Thus, reversing the usual polarity of such comparisons, I suggest below that debate over the Second Reform Bill was so intense because it represented the entrance, however surreptitiously, of a new discourse of racial formation into the social fabric of England.

The 1860s were a time when constructions of race and class were undergoing substantial changes. A new scientific interest in race and descent combined with renewed political emphasis on equality of birth and the "rights of man" to produce a highly contradictory, unstable situation. An older discourse of "blood" and "breeding," associated with the "feudal and aristocratical constitution of society," as Arnold put it, was being replaced by a newer rhetoric of "citizenship" and "rights," a rhetoric which, nevertheless, incorporated elements of the older discourse in its emphasis on the "natural" disposition of particular groups, especially those which could be marked as racially other. Thus, by a circuitous route, "blood" made its reappearance in the new science of anthropology at precisely the moment it appeared to have lost its explanatory value in descriptions of English society: to quote Arnold again, "science has now made visible to everybody the great and pregnant elements of difference which lie in race".

The career of George Eliot exemplifies this transition, I might suggest, as she moved from the early novels' engagement with the domestic inheritance plot to the emphasis in her last novel, *Daniel Deronda,* on international and racial questions in which, paradoxically, individual destiny is more a question of blood and breeding than it ever was in *Silas Marner*. In the penultimate section of this essay I analyse her 1866 novel, *Felix Holt*, as enacting this transition from one literary and intellectual mode to the other.

This is also the movement that Etienne Balibar charts so accurately in an essay on the complex relationship between race and class in modern Europe:

The "bourgeois revolutions"... had raised the question of the political rights of the masses in an irreversible manner.... The idea of a *difference in nature* between individuals had become juridically and morally contradictory, if not inconceivable. It was, however, politically indispensable, so long as the "dangerous classes"... had to be excluded by force and by legal means from political "competence" and confined to the margins of the polity—as long, that is, as it was important to *deny them citizenship* by showing... that they constitutionally "lacked" the qualities of fully fledged or normal humanity. Two anthropologies clashed here: that of equality of birth and that of a hereditary inequality which made it possible to re-naturalize social antagonisms. ("Class Racism" 209-10, emphasis in the original)

A quick glance at the pages of the *Anthropological Review* (founded 1863) will confirm that forcefully racist arguments were being made that people of African descent in particular "lacked the qualities of fully fledged or normal humanity." One effect of these arguments was to produce a racialized white Englishness, which allowed the white working class to be enfranchised at the expense of the black working class: citizenship and its concomitant rights were defined by racial (as well as national and class) demarcation. This is what Balibar means when he goes on to say that "the introduction of universal suffrage is moving the boundary line between 'citizens' and 'subjects' to the frontiers of nationality".

The Morant Bay rebellion, occurring at a moment of intense debate over the status and characteristics of "the negro," ensured the subjection of the Afro-Jamaican labouring classes; I hope to show that this is intimately connected to the granting of citizenship to English working-class men.

MORANT BAY AND THE EMERGENCE OF "HEREDITARIAN RACIALISM"

The revolt of October 1865 in and around the town of Morant Bay, on the southeastern coast of Jamaica, has garnered increasing attention from cultural critics and historians. Belatedly, critics have begun to move away from earlier polemics that hinged on the actions and character of the governor, Edward Eyre, in the suppression of the revolt. Philip Curtin, Bernard Semmel, and, more recently, Catherine Hall and Gad Heuman have laid the groundwork for a more careful analysis of the events in Jamaica and their aftermath that situates them in the context of contemporary debates over race, slavery, labour, and empire—debates in which Eyre himself appears more as symptom than as cause.

Such analyses, while avoiding the histrionics of earlier readings of "the Governor Eyre controversy," tend to agree that Morant Bay was an extremely significant event in British imperial history, despite being relatively minor in terms of numbers of casualties. Although the Sepoy Rebellion (the so-called Indian Mutiny) of 1857 and the New Zealand Land Wars (once called the Maori Wars) of the mid-1860s were far bloodier, it was Morant Bay that crystallized debate in Britain about the imperial mission itself.

Thus postcolonial scholars are coming to accept that Morant Bay was as important as people believed it to be at the time. The journalist and historian Justin McCarthy remembered in the 1870s that back in 1866, "for some weeks there was hardly anything talked of, we might almost say hardly anything thought of, in England, but the story of the rebellion that had taken place in the island of Jamaica, and the manner in which it had been suppressed and punished" (qtd. in Semmel 13).

This was not mere journalistic hyperbole: it is indeed remarkable the extent to which a local rebellion in a British colony that had long ceased to be of the highest economic significance galvanized most of the major public figures of the day to take a stand on one side or the other. Defending the governor's methods on the executive committee of the Eyre

Testimonial and Defence Fund were Ruskin and Carlyle, with Dickens offering vocal but more passive support.

On the other side, the chairman of the Jamaica Committee, set up to condemn the slaughter by British and Jamaican troops that followed the initial rebellion, was John Stuart Mill, who spent much of the next two years trying unsuccessfully to bring Eyre to trial on murder charges for the execution under martial law of the Jamaican politician George William Gordon. Supporting Mill were Huxley, Darwin, and Goldwin Smith, among others.

The events in Jamaica generated such an intense response, I would suggest, because they connected a longstanding concern in English middle-class society over the consequences of the abolition of slavery with newer debates around working-class enfranchisement and citizenship. Of course, these issues had never been entirely separable, as the ubiquity of the rhetoric of slavery and freedom in Chartist texts of the 1840s amply demonstrates. Indeed, the period of agitation leading up to the first Reform Bill of 1832 exactly coincided with the movement towards the abolition of slavery in all British territories (which itself followed a major slave revolt in the west of Jamaica).

This connection was sharpened by English responses to the U.S. Civil War, which was all too easily coded as a struggle between a modern, industrialized North and an antiquated, paternalistic South, in which the abolition of chattel slavery came to represent the triumph of all the forces of Progress, that imaginary Victorian behemoth. But beyond this historical link between abolition and liberal progress, what was new in the conjuncture of the mid-1860s was a widespread interest in questions of race, heredity, and breeding, which were then, after the publication of Darwin's *On the Origin of Species* in 1859, being transformed into *scientific* questions.

However, this was a moment of transition, and these scientific concerns continued to be marked by their former prominence in the realm of the literary romance genre, their realization in the tropes of inheritance, bloodlines, and genealogy. And it could even be argued that these new theories were doubly literary, because, as Gillian Beer argues in her magisterial analysis of the Darwinian revolution:

Most major scientific theories rebuff common sense. They call on evidence beyond the reach of our senses or overturn the observable world. They disturb assumed relationships and shift what has been substantial into metaphor.... When it is first advanced, theory is at its most fictive. The awkwardness of fit between the natural world as it is currently perceived and as it is hypothetically imagined holds the theory itself for a time within a provisional scope akin to that of fiction. (*Darwin's Plots* 3).

It is this instability in meaning that allows us to locate and analyse these discourses of descent—of species, races, nations, families, individuals—in a whole range of mid-Victorian texts, from novels and cultural criticism to popular journalism and scientific articles. Such an analysis will serve as a kind of cross-section of a crucial moment in modern British history.

Morant Bay occurred at a moment when what we might call the "romantic" and the "scientific" understandings, to risk a convenient shorthand, of blood, race, and inheritance still overlapped. And at their point of intersection in the mid-1860s stood the figure of "the negro." Africans—especially those Africans who laboured under the legacies of chattel slavery—occupied a particular place in the emergence at this moment of what George Stocking has aptly called "hereditarian racialism" (*Victorian Anthropology* 142): that is, the notion that difference is hereditary (and therefore more or less fixed) and that the name for that difference is "race."

In 1863, a group of scientists led by James Hunt founded the Anthropological Society of London, bringing into the open a split within the older Ethnological Society of London, a division explicitly based on the status of "the negro," in particular, and on the importance of "race" in general. Hunt's inaugural address to the new body was at pains to stress the scientificity of the new discipline of anthropology, its adherence to a Gradgrindian positivism that sought only the facts and resisted the charms of non-scientific prejudices.

Hunt's speech staked a claim for a huge field of inquiry: "Anthropology is... the science of the whole nature of Man," he declared ("Introductory Address" 2). But within this field, the position of "the negro" is closed off before the inquiry has even begun:

> Whatever may be the conclusion to which our scientific inquiries may lead us, we should always remember, that by whatever means the Negro, for instance, acquired his present physical, mental, and moral character, whether he has risen from an ape or descended from a perfect man, we still know that the Races of Europe have now much in their mental and moral nature which the races of Africa have not got.

As Hunt continued his address, he made it clear that when it came to "negroes" his fellow scientists were at liberty to disregard the conclusions to which their scientific inquiries might lead them—in particular, he wanted to avoid the "vulgar error that the Negro only differs from the European in the colour of his skin and peculiar hair". Quickly, the disingenuousness of that "for instance"—as in "the Negro, for instance"—becomes clear. The "negro" (and, as we shall see, the Jamaican "negro" in particular) was not merely one example among many in this new science; "he" became the very foundation of the science itself, in his exclusion from the project of civilization.

The political goals of the Anthropological Society were thus explicit from the start: the society claimed the mantle of science in an overt rejection of an older discipline linked to the antislavery movement. The Ethnological Society from which Hunt and his followers felt compelled to distance themselves had been founded back in the 1840s as an offshoot of the Aborigines Protection Society, one of the abolitionist and philanthropic organizations that formed the backbone of middle-class dissenting culture from the late eighteenth century onwards.

The motto of the APS was "*ab uno sanguine* " (of one blood), a reference to the biblical emphasis on the essential unity of humankind. There is obviously much common ground between this sentiment and the better known slogan of the abolitionist movement in Britain: "Am I not a man and a brother?" (inscribed on images of an African man kneeling in chains). But by the time of Morant Bay in the mid-1860s a new idea of race had arrived to disrupt the Victorian antislavery consensus; the founding of the Anthropological Society was one example of this cultural shift.

Homilies on the oneness of the human race were out of fashion. *The Morning Herald*, finding the time for analysis of the events in Jamaica as early as November 1865, discovered that a great change had taken place in English attitudes, because "the world-renowned question, once thought so convincing, of 'Am I not a man and brother?' would nowadays be answered with some hesitation by many—with a flat negative to its latter half by those who regard the blacks as an inferior race" (qtd. in Lorimer 198-9).

Delivering his annual presidential address to the Anthropological Society of London shortly after the outbreak at Morant Bay, James Hunt declared that:

> We anthropologists have looked on, with intense admiration, at the conduct of Governor Eyre.... The merest novice in the study of race-characteristics ought to know that we English can only successfully rule either Jamaica, New Zealand, the Cape, China, or India, by such men as Governor Eyre.
>
> Such revolutions will occur wherever the Negro is placed in unnatural relations with Europeans. Statesmen have yet to be taught the true practical value of race-distinctions, and the absolute impossibility of applying the civilisation and laws of one race to another race of man essentially distinct. Statesmen may ignore the existence of race-antagonism; but it exists nevertheless. ("Presidential Address" lxxviii)

This period witnessed the re-emergence of the long discredited theory of polygenism, which held that the various races of humankind had separate origins, and had developed as separate species which, all evidence to the contrary notwithstanding, were not fertile with one another. The ASL expended a great deal of intellectual energy on proving that races—especially the black and white races—were "essentially distinct." The irony, however, was that the hereditarian racialism peddled by the likes of Hunt relied heavily on the romantic concept of blood so central to the abolitionist movement they despised, and to the ethnologists they had split from.

A cartoon from *Punch*, contemporary with the Morant Bay controversy, conflating race, class, affiliation and national duty.

So analysis of the Jamaica events often had more in common with the inheritance plot of the romance novel than with the science of anthropology. *The Times* declared on November 18, 1865 that "though a fleabite compared with the Indian mutiny, it [Morant Bay] touches our pride more and is more in the nature of a disappointment.... Jamaica is our pet institution, and its inhabitants are our spoilt children" (qtd. in Bolt 77). A fortnight earlier, on November 4, 1865, as the first sketchy reports of the events in Jamaica were arriving in Britain, *The Times* recoiled at the ingratitude of the "negro":

> He, who has come in as the favoured heir of a civilization in which he had no previous share—he, petted by philanthropists and statesmen and preachers into the precocious enjoyment of rights and immunities which other races have been too glad to acquire by centuries of struggles, of repulses, and of endurance—he, dandled into legislative and official grandeur by the commiseration of England,—that he should have chosen... to revolt... this is a thing so incredible that we will not venture to believe it now. (qtd. in Bolt 87)

A great deal is condensed in this quotation. Since Carlyle's now notorious "Occasional Discourse on the Nigger Question" (1849) had popularized the figure of "Quashee" eating pumpkins and refusing to work, the myth of the lazy freedman had rapidly gained ground in Britain, carrying with it the literally incredible notion that Africans in the Caribbean had been "favoured" by emancipation. Included in this potent myth was the false perception that Africans had been given the vote in large numbers in those Caribbean islands, such as Jamaica, where some form of representative government was in operation ("dandled into legislative and official grandeur").

This motif of favouritism also refers to the idea that British abolitionism and philanthropy had concerned themselves with the poor and dispossessed overseas while ignoring British poverty "at home" (the ridiculous figure of Mrs. Jellyby in Dickens' *Bleak House* being the perfect example of this). Here the whole question of Caribbean wage labour in the post-emancipation period is displaced onto the discourse of family inheritance, with Afro-Jamaicans as the "favoured heirs" of British middle-class culture who fail to recognize their privilege.

Their "precocious" access to the "rights and immunities" of civilization is explicitly contrasted with the hard labour ("struggles... repulses... endurance") of other, white races. Here the language of filiation and inheritance sits uneasily with the language of citizenship and rights; the romance novel vies with the science of political economy.

Thus we can begin to see how complicated is the relationship between the discourses of racial difference and working-class enfranchisement. The debate over the decline of the Jamaican economy, which was engaged once again after Morant Bay, concerned itself fundamentally with questions of capital and labour: after emancipation, did sugar plantations continue to fail because Afro-Jamaicans were unused to the discipline of wage labour, or because the planters failed to pay wages regularly and failed to invest capital in modernizing agricultural and industrial practices?

When the black population withdrew its labour from the estates, were they working against their own economic interests or were they establishing themselves as an independent peasantry by saving money to buy small parcels of land and growing their own crops to sell in the Jamaican internal market?

However, these economic questions were constantly being supplemented by questions of race—did the Afro-Jamaican "character" disprove the fundamental tenet of political economy, that men would work to further their economic self-interest? And the emergence of the dogmatic physical anthropology of writers like James Hunt meant that this "character" could now be scientifically explained as a question of unmodifiable racial inheritance—Stocking's "hereditarian racialism." Such theories left "the negro" doomed by bloodlines to remain at the bottom of a static taxonomy of racial "types."

It is important to recognize that such a taxonomy implies the racialization of the white English also, and that the intersection of Reform and Jamaica only makes sense when viewed in this light. Edward Beesly, a prominent figure both on the Jamaica Committee and in the labour movement (and a close associate of Marx's in the First International), wrote to the labour newspaper *The Bee-Hive* in November 1865 the following response to the uprising in Morant Bay:

I protest I am no negro-worshipper. I don't consider a black man a beautiful object, and I daresay he sings psalms more than is good for him. Some negroes may be men of ability and elevated character, but there can be no doubt that they belong to a lower type of the human race than we do, and I should not really like to live in a country where they formed a considerable part of the population. But there is no reason why the negro should work cheaper for us because he is ugly. If the white labourer has a right to put a price on his labour, so has the black labourer. (qtd. in Lorimer 191)

The identity of the white and black labourers—the fact that capital treats them both as labour power from which value can be extracted—is riven by the assumption that black labourers "work for us," where "we" includes the white labourers whom Beesly claimed to represent. Thus Beesly can consider himself fortunate that he lives in a country where white labourers form a considerable part of the population. Here we might recall Etienne Balibar's contention that the extension of the franchise was "moving the boundary line between 'citizens' and 'subjects' to the frontiers of nationality" ("Class Racism" 210); the subjection of the Jamaican workers, who are of a lower racial "type," ensures the fantasmatic stability of the frontier of the country of England (from which blacks are happily absent). And inside these racial and national frontiers there opens up the possibility of citizenship for "white labourers."

GENEALOGY, ANTHROPOLOGY, AND HYBRIDITY

Ten years after Edward Beesly's comments in *The Bee-Hive*, George Eliot published *Daniel Deronda*, in which the following passage occurs, with its odd echoes of Beesly's letter:

The talk turned on the rinderpest and Jamaica.... Grandcourt held that the Jamaican negro was a beastly sort of baptist Caliban; Deronda said he had always felt a little with Caliban, who naturally had his own point of view and could sing a good song; Mrs Davilow observed that her father had an estate in Barbadoes, but that she herself had never been in the West Indies; Mrs Torrington was sure she could never sleep in her bed if she lived among blacks; her husband corrected her by saying that the blacks would be manageable enough if it were not for the half-breeds; and Deronda remarked that the whites had to thank themselves for the half-breeds.

This passage provides striking evidence of the prominence of the debate over Morant Bay at the time: ten years after the controversy had died down, Eliot could be reasonably sure that a brief allusion to Jamaica would allow her readers to date the conversation at Grandcourt's estate as late 1865 or early 1866, the last time that Jamaica had taken centre stage in British culture. Many of the issues addressed in this essay are contained within this intellectually allusive piece of narrative.

It is especially important here to trace the discourse of the inheritance of the "estate" in the debates over Jamaica, since this connects with my earlier claim that this older language of a caste privileged by blood returns in descriptions of racial formation in the 1860s. I think this language can be glimpsed in Beesly's patrician assumption that Afro-Jamaicans should be working "for us." And in Eliot's passing reference to Morant Bay in *Daniel Deronda* we can clearly see how the polite chatter at Grandcourt's estate connects plantation life in the West Indies with the world of the English aristocracy (and lesser gentry), in which the question of breeding and pedigree intersects with the question of miscegenation ("the whites had to thank themselves for the half-breeds").

This George Eliot passage bears striking witness to the

mid-Victorian fascination with hybridity, in all its forms. In his book *Colonial Desire*, Robert Young has assembled a mass of cultural and historical evidence as proof that across a wide range of discourses, from the biological sciences to Victorian poetry, the spectre of the "hybrid" haunted the mid-nineteenth-century imagination in Britain. In particular, the new scientific racism dwelt at length on the troubling figure of the "mulatto." Paul Broca's influential work on human hybridity laboured mightily to show that the offspring of unions between Europeans and Africans were infertile with each other, although they were said to be fertile with either "parent race" (Broca 28-39).

This was a variant on the popular theory that hybrid human forms "reverted" to pure races after two or three generations, a theory invoked in an attempt to prove the permanence of racial "types," or, in extreme versions of this argument, to prove that different human "races" were in fact different species (the theory of polygenism). James Hunt, who modelled the Anthropological Society of London on Broca's Société anthropologique de Paris, argued torturously that it was not yet proven that "the offspring of all the mixtures of the so-called races of man are prolific.... At present it is only proved that the descendants of some of the different races of man are temporarily prolific; but there is the best evidence to believe that the offspring of the Negro and the European are not indefinitely prolific" (*Negro's Place* 24-5).

For Hunt, however, this desire to wish away the offspring of mixed race unions clashed with his belief in the improving powers of European blood. He explained the intelligence of Africans in the United States (which he "fully admit[ted]") as "owing to the mixture of European and Negro blood" rather than being explicable by environmental factors (*Negro's Place* 33), since the theory that human racial groups developed because of the social and climatic conditions they lived in was associated with the liberal abolitionist movement he so strenuously opposed. The debate between these two positions on racial formation was engaged most frequently and most explicitly at this time in writings on the Caribbean; we can see both sides of the argument conflated in Anthony Trollope's travelogue *The West Indies and the Spanish Main* (1859), which provides further evidence of this mid-Victorian obsession with the mulatto:

My theory... is this: that Providence has sent white men and black men to these regions in order that from them may spring a race fitted by intellect for civilization; and fitted also by physical organization for tropical labour....

When civilization, commerce, and education shall have been spread; when sufficient of our blood shall have been infused into the veins of those children of the sun; then, I think, we may be ready, without stain to our patriotism, to take off our hats and bid farewell to the West Indies.

Trollope, in his outlandish celebration of the Jamaican "coloured" class, seems unable to decide between explanations based on environmental factors (civilization, commerce, education) and those based on mixing of blood. He is unsure whether to adopt an analytic framework based on the English class system, in which the "coloureds" would play the heroic role of a rising bourgeoisie, and one based on the new science of race, in which blood determines character and destiny.

Trollope's position may have appeared idiosyncratic, but in fact it was essentially the same as the Jamaica policy followed by the Colonial Office after emancipation was completed in 1838, although the ultimate goal of the British government was undoubtedly not Jamaican decolonization, as Trollope here suggests. Tired of the West India lobby's power in Parliament, and of the constant clashes between the Jamaican planters (who dominated the local House of Assembly) and the governor about who should have day-to-day control over the island's affairs, the Colonial Office tried to promote the interests of the island's merchant and professional class, the majority of whom were "coloureds," as a counterweight to the anachronistic power of the white planters.

This involved a delicate balancing act, since extending the franchise, for instance, to include more "coloureds" also risked empowering those elements in Jamaican society more sympathetic to the interests of the black peasantry. Thus there developed the anomalous situation that while the property qualifications for voting rights were gradually reduced (although the percentage of the population eligible to vote in Assembly elections remained minuscule at the time of Morant Bay), the restrictions on who could stand as candidates remained as onerous as ever. The number of African and multiracial Jamaicans holding Assembly seats never rose above fifteen out of 45; at the time of the 1865 rebellion, that number had been reduced still further, to twelve.

The controversy surrounding the events in Jamaica in October 1865 hinged on the execution of George William Gordon, a wealthy merchant and landowner renowned in Jamaica for his outspoken support for the black masses. Gordon was the representative in the House of Assembly of the district of St. Thomas-in-the-East where the uprising took place, an ardent and vocal opponent of the governor, Edward Eyre, and, significantly enough, a "coloured." After the governor had imposed martial law in the east of the island on hearing of the uprising, he had Gordon arrested in Kingston (where martial law was not in place) and transported by boat to Morant Bay where he stood trial before a court martial, with the flimsiest of evidence against him, was sentenced to hang, and then duly executed on Eyre's personal orders.

It was Eyre's scant regard for legal niceties, the perception that he had taken advantage of a chaotic situation to rid himself of a troublesome adversary, that outraged liberals and radicals in England and Jamaica. Thus the debate tended to focus on the character, and especially the family history, of George William Gordon, son of a planter father and a slave mother, who had been cast out of his father's house, had pulled himself up by his bootstraps and made his fortune at an early age, and then rescued his father from ruin when his sugar estate fell into bankruptcy. The uprising, about which Gordon apparently knew nothing in advance, was characterized crudely as a kind of personal feud between the governor and the radical politician.

The real story of the rebellion remained all but untold:

the severe drought that had brought St. Thomas-in-the-East to the brink of famine; local dissatisfaction with the magistrates, who all represented planter interests, and punished petty crimes like crop theft severely (crimes that had increased as poverty grew); the desire of poor smallholders to maintain their tenuous hold on land to which they often held no legal title, versus wealthy landowners' attempts to extract rent from them and evict them if rent was not forthcoming.

All of this was lost in the polemics over Gordon's execution. His final letter to his wife (a highly respectable white woman) was a major propaganda coup for Eyre's critics in England; in it he declared his allegiance to the Queen, demonstrated Christian forgiveness for his persecutors, and generally behaved himself like a gentleman. The Baptist minister Wriothesley Noel felt "compelled to conclude that the hatred which hunted him to death was like that which crucified the Lord of glory as a blasphemer and a traitor". In only marginally more prosaic terms, Noel quotes Gordon's mother-in-law: "The late Mr. Gordon was bold as a lion in the cause of truth, but in domestic life, few, if any, could surpass him in urbanity of manner and kindness of disposition".

Rev. David King cites a fellow Presbyterian minister, Rev. H. Renton, as saying, "I never knew a man who seemed to me actuated by more honourable and unselfish and purer motives. He had an enthusiastic admiration of the British Constitution, and an exalted estimate of the dignity, rights, and privileges of British citizenship" (qtd. in King 8). Men such as these had no doubt, as an anonymous member of the Jamaican Assembly put it in a letter to the *Daily News* on February 5, 1866, that "Jamaica had a worthy and faithful son in him" (qtd. in Noel 6).

The language of filiation and inheritance seemed inescapable in the furor over Gordon's death. In particular, opinion was sharply divided over Gordon's relationship with his father. On one hand, there were accounts of Gordon's filial devotion, despite his father's alleged hostility to his non-white children (which some claimed included banishment from his house). David King asserted that: "Through the reverses of the colony the father, from being very rich, came to lose all; and the coloured son bought his estate: not, however, to deprive him of it, but to leave him in occupancy, surrounded by the comforts he had been accustomed to enjoy. He always spoke to me with deferential regard for his father" (qtd. in Noel 3-4).

On the other hand, in an anonymous letter to *The Times,* "one who knew him for 21 years" claimed that "Mr. G.W. Gordon was a singular compound of opposites, a great pretender in religion, but one who altogether ignored the claims of truth and honesty. One who could expatiate eloquently on the sins of the people, and at the same time beat his own father and defraud all those who were so unfortunate as to place confidence in him" (Great Britain 245). And, as if to demonstrate that Gordon's dubious lineage had its corollary in his willingness to disinherit a child, Governor Eyre included among the 170 pages of documents vilifying Gordon that he gave to the Royal Commissioners a copy of an anonymous letter to the Jamaican *Colonial Standard,* claiming that Gordon had purchased half of "a thrown-up sugar estate," the other half of which was being held in trust "on behalf of an infant."

The letter maintained, moreover, that Gordon had proceeded to dismantle the sugar works and everything else "that was convertible into money" without even informing the trustees of his actions. The letter writer narrated this story to "expose what is really known of this said-to-be martyr." He concluded: "All feelings of delicacy towards Gordon's family must subside" (Great Britain 174).

This letter, showing by negation at least that the Gordon family romance was a story in the public domain, was published in Kingston on January 13, 1866. Three days later, on January 16, the gentlemen of the Anthropological Society of London held their fortnightly meeting (ladies were not allowed to become members of the ASL; in fact, the proposal that the Ethnological Society permit women to join had been one of the reasons for the split that had produced the ASL in 1863). There President Hunt informed the gathering that ASL stalwart William Pritchard "had been appointed special commissioner from the Anthropological Society of London, to inquire into the causes of the recent negro insurrection in Jamaica" ("Minutes" lxxxii).

Reassured that their views on the rebellion would be made known in official circles, therefore, the members sat back to listen to a scholarly paper entitled "Remarks on Genealogy in Connexion with Anthropology," by George Marshall. In his paper, later published in the *Memoirs* of the society, Marshall claimed that: "Genealogy, or the tracing of descent of individuals, and through them of nations, from some common progenitor, is a subject of vital importance to a society which includes among its various objects that of investigating the laws of man's origins and progress" (Marshall 68). It is no coincidence, I would maintain, that the public fascination with George William Gordon's "pedigree" is mirrored in this exactly contemporaneous debate on the uses of genealogy, as mid-Victorians attempted to work through the connection between the "descent of individuals" and of races and nations.

Balibar argues in his essay "The Nation-Form" that one of the striking features of a modern national culture is that, "except for a few genealogy 'fanatics' and a few who are 'nostalgic' for the days of the aristocracy, genealogy is no longer either a body of theoretical knowledge or an object of oral memory.... Today *it is the state which draws up and keeps the archive of filiations and alliances*" (101; emphasis in original). While this statement seems more persuasive in the French than the British context, as a general description of an historical shift it is unarguable. What are we to make, therefore, of Marshall's assertion that "a taste for genealogy is a passion inherent in the whole human race. In all nations, civilised and uncivilised, in all times, ancient as well as modern, we find mankind carefully preserving the names and relationship of those from whom they claim descent"?

In fact, it seems clear that Marshall's paper is an attempt to graft a discipline in decline onto the new science of anthropology—another indication that the new scientific racism buttressed itself with the narratives of a passing hereditary aristocracy (which we can properly call "nostalgic"):

It is admitted that ethnology is an important part of anthropology; and are not ethnology and genealogy essentially the same? Have not the ethnologist and the genealogist the same object in view? If they differ, is it not only in this, that the ethnologist studies man by grouping him into different large races; whilst the genealogist seeks to know him more completely by studying him in individual families? The genealogist is, in fact, the architect who builds up the structure of the science of man, stone upon stone, and story upon story. He is the author who compiles the history of man, of which the ethnologist, like a reviewer, presents to the public a general sketch of the contents.

The literary metaphors ("author," "reviewer") and the emphasis on "story" demonstrate once more the superimposition of the "romantic" and "scientific" accounts of human descent.

The responses to Marshall's paper—as recorded in the minutes of the ASL—make fascinating reading. "Dr. Beigel observed that genealogy... was in reality anthropology. What had hitherto been considered genealogy was nothing more than the determination of what man was the ancestor of another; what relation, in short, Tom was to Harry. But when they proceeded to consider what the physical condition of Tom was, that subject of inquiry became anthropology" ("Minutes" lxxvi). Rev. Dunbar Heath disagreed: "In considering the question, they should view the influence of lineal descent, as well as other influences distinct from it.... The external life of the mother, independent of the father, had no doubt great influence, but was there not something more than that? Was there not something in the race?" (lxxxvi-lxxxvii).

The role of the mother, so rarely even acknowledged in these discussions, is something I will return to in my analysis of *Felix Holt*; here it serves momentarily to break apart the constellation of individual and "racial" descent, the bizarre assumption that heredity is a question of paternity only. But other participants in the meeting failed to take up Heath's point, and continued to conflate the history of noble families with the make-up of human groups or "races." Augustus

Goldsmid thought genealogy could usefully "show what influences that affect man's nature may be said to depend on external circumstances, and what are innate properties" (lxxxviii). The cases that he suggested might benefit from this genealogical analysis were, not surprisingly, those of noble families:

> One fact deserving of notice... he would mention, the thickness of the lip of the members of the House of Hapsburg... [which] was observable in almost every branch of the family. Another instance was that of a gentleman belonging to a great aristocratic family, who had one white lock of hair, though his hair was generally dark, which peculiarity had been transmitted to him from a distant ancestor. ("Minutes" lxxxviii)

Goldsmid's suggestions were immediately taken up by William Pritchard (who had just been appointed to take charge of the ASL's special mission to examine the causes of the Morant Bay rebellion, of course), who executed an apparently seamless transition from great aristocratic families to "natives":

> Mr. Pritchard stated that among the natives of the Pacific he had met with individuals who had a white lock amongst the surrounding dark hair, which was said to be hereditary. With respect to the question of consanguinity, he stated that there are many of the small or *atoll* islands in the Pacific where the natives trace back their origin through three or four hundred years to the few persons who, drifting from their homes, originally landed there. (lxxxviii)

Despite Dunbar Heath's note of caution, most of those present found no difficulty in marrying their brand of physical anthropology (based largely on questions of blood and breeding) to the protocols of genealogical research. The meeting then adjourned, with President Hunt calling the members' attention to a special meeting of the ASL, "at which Captain Bedford Pim would read a paper on the causes of the Negro insurrection in Jamaica" ("Minutes" lxxxix). Demand for tickets had been so great that a larger room would have to be obtained for the meeting, Hunt proudly declared.

This intersection of genealogy, anthropology, and responses to the Morant Bay rebellion, I am suggesting, rests on more than a temporal coincidence. The flood of pamphlets, letters, and speeches about Jamaica in late 1865 and throughout 1866 occurred in the context of existing debates about the relation between the descent of individuals and races/nations. As William Pritchard suggested, the "question of consanguinity" became critical at this moment, where inheritance through blood was perceived to explain human culture in all its variety.

Thus, at the moment when the Reform movement and the opposition to Governor Eyre were giving public weight to the figure of the citizen-subject and the rights of man, others were falling back on the premodern discourse of bloodlines and inheritance, which, after Darwin, bore the modern stamp of scientific method and enabled the citizen and the subject to be prised apart on the basis of racial difference. I want to turn now to an examination of George Eliot's novel *Felix Holt,* a text in which this constellation of genealogy, inheritance, political rights, and race is everywhere strikingly apparent without ever being resolved into the simple binary oppositions that marked the polemics of the pamphleteers and anthropologists with whom she shared the public sphere.

READING FELIX HOLT AFTER MORANT BAY

George Eliot's novel *Felix Holt, the Radical* was first published in May 1866, at the height of the controversy over the suppression of the Morant Bay rebellion. By turning to *Felix Holt,* we can shed light on some of these entangled problems of race, genealogy, and descent. We can also show that this complex tale of English Reform intersects in more than fleeting ways with the questions raised by the events in Jamaica, despite the fact that Eliot never refers to the Caribbean in the novel.

Eliot's engagement with the debate over the extension of the franchise turns, I argue, on the racially hybrid figure of Harry Transome, who inherits the country estate in the novel but cannot be allowed to inherit that larger and more precious estate, England. Thus this essay will return to the relationship between "slaves" and the "rank and file" with which it began.

Critics, if they have paid attention to *Felix Holt* at all, have tended to see it as a flawed, transitional novel of Eliot's, the subsidiary term in comparisons to the better novels which come before and after it. Thus the discovery that Esther is the true heir to the Transome estate, despite her humble station as Rev. Lyon's adopted child, is a recapitulation of Eppie's story in *Silas Marner*. Eliot's attempt to capture the web of relations in the provincial town of Treby Magna in the period of the First Reform Bill is seen as a precursor to the magnificence of *Middlemarch*. Raymond Williams expresses well the dissatisfaction most modern critics have felt in reading *Felix Holt*.

He observes that the novel "is made to turn on the inheritance of an estate, and this is a crucial surrender to that typical interest which preoccupied the nineteenth-century middle-class imagination". But this "surrender" is not the same as the easy, casual way that Trollope, for instance, handles the traditional settlements of the romance genre; rather it deforms the structure of the novel: "George Eliot, by contrast [with Trollope], questioning in a profoundly moral way the real and assumed relations between property and human quality, accepts the emphasis of inheritance as the central action, and then has to make it external, contradictory, and finally irrelevant".

The basic point here is that it is the very convolutedness of the inheritance plot that reveals its failure, in the 1860s, as symbol of the transmission of the national heritage. In Disraeli's *Sybil, or the Two Nations,* to which *Felix Holt* is often compared, the hidden aristocratic lineage of Sybil must lead to the restitution of the estate to her: blood eventually "tells." In Eliot's novel, by contrast, the relationship between property and virtue has been irrevocably severed, and the whole edifice of patrilineal inheritance appears to be crumbling.

Not only does Esther ultimately reject her inheritance of the Transome estate, preferring the virtuous existence of an artisan's wife, but she is not even "really" a Transome, her legal claim stemming from her descent from the Bycliffe family, who have no "natural" claim to inherit the Transome estate. As Catherine Gallagher writes, in the best modern reading of the novel:

Indeed, Frederic Harrison, who advised Eliot on the legal intricacies of the plot, implored her to make Esther a real Transome so that her claim would carry the weight of nature as well as that of legality, but Eliot insisted on grounding Esther's claim also in legal conventions. Thus, although *Felix Holt* resembles *Sybil* in that a young woman is discovered, in the aftermath of a popular uprising, to be the heir to an estate, it reverses *Sybil* by making that young woman no more the natural heir to the estate than is the family she has the power to dispossess.

Disraeli needed to bind the naturally virtuous status of Sybil and her Chartist father to the institutional structures of the hereditary aristocracy; twenty years later, by contrast, George Eliot felt no compunction in poking fun at the claims of good breeding. The last surviving real Transome, poor, mad Tommy Trounsem, claims that "'I allays felt it inside me as I was somebody, and I could see other chaps thought it on me too'". However, this is patently false in the logic of the novel: although a certain pathos clings to Tommy, his fundamental role is to be trampled to death in the election-day riot so that Esther's non-natural right to the estate can be established.

Thus Eliot disregarded the advice of Frederic Harrison, a young barrister whom she met while working on the novel, and who advised her, as Gallagher notes, on the law of entail (that branch of inheritance law on which the plot of *Felix Holt* depends). The extended correspondence between the two is well known: not only does it provide rare insights into Eliot's thoughts during the composition of a novel, it also engages some key intellectual concerns of both Eliot's and Harrison's, especially the question of Comtism.

But critics have failed to notice the fact that at exactly the same time as Harrison was providing legal counsel to George Eliot, he was also serving on the executive committee of the Jamaica Committee, the body led by John Stuart Mill that protested the suppression of the Morant Bay uprising. Soon after *Felix Holt* was published, Harrison began his series of essays on martial law—a key question in the Jamaica events—later published as number 5 in the Jamaica Papers series: *Martial Law: Six Letters to the "Daily News"* (1867). So although Eliot and Harrison do not refer to the Jamaica rebellion in their letters, there is strong circumstantial evidence that the inheritance of the Transome estate in *Felix Holt* and the troubles in Jamaica must be connected.

The novel opens with Mrs Transome nervously awaiting the return from "the East" of her son Harold to take over the running of the Transome estate, now that her wild, "savage" older son Durfey has finally died and Harold is the heir apparent. (Harold has spent the last fifteen years acquiring a fortune in Smyrna, technically part of the Ottoman Empire but under de facto British control.) Mrs Transome's anxiety is magnified because Harold has only recently informed her "that he had been married, that his Greek wife was no longer living, but that he should bring home a little boy, the finest and most desirable of heirs and grandsons"; his mother's response to Harold's revelation of this long-kept secret was to tear up the letter "in a rage".

Mrs Transcme's anger at this suppression of the place of women in questions of descent is in fact bitterly appropriate, since the reader eventually discovers that the arriviste lawyer Jermyn is Harold's biological father, and thus Harold's (and Harry's) descent and inheritance are entirely dependent on Mrs Transome. Thus right at the outset the novel undermines the traditional claims of patrilineal inheritance—Harold's belief that his mother was "a good elderly lady, who would necessarily be delighted with the possession on any terms of a healthy grandchild". The return of the prodigal son to take over the estate and save the nation is made possible by the relegation of Mrs Transome, who has been managing the estate up to this point, to the role of domestic ornament. Harold says to his mother, "'Ah, you've had to worry yourself about things that don't properly belong to a woman.... We'll set that right. You shall have nothing to do now but to be grandmamma on satin cushions'". Behind this suppression is the silent (and convenient) death of Harold's Oriental wife.

Harold returns from the Orient darker, wealthier, with a taste for spicy food, and with new ideas about politics and the role of women. These threads are all entangled in Eliot's Orientalism: Harold's decision to become a Radical shocks his Tory mother "as if her son had said that he had been converted to Mahometanism at Smyrna, and had four wives, instead of one son". Similarly, Harold's corruptibility, the fact that his Radicalism (unlike Felix Holt's) is veneer rather than a deeply held commitment, is signalled by his seduction by the delights of Oriental women: "Western women were not to his taste.... Harold preferred a slow-witted, large-eyed woman, silent and affectionate, with a load of black hair, weighing more heavily than her brains.

He had seen no such women in England, except one whom he had brought with him from the East". The narrator makes this observation at the moment when the possibility arises of Harold and Esther getting married, thus resolving the problem of the inheritance plot with a union straight out of the romance genre. But Eliot refuses the easy way out: Harold's Orientalism is utterly incompatible with Esther's independence of spirit. She is tempted, "but it was a fact that Harold's previous married life had entered strongly into her impressions about him. The presence of Harry made it inevitable". Harold tries to woo her: "'You don't suppose, I hope, that any other woman has ever held the place that you could hold in my life?'"; as proof of this sentiment he delivers the revelation that opens up *Felix Holt* to the debates over Morant Bay: "'Harry's mother had been a slave—was bought, in fact'".

The careful use of the pluperfect tense—"had been"—and the passive voice—"was bought"—leaves nicely ambiguous Harold's proprietary relationship to his wife. On the one hand, Harold is aligned squarely with the slaveholding planters of the Caribbean who kept, and indeed owned, black mistresses but eventually married respectable white women of their own class. On the other hand, the syntax allows the reader to interpret Harold's relationship with his wife as an act of abolitionist philanthropy, a white man saving a native woman from Oriental despotism.

Although slavery is displaced from the Caribbean to Turkey in Eliot's novel, the "presence of Harry" in the novel comes from the same source as the controversy over George William Gordon and the Jamaica uprising. In February 1866, while George Eliot was finishing *Felix Holt* and England was convulsed by the Governor Eyre case, Dr. Hyde Clarke delivered a paper at the Anthropological Society of London entitled "On Anthropological Investigations in Smyrna," where he was the ASL's local secretary and where Harold Transome made his fortune and met his wife:

Many examples of mixed races are found here, particularly of Negro mulattoes and Levantines, or the mixture of Europeans with the natives of the country. The latter afford the most beautiful women in the first, and occasionally in the second, generation; but there is undoubted evidence that neither of the mixed races is permanent.... It is curious that, though the Levantine is a cross-breed chiefly among the Indo-Europeans, the third and fourth generations produce many of the phenomena of Negro cross-breeds, as seen in the West Indies and South America.

Unwittingly, no doubt, George Eliot finds herself sharing the same field as the new physical anthropologists, with their heavy-handed Orientalism and their fascination with the figure of "the negro." In other words, the trouble with Harry is that he is a mulatto. Eliot gives very little narrative time to the ultimate heir of the Transome estate, but in Harry's irregular appearances he is consistently portrayed as violent and wild. We see him first through the eyes of the Debarrys (sole representatives of the old aristocracy in *Felix Holt*): Lady Debarry initially mistakes him for "'a charming little fellow...[a] round-cheeked cherub'".

But she is soon disabused, as Harry sinks his teeth into Mrs Transome's arm: "'What a little savage!'", Lady Debarry quickly corrects herself; and then, when she has had time to reflect a little: "'That savage boy—he doesn't look like a lady's child'". Lady Debarry is right the second time around. It may no longer be possible, in the age of Reform and industrialization, to be sure what a lady's child looks like; we cannot rely on genealogy to tell the truth about good breeding any more. But there can be no doubt, in the age of anthropology, as to the characteristics of the savage.

The problem this poses for the novel, however, is insuperable. Although Harry's filiation is almost the only line of descent in the book that is not in doubt, there is such uneasiness about Harry that he and his father almost never appear together. When Harold first arrives back at Transome Court and his mother asks him about his son, Harold replies casually, "'O, I left him behind in town.... My man Dominic will bring him, with the rest of the luggage'". In this narrative distancing, I think we can read the trace of George William Gordon's expulsion from his father's house.

The overelaborate inheritance plot that takes up so much of *Felix Holt* is ultimately resolved by the estate being passed on to Harry, but the novel makes so little of this denouement that the reader is forced to conclude that this half of the book's plot is finally irrelevant, as Raymond Williams put it. Once we recognize that Harry is the son of a slave, however, we are in a better position to read this narrative incoherence. In a climate in which *The Times* could write scathingly of Afro-Jamaicans as the "favoured heirs" of British middle-class culture, George Eliot shows the ultimate worthlessness of the country house as a symbol for the national heritage by having its heir be the son of a slave mother.

Thus *Felix Holt* ends by proving the truism delivered by the coachman in the "Author's Introduction" to the novel, that "property didn't always get into the right hands". Such a reading would seem to divide the novel in two: first, the Transome Court plot, with its roots in the traditional inheritance narrative and its branches intersecting with contemporary race theory; second, the Felix and Esther plot, which concerns itself most directly with Reform and political rights for the English working classes. But, as I have argued throughout this essay, questions of class and citizenship in the mid-1860s cannot be kept separate from questions of race and breeding.

Thus Felix applauds the Chartist speaker who gets up in

front of the crowd at Treby Magna and denounces the "slave's share" the workers have at present, calling instead for a "freeman's share" of the nation's wealth. However, for Felix Holt, and for George Eliot, rights ought not to accrue to men simply on the basis of their being born free. Felix follows the Chartist speaker up on to the podium and proceeds to lecture the assembled masses on the dangers of premature democracy, exhorting them not to mistake the benefits of the vote—which he calls, in perfect Arnoldian language, a mere "engine"—for the more lasting gifts of wisdom, education, and virtuous living.

As he comments to Esther a little while earlier, "'I want to be a demagogue of a new sort; an honest one, if possible, who will tell the people they are blind and foolish, and neither flatter them nor fatten on them'". Catherine Gallagher argues that Felix represents a vision of Matthew Arnold's "best self," the man of culture he idealizes in *Culture and Anarchy* (Gallagher 244). And this speech of Felix's sounds uncannily like the lecture Matthew Arnold delivered a year later at Oxford, entitled "Culture and Its Enemies," later to become the first chapter of *Culture and Anarchy* :

Culture... does not try to teach down to the level of inferior classes; it does not try to win them for this or that sect of its own, with ready-made judgments and watchwords. It seeks to do away with classes; to make the best that has been thought and known in the world current everywhere.... This is the social idea; and the men of culture are the true apostles of equality.

However, Felix differs from Arnold's man of culture in that he does not become the déclassé "alien" of *Culture and Anarchy*. Instead, Felix continually insists on his class identity; his virtue lies in his determination to remain an artisan: "'I mean to stick to the class I belong to'". His status as *artisan* is crucial here. The factory hands and agricultural labourers of Treby Magna represent the emergence into the public sphere of a new class, the proletariat; George Eliot's worker-hero represents an anachronistic understanding of caste that owes more to the outmoded language of blood and breeding than to the language of rights and citizenship that accompanies advanced capitalism.

So that when Felix continues his speech to Esther about wanting to be a new type of demagogue by saying "'I have my heritage—an order I belong to. I have the blood of a line of handicraftsmen in my veins'", we know that this is an anachronistic sentiment, a trace of nostalgia for a vanishing segment of the population. But I want to push this line of thinking one step further. The invocation of blood here, in the section of the novel primarily concerned with domestic Reform, is also a statement transposed from the new hereditarian discourses of race that I analyzed above.

And so we can argue that the two halves of *Felix Holt* are not as distinct as they have seemed to most critics and readers. The "blood of a line of handicraftsmen" that Felix embodies is not so different from the wild blood that determines the character of young Harry, whose inheritance of the estate is eclipsed by the birth of "a young Felix" on the last page of the novel.

The new way of talking about race in the mid-1860s allows "blood" to resurface as a meaningful concept; it even reflects back onto those class distinctions it would seem unable to explain now that "family" and "breeding" are no longer self-evidently positive. Thus the narrator comments on Esther's anticipation of the problems she will encounter in talking to Harold Transome about Felix:

She had a native capability for discerning that the sense of ranks and degrees has its repulsions corresponding to the repulsions dependent on differences of race and colour; and she remembered her own impressions too well not to foresee that it would come on Harold Transome as a shock, if he suspected that there had been any love-passages between her and this young man, who to him was of course no more than any other intelligent member of the working class.

The differences between Harold Transome, who represents the English gentry's inability to adjust to the changes associated with Reform, and Felix, the new symbol of honest, hard- working Englishness, can most easily be explained by comparison with "differences of race and colour"—and these distinctions, the narrator implies, are not open to question. This is the equivalent of Matthew Arnold's statement that "science has now made visible to everybody the great and pregnant elements of difference which lie in race", a statement, we should recall, in the service of the author's classification of the English class system into Barbarians, Philistines, and Populace.

Thus we have found, in the unlikely setting of *Felix Holt* 's study of provincial life, proof of the saturation of discourses of citizenship and Reform by questions of race, genealogy, and descent. We have traced the outlines of the debate over the Jamaica rebellion in George Eliot's novel, providing further evidence of the complex and interlocking relationship between "slaves" and "the rank and file" in the British Empire of the mid-1860s.

INHERITING THE EMPIRE

The third quarter of the nineteenth century often used to be characterized by historians as the period of "anti-imperialism," when prominent intellectual figures like John Bright and Goldwin Smith publicly called for the independence of "the Colonies," which were seen as a financial and military drain on the resources of England. This notion of anti-imperialism has more recently given way to an understanding of the continuities in British imperial policies, the fact that the empire expanded throughout the nineteenth century (in both its formal and informal incarnations), and a recognition that those who advocated the independence of the white settler colonies never even considered the possibility that British dependencies peopled predominately by non-whites ought to govern themselves.

However, without wanting to endorse the idea of mid-Victorian anti-imperialism, I would suggest that this period needs to be rethought once more in the light of the Jamaica events and the responses to them. In short, it is my argument here that when the possibility emerges of the end of British rule over the declining colony of Jamaica, the spectre of the end of imperial hegemony arises. And the response to this threat is to conceive, for the first time, of the Empire as a whole, no longer insisting on the distinctions between the Colonial Empire, the Indian Empire, Crown Colonies, and other dependencies.

It is only in the mid-1860s that Victorian writers began to talk of the British Empire in the sense that seems so familiar to us now. Richard Koebner, in his meticulous study of the changing significance of the word "imperialism," notes that during the first 30 years of Queen Victoria's reign the term "British Empire," if it was used at all, "was governed by the interpretation which related the name to the United Kingdom of the British Isles and to England in particular" (Koebner and Schmidt 45). The common phrase "Imperial Parliament" referred primarily to England's hegemony over Scotland, Wales, and, more particularly, Ireland, which after the Act of Union of 1800 sent "representatives" to sit in the House of Commons in London.

Thus, in a way which seems distinctly counterintuitive to those of us at the other end of the British Empire, "the Colonies and the Indian Empire were regarded as dependent on the British Empire rather than being parts of it" (Koebner and Schmidt 37). In 1865, Jamaica was in the anomalous position of being a colony not generally included in the phrase "the Colonies," which tended to encompass only the white settler territories (although administratively it was part of the domain of the Colonial Office). Paradoxically, therefore, the fact that Jamaica was unassimilable to the standard contemporary discourses of imperialism enabled it to become the locus of the construction of the Empire.

The Morant Bay uprising, far more than the Sepoy Rebellion of 1857 to which it was (and is) often compared, crystallized concern on questions of governance, citizenship, and rights, both "domestic" and "imperial," and in so doing inaugurated the new era of "the Empire." Perhaps we can read this awkward transition in the letter from Carlyle I alluded to in the opening paragraph of this essay. After opining that "penalty and clamour are not the thing this Governor merits from any of us, but honour and thanks, and wise *imitation* (I will farther say) should similar emergencies arise, on the great scale or on the small, in whatever we are governing!" (Workman 91-2), Carlyle goes on to pledge his active support for the campaign so that

> by wise effort and persistence, a blind and disgraceful act of public injustice may be prevented [i.e., the prosecution of Eyre brought by the Jamaica Committee]; and an egregious folly as well,—not to say, for none can say or compute, what a vital detriment throughout the British empire, in such an example set to all the colonies and governors the British Empire has.

Here, as Carlyle piles clause upon clause with his characteristic rhetorical abandon, we can detect the instability of meaning between the lower-case "empire"—which seems to approximate the more modern concept—and the capitalized "Empire"—which "has" colonies and governors that, nevertheless, do not seem to be a part of it.

The solution that Carlyle proposes to this crisis of British imperialism is a throwback to the romance inheritance plot that George Eliot struggled to leave behind in *Felix Holt*. In *Shooting Niagara: And After?* (1867), his tirade against democratic government and the "knot of rabid Nigger-Philanthropists" who made up the Jamaica Committee, Carlyle devotes several pages to the island of Dominica. ("Jamaica," he claims implausibly, "is an angry subject, and I am shy to speak of it".) He elaborates a fantasy scenario, in which

> the Queen "in Council"...[will] pick out some gallant-minded, stout, well-gifted Cadet, - younger son of a Duke, of an Earl, of a Queen herself... and say to him...., "See, I have scores on scores of 'Colonies,' all ungoverned, and nine-tenths of them full of boa-constrictors, rattlesnakes, Parliamentary Eloquences, and Emancipated Niggers ripening towards nothing but destruction: one of them *you* shall have, you as Vice-King; on rational conditions, and *ad vitam an culpam* it shall be yours (and perhaps your posterity's if worthy)."

Carlyle suggests a model of governance based on the protocols of inheritance rooted in the structural power of the hereditary aristocracy in England; I have argued in this essay that this residual conception of society fueled the emergent discourses of anthropology and racial science. However, the new concept of Empire marks the beginning of the end of the inheritance plot as a trope for what we must now call governmentality. Joseph Howe, in a little pamphlet called *The Organization of the Empire* (1866), signals the end of this older discourse of empire, one which assimilates the relationship between "mother" country and colony to a family affair. Some people, he says, argue that colonies "grow up" and should therefore receive independence:

The parental relationship is assumed to sanction this policy. Young men grow, and, when they are of age, marry and set up for themselves, and why should not colonies do the same. But the analogy is not perfect. One house would not hold all the married members of a large family, nor one estate maintain them. They scatter that they may live. They are kept in friendship by the domestic affections, and personal ties, which in respect of distant communities, do not exist, and at the death of the founder of the family there is an estate to divide.

Not so with Colonies. Their life begins at a distance from the homestead. There are few personal attachments. There is no estate to divide, and no security that when they separate they may not drift into antagonism to each other, and to the parent colony.

The old metaphors are worn out, Howe is arguing. The inheritance of an estate, be it Transome Court, an "ungoverned colony" like Jamaica, or the estate of "the Empire," can no longer signify the mode of English power after the 1860s. Instead, the practice of imperialism, in its late Victorian manifestation of a mission to educate and civilize "backward peoples," emerges, paradoxically enough, in the writings of those mid-Victorian liberals who advocated equal rights for whites and blacks and the extension of the franchise and citizenship to the working classes in England. Frederic Harrison, for instance, George Eliot's collaborator on *Felix Holt*, can be heard bringing this new Empire into being in his treatise on martial law written to protest the suppression of the Jamaica revolt:

In the name of the people, of the great family of citizens of the British empire, it again becomes vital to crush the pretensions of the executive abroad; it becomes necessary to vindicate beyond the seas the first principles of civil liberty.... This is why an association of Englishmen has undertaken to bring this cause to an issue [i.e., by prosecuting Eyre]... simply to hear from the lips of an English judge what is the right to civil justice of English citizens, what are the safeguards of life throughout the breadth of our vast empire.

The repetition of Englishness here (Englishmen, English judge, English citizens) appears to be in opposition to the principle of formal equality that Harrison celebrates. The "people," the "family of citizens"—the genealogical term persists as a link to the discourses Harrison was ostensibly refuting—for whom these "Englishmen" speak are marked as subjects as well as citizens in this unstable equation. Defended against the unlawful force of the executive power, they become subject to a new kind of discipline, one formed through education, church missions, public health policies, and the apparatus of civil law: "The precise issue we raise is this—that throughout our empire the British rule shall be the rule of law; that every British citizen, white, brown, or black in skin, shall be subject to definite, and not to indefinite powers".

In this strategy for managing what he calls "our vast unresting empire", Harrison is taking up the definition of empire of his fellow executive committee member of the Jamaica Committee, Goldwin Smith. Back in 1863, Smith had written in the foreword to a collection of his pieces from the *Daily News*, given the title *The Empire* for its book publication:

The term Empire is here taken in a wide sense, as including all that the nation holds beyond its own shores and waters by arms or in the way of dominion, as opposed to that natural influence which a great power, though confining itself to its own territories, always exercises in the world. In the case of our Empire this definition will embrace a motley mass of British Colonies, conquered Colonies of other European nations, conquered territories in India, military and maritime stations, and protectorates, including our practical protectorate of Turkey [where Harold Transome struck it rich, of course], as well as our legal protectorate of the Ioanian islands. These various dependencies stand in the most various relations to the Imperial country.

Koebner and Schmidt comment on the novelty of this definition, arguing that "by making the name of Empire the comprehensive headline of a critical survey of colonial, Indian, and certain external affairs, the author [Smith] was not so much referring to an established terminology as intending to create such usage on his own account". I would argue that the better known beginnings of the imperial federation movement in the late 1860s—for instance the founding of the Colonial Society in 1868, with its motto "United Empire"—are made possible by the efforts of liberal thinkers such as Smith and Harrison; that the call for an integrated empire begins with the invocation of formal equality before the law.

This gesture may even be explicitly anti-imperialist, as when Goldwin Smith argues for the independence of Canada, but covertly the expansion of English law around the empire works to consolidate the very inequalities that English rule works by at the same time as it establishes a formal discourse of equality, rights, and citizenship. That this new imperial apparatus of discipline and surveillance emerges in the aftermath of the controversy over Morant Bay can be seen clearly in the writing of Charles Roundell, who had acted as secretary to the Royal Commission of inquiry while it collected its thousands of pages of evidence in Jamaica in 1866.

Later that same year, he published a pamphlet of his own, *England and Her Subject Races, with Special Reference to Jamaica,* in which he extrapolated from the Jamaica situation to provide a blueprint for the organization of the Empire as a whole. The rebellion of 1865, he concluded, showed the need for "an impartial and trusted administration of justice" and a system of "regulating native settlements":

The principal agents for effecting these primary requirements will be an efficient police, the enactment of a bastardy law, a systematic registration of births and deaths, the establishment of hospitals and a well-organized system of medical supervision, the construction of roads, the instruction of the people in improved methods of agriculture, and, above all, a system of industrial, compulsory, unsectarian education.

The problem of descent, inheritance, and miscegenation will be handled by a bastardy law, the state will take over the genealogical enterprise of recording births and deaths, and the emphasis on compulsory state education is in line with the thinking of Matthew Arnold; here we can see the outlines of a theory of late Victorian high imperialism. From the minor rebellion at Morant Bay, via the agitation for parliamentary reform, there emerges this checklist for the constitution of a new (but to us familiar) figure: the citizen-subject of the British Empire.

Following the critical and popular success of *Scenes of Clerical Life* in 1858, George Eliot (pseudonym of Mary Ann, or Marian, Evans) published *Adam Bede* to further acclaim. Having gained recognition for the realistic characters and situations in the three sketches comprising *Scenes*, Eliot again sought to create complex characters who display a range of traits, neither all good nor all bad. A pastoral novel, *Adam Bede* is set at the turn of the nineteenth century and presents realistic images of daily life in a quiet rural community. However, within this apparently peaceful, simple country world, Eliot's character-narrator tells a story of unfulfilled love and selfishness resulting in tragedy and hard-won self-awareness. Through the narrator, the middle-class reading audience is encouraged to look upon the novel's lower-class characters with the same sensibility and sensitivity as they would their peers. Rather than expressing superiority or contempt for the rural people in the novel, readers are invited by the narrator to set aside class or economic biases and view the characters in *Adam Bede* in light of their humanity and goodness.

Discussing *Adam Bede* in her personal journals, Eliot cautiously confessed that the character of Adam was inspired by her own father's early life, and the character of Dinah was drawn from her Methodist Aunt Samuel. She insisted, however, that the novel was not biographical beyond those initial inspirations. These same journals, along with her published essays and reviews, have led critics to argue that *Adam Bede* reflects themes in other literary works with which she was familiar, including Milton's *Paradise Lost*, Hawthorne's *The Scarlet Letter*, and the Greek Tragedies, among others. However, according to Eliot, she did not intend *Adam Bede* as a memoir or even as historical fiction; it was her most earnest intent to write realistic fiction at a time when realism was "out of fashion." *Adam Bede*, considered by her contemporaries to display "a touch of genius," has been overshadowed in twentieth-century criticism by the more mature *Middlemarch*. Nevertheless, its reputation has remained untarnished and many scholars regard *Adam Bede* as one of the finest examples of realistic fiction of its time.

Adam Bede is set in the rural community of Loamshire, England, in the summer of 1799. Adam Bede, the eponymous main character, and his younger brother Seth are employed as carpenters. Seth is well-meaning and generous while Adam, who serves as foreman to the crew of rustics who assist him, is serious and hard-working. Outwardly, Adam is a role model for the community, but inwardly he is plagued by resentment towards his alcoholic father and annoyance with his ever-complaining mother. Seth is a devout Methodist who practices his religion over the objections of both his family and the larger community.

He is in love with Dinah Morris, a solemn Methodist preacher who, though demure and feminine, refuses to allow her religious mission to be compromised by her gender. Her quiet confidence attracts significant attention in Loamshire, and, in part, fuels Seth's affection. Meanwhile, Adam hopes one day for the financial security to be able to ask Hetty Sorrel, a distractingly beautiful and childishly self-centered young woman, to be his wife. While Dinah refuses Seth's romantic affections believing her duty is to minister to the unsaved, Hetty is deliberately distant and coquettish, while at the same time encouraging Adam's hopes for an eventual union. Although the two women are entirely different in character and morals, their lives are nevertheless entwined; both are orphaned cousins staying with their relations, the Poysners, a prominent tenant farming family.

Like the Poysners, the entire community operates under the patronage of the elderly landowner, Squire Donnithorne. His grandson Arthur, without an income of his own as long as his grandfather remains alive, looks benevolently upon Loamshire as his birthright. He imagines himself making improvements to the land and gaining the love of all his tenant farmers through his generosity and earnestness. But until he gains his inheritance, he is powerless and becomes bored and frustrated with his grandfather's mismanagement of the land. Seeking distraction, he discovers Hetty. While he is drawn to her beauty, she is equally drawn to his social position and the promise of being rescued from domestic servitude to live as the wife of a wealthy, respected man.

Hetty becomes deluded about the nature of their relationship, and Arthur is torn between his determination to live up to his social position and his desire for the young woman. At a pivotal moment, the couple is caught in an embrace by Adam who, despite his inferior social standing, challenges Arthur over the indiscretion. Adam, heartbroken, loses his faith in his long-time friend Arthur, but becomes more protective of Hetty. Shortly after Adam's discovery, Arthur ends the affair and leaves town, and Hetty turns to Adam for comfort. He takes her back, and joyously plans their life together. However, haunted by her scandalous behaviour, Hetty discovers that she is pregnant and, unable to take responsibility for her actions, runs away.

Alone, Hetty gives birth to a child, whom she abandons in the wilderness. Her crime is discovered, and she is sentenced to death for infanticide. Adam refuses to believe she could have committed such a crime, and Hetty herself refuses to confess. Arthur, who left the country immediately following the affair, has not been heard from, and Hetty is left with only the comfort of her cousin Dinah. Arthur returns with a stay of execution just in time to save Hetty from death. Through the course of his love and loss of Hetty, Adam learns sympathy and forgiveness, and thus becomes a better person than he was at the start of the novel. With this change, Adam is rewarded with marriage to Dinah, who gives up her ministry in favour of domestic life.

While *Adam Bede* centers around the title character's progress from a calloused sense of moral superiority to a state of sympathy and understanding for others, there are several other significant themes. *Adam Bede* is widely recognized as a pastoral novel dealing with rural farm life and country people. Attentions to the everyday details of butter-making, berry-picking, and cattle-herding, far away from the political and economic changes of an industrialized society, lend the story a sense of innocence and peacefulness. However, as England crossed from the eighteenth to nineteenth century, the pastoral peace enveloping the Loamshire countryside is disrupted by Hetty and Arthur's affair. The pastoral setting underscores the transition of English society from relative innocence to experience, leaving Eliot's readers nostalgic for simpler times.

In addition, issues of religion, while not at the forefront of the novel, are nonetheless present. Dinah's evangelical Methodist preaching is set against Reverend Irwine's staid traditional church leadership. In the midst of this doctrinal difference, moral weaknesses abound and neither religious leader is able to save Hetty and Arthur from their lack of moral judgement. While Eliot avoids religious sermonizing, the lack of spiritual intervention on behalf of the lovers demonstrates her greater concern with the state of religion in nineteenth-century England and hints at her own religious dissent.

Eliot's use of realism in the novel is also significant. The realistic portrayal of both her characters and situations is reinforced by her pointed description of Dutch genre painting in Chapter 17 of the novel. Dutch painting was considered a low art form by Eliot's contemporaries, not because the technique was inferior, but because the subject matter failed to conform to the aesthetic ideal of beauty so favored by critics and consumers alike. By embracing this genre of painting, where commoners engaged in common tasks were presented in great detail, Eliot attempted to justify her own representation of "common, coarse people." Immediately recognized as a significant literary work, *Adam Bede* has enjoyed a largely positive critical reputation since its publication.

An anonymous review in *The Athenaeum*in 1859 praised it as a "novel of the highest class," and *The Times* called it "a first-rate novel." Contemporary reviewers, often influenced by nostalgia for the earlier period represented in *Bede*, enthusiastically praised Eliot's characterizations and realistic representations of rural life. Charles Dickens wrote: "The whole country life that the story is set in, is so real, and so droll and genuine, and yet so selected and polished by art, that I cannot praise it enough to you." In fact, in early criticism, the tragedy of infanticide has often been overlooked in favour of the peaceful idyllic world and familiar personalities Eliot recreated.

Other critics have been less generous. Henry James, among others, resented the narrator's interventions. In particular, Chapter 15 has fared poorly among scholars because of the author's/narrator's moralizing and meddling in an attempt to sway readers' opinions of Hetty and Dinah. Other critics have objected to the resolution of the story. In the final moments, Hetty, about to be executed for infanticide, is saved by her seducer, Arthur Donnithorne. Critics have argued that this deus ex machina ending negates the moral lessons learned by the main characters. Without the eleventh hour reprieve, the suffering of Adam, Arthur, and Hetty would have been more realistically concluded. In addition, some scholars feel that Adam's marriage to Dinah is another instance of the author's/narrator's intrusiveness. These instances have been found to directly conflict with the otherwise realistic images and events of the novel.

This act of textual suppression was singularly unsuccessful, because J. Dover Wilson restored the excised lines in the edition of *Culture and Anarchy* that has remained the most popular since its publication in 1932. Arthur Penrhyn Stanley was Thomas Arnold's biographer. The letter in question does not appear in Stanley's *Life and Correspondence*

says a great deal about descent in general: "Propinquity of descent,—the only known cause of the similarity of organic beings,—is the bond, hidden as it is by various degrees of modification, which is partially revealed to us by our classification". Although, as Beer points out in *Darwin's Plots,* this theory actually "muddied descent, and brought into question the privileged 'purity' of the 'great family'", opening up the possibility of "an uncouth progenitor hard to acknowledge as kin", many of the new race theorists adapted a crude version of natural selection to their notions of fixed racial "types" defined by blood relations.

This series of pamphlets was published by the Jamaica Committee in an attempt to influence public opinion in Britain over Morant Bay. Other Executive Committee members included Mill, Huxley, Spencer, and E.B. Underhill, whose letter to Governor Eyre in early 1865 about the desperate condition of the island's population had led to the so-called Underhill meetings throughout the island, at which grievances were expressed and the beginnings of a resistance movement can be discerned.

There is only one, fleeting, reference to Harrison's work with the Jamaica Committee in their correspondence: on February 5, 1867, Harrison wrote to Eliot, "I sent you as you asked the letters on Martial law. The Prosecution commences at once". When Eliot replied a fortnight later, she did not even acknowledge receipt of Harrison's pamphlet. The prosecution Harrison was referring to was the private case brought by the Jamaica Committee against Colonel Alexander Nelson and Lieutenant Herbert Brand, the presiding officers at George William Gordon's trial, on charges of wilful murder. Although the Lord Chief Justice, Sir Alexander Cockburn, delivered a famous address to the grand jury virtually instructing them to proceed with the trial, the jury refused to indict the two officers. In March, the Committee began the first of its two unsuccessful attempts to secure a conviction of Edward Eyre, the first time on murder charges, the second time for "high crimes and misdemeanours".

Of course, this does not prevent Mrs Transome herself

clinging to the very notion of breeding that the novel in general, and her own life in particular, renders obsolete: "Poor Mrs Transome, with her secret bitterness and dread, still found a flavour in this sort of pride [of family and blood]; none the less because certain deeds of her own life had been in fatal inconsistency with it. Besides, genealogies entered into her stock of ideas, and her talk on such subjects was as necessary as the notes of the linnet or the blackbird. She had no ultimate analysis of things that went beyond blood and family—the Herons of Fenshore or the Badgers of Hillbury".

Gillian Beer comments: "The book opens with the suppression of a woman's [Mrs Transome's] independence, a suppression which has been previously put at her [Eliot's] works' conclusion, and therefore out of reach of question". Harold's deceased wife has attracted little or no attention from critics.

This revelation also raises the intriguing possibility that the "woman from the East" whom Harold brings to Transome Court—who is mentioned nowhere else in the novel, and is certainly never seen—is in fact Harry's mother, and that the story about her death is a convenient fiction. This suppressed narrative of the "native" woman hidden in the country house would make *Felix Holt* an explicit reworking of *Jane Eyre*, and would consolidate the claims made here for the connections between George Eliot's novel and Jamaica. Unfortunately, pursuing this comparison is beyond the scope of this essay.

The imaginary stagecoach of the Introduction makes its way through Treby Magna and on to the reader's first view, through the eyes of the coachman, of "Transome Court, a place there had been a fine sight of lawsuits about. Generations back, the heir of the Transome name had somehow bargained away the estate and it fell to the Durfeys, very distant connections, who only called themselves Transomes because they had got the estate. But the Durfeys' claim had been disputed again and again; and the coachman, if he had been asked, would have said, though he might have to fall down dead the next minute, that property didn't always get into the right hands". Characteristically, this information is conveyed through an unnamed, minor character. Bruce Robbins' groundbreaking book *The Servant's Hand,* which analyzes the centrality of these apparently marginal figures in English fiction, contains a fine reading of *Felix Holt* : "Throughout the novel, the news that 'property doesn't always get into the right hands,' as the coachman of the introduction puts it, is specifically and almost obsessively placed in the hands of propertyless servants".

It would be more accurate, in fact, to say that writers began to use the term "British Empire" once again, since it had been current before the American Revolution in discussions about the possible loss to England of the thirteen colonies although it is doubtful whether the term encompassed all of England's dependencies overseas, including what was coming to be known as the Indian Empire. I believe that this point in fact strengthens my argument that it is only at the moment of possible loss of imperial hegemony that the Empire as such comes into being

Bibliography

Ackroyd, Peter. *T.S. Eliot: A Life.* New York: Simon and Schuster, 1984.

Drew, Elizabeth. *T.S. Eliot: The Design of his Poetry*. New York: Charles Scribner's Sons, 1949.

Eliot, T.S. *Old Possum's Book of Practical Cats*. New York: Harcourt Brace Jovanovich Publishers, 1982.

Eliot, T.S. *The Waste Land and Other Poems*. San Diego: Harvest/HBJ, 1930.

Kenner, Hugh ed. *T.S. Eliot: A Collection of Critical Essays.* New Jersey: Prentice-Hall, Inc., 1962.

Larkin, Philip. *The Oxford Book of Twentieth-Century English Verse.* Oxford: Clarendon Press, 1973.

Matthews, T.S. *Great Tom: Notes Towards the Definition of T.S. Eliot*. New York: Harper & Row, 1973.

The Merrill Guide to T.S. Eliot. Columbus: Charles E. Merrill Publishing Company, 1970.

Onsby, Ian, ed. *The Wordsworth Companion to Literature in English.* Great Britain: Cambridge University Press, 1994.

Reffel, Burton. *Possum and Ole Ez in the Public Eye: Contemporaries and Peers on T.S. Eliot and Ezra Pound 1892-1972.* Conneticut: Archen Books, 1985.

Sencourt, Robert. *T.S. Eliot: A Memoir*. New York: Dodd, Mead and Company, 1971.

Southam, B.C. *A Guide to the Selected Poems of T. S. Eliot.* New York: Harcourt, Brace & World, Inc., 1968.

Southam, B.C. *A Student's Guide to the Selected Poems of T.S. Eliot*. London: Faber & Faber, 1990. (5th edition)

Williams, Oscar. *Master Poems of the English Language.* New York: Trident Press, 1966.

The cat drawings are by Edward Gorey for the 1982 printing of *Old Possum's book of Practical Cats* and remain Mr. Gorey's property.

The photograph of T.S. Eliot on the main page is from The Bettman Archive, and was scanned out of *Master Poems of the English Language.*
